S·E·W

SEW EVERYTHING WORKSHOP

The Complete Step-by-Step

Beginner's Guide

by diana rupp

illustrations by lena corwin · photographs by andrea chu

WORKMAN PUBLISHING · NEW YORK

Dedication

This book is for my mom and my great-grandma Hallie,
for teaching me how to sew.

This book references websites that may be of interest to the reader. Every effort has been made
to ensure that the information about these websites is correct and up to date as of press time.

Library of Congress Cataloging-in-Publication Data

    Rupp, Diana.
      S.E.W. : sew everything workshop : the complete step-by-step beginner's guide
    with 25 fabulous original designs, including 10 patterns / by Diana Rupp. -- 1st ed.
        p. cm.
      "Box of patterns attached to book."
      ISBN-13: 978-0-7611-3973-7 (hc.)
      1. Sewing--Amateurs' manuals. 2. Dressmaking--Patterns. I. Title.
      TT705.R74 2007
      646.2--dc22

                                    2007025160

Design: Janet Vicario with Munira Al-Khalili

Workman books are available at special discounts when purchased in bulk for premiums and
sales promotions as well as for fund-raising or educational use. Special editions or book excerpts
can also be created to specification. For details, contact the Special Sales Director at the address below.

WORKMAN PUBLISHING COMPANY, INC.
225 Varick Street
New York, NY 10014-4381
www.workman.com

Printed in China
First printing October 2007
10 9 8 7 6 5 4 3 2 1

acknowledgments

I would like to thank everybody who helped me produce this book, especially:

My friend and agent Nina Collins for believing in me and standing by me, no matter what.
I am inspired by your generosity and will be forever grateful. I OWE YOU. Matthew Elblonk of
the Collins Literary Agency (when are we going for drinks?). Editor extraordinaire Ruth Sullivan
and everybody at Workman Publishing, especially Maisie Tivnan, Munira Al-Khalili, and Janet
Vicario for all their hard work and for making a dream come true. Jessica Vitkus for her mad
editing and writing skillz. (I've said it once, and I'll say it again: Lady, you are so talented!)
Teva Durham of loop-d-loop for being a kick-ass designer and one of my favorite storytellers.
My friends Andrea Chu and Lena Corwin for their visual genius—I couldn't imagine a better team.

To the teachers and students of Make Workshop for their continued support and understanding
while I was hard at work on this book—you make me feel very lucky to do what I do!

Cal, Michelle, and Nikki for helping me with the making.

Fernanda Franco for designing the original book proposal that got this whole thing started.
Put simply: You rock.

Christine Brenneman for spending a week with me in SF just writing. Oh, and for introducing
me to Dr. Dolphin. I majorly heart you.

I'd also like to give a big shout out to all my family and friends:

Dad, for telling me from day one that I could do anything I set my mind to.

Paula, as always, thank you for listening.

Marnie, Petr, Zoe, Robin, Jeanie, Alex, and Zach—I love you guys!

Emily, Ford, Kristin, Megan, Sasha, SB, Andrea Y., Gay, David, Don,
Christine Z., and Stacie for being the best friends EVER.

Dan Golden—without you I am nothing.

Rita for comforting me through all those really hard times.

And Joel Tippie, for inspiring me to be that much better.

contents

Part 1 Learning to Sew

Preparing Your Space • Getting Organized • Building a Sewing Kit: The Essential Tools • Shopping for Your Dream Machine • Playing Matchmaker: (Wo)man and Machine

The Anatomy of a Sewing Machine • Parts at Play • Hands-on Practice • Start Your Engines: Your First Seam • Meet the Stitches • Conquering Tension • Zen and the Art of Sewing Machine Maintenance • Quiz

Fiber First • Like a Virgin: Shopping for Your First Projects • Thinking Outside the Bolt • Pushing Your Skills • Drape Expectations • Lessons from the Color Wheel • The Ten Fabric Commandments • Sometimes a Great Notion • Fabric Store Treasure Hunt

Anatomy of a Pattern • How to Measure Up • The Eight-Step Program: From Prepping the Material and Pattern, to Layout, Pinning, Cutting, and Marking • Working with Directional Fabrics • Cheat Sheet of Pattern Symbols

Seam-ingly Beautiful • Pressing Matters • Finishing School: Trimming, Clipping, and Notching • Shaping Up: Making Darts, Easestitching, Gathering, and Interfacing • Tailoring and Fitting • Cheating the Pattern • Getting Closure: Hems, Zippers, and Buttons

Part 2 # The Projects

Learning to Sew

introduction

Sewing touches you every day. Literally. Look at the clothes you are wearing. Look at the seams. Can you see where the line of stitches dips a little? Or maybe the thread broke, so there's backstitching where the new thread starts. Quirks like these are signs that a person once sat at a sewing machine, easing the fabric through and leaving a physical trail of thread from that real moment in time. And thanks to that seamstress (chances are it was a woman), you are now warm or cool, stylish or comfortable.

As long as humans have been wearing clothes, people have been sewing them. Cave dwellers stitched furs together with bone needles and thread made of animal sinew. (It's possible that sewing predates cooking as a household skill!) After civilization set in, dressmakers, tailors, and moms hand-stitched clothes for clients, kings, and loved ones—a time-consuming task at best. But now mass production allows everyone to buy clothes in stores, and few people know how to sew—home ec classes have been phased out or are offered only as an elective. Just the phrase "mass production" makes clothing sound about as poetic and enjoyable as a hunk of steel. So I am thrilled to put the "hand" back into "handmade" and the "home" back into "homemade."

I own and run a studio called Make Workshop in New York City, and I teach sewing classes. People come to me with all levels of sewing experience and sometimes a little baggage, too. I have students who tried to learn from their moms, but it didn't go well (which I understand when I think of the times my mom tried to teach me to drive). I have students who are baffled by the machine. For many, it's just scary to learn a new skill as an adult. But like a roller coaster or a

I'm happiest at my sewing machine.

first date, things that are scary are also exciting. Sewing is exciting! It's the whir of the motor and the power to create.

Sewing has brought me much joy, so I know it's worth helping my students—and you, dear readers—get through those first projects. That's why I wrote this book. My workshops only have room for so many newbie seamsters; I can't teach everyone at once. But if you read this book, it's like taking my workshop at home—in your own time, on your own machine. I walk you through all the basic steps of garment making, from setting up your space to stitching the final hem. Each chapter along the way includes "Make It" assignments to help you practice and get comfortable. When you've worked through the first half of the book, you'll know every technique you need to make all my projects (the second half of the book). And guess what? It's not that hard! With a little patience and practice, anyone can sew. I promise.

My Personal Sew-ography

Mom looking glam in her handmade prom dress.

I have sewn for as long as I can remember. Sewing runs on both sides of my family. My great-grandmother Hallie, on my mother's side, was a professional milliner and an accomplished quilter. I remember sitting with her and embroidering when my fingers weren't much bigger than the needles.

My mom taught me to sew on a machine. She had taught herself as a kid. On her thirteenth birthday, my mom got a Singer sewing machine and some paisley fabric (the semiofficial state fabric of Southern California). She and her dad, my grandpa Gordon, took it upon themselves to make a pair of Capri pants (the semiofficial garment of Southern California in the early '60s). The project bordered on disaster. They sewed the inseams together to make something resembling the world's narrowest skirt. They ripped the seams out and, by and by, they figured out the pattern. Undaunted, my mom went on to make all her own clothes, including her high school prom dress—a glammy number in iridescent blue moiré that cinched her twenty-one-inch waist. She even made a matching jacket with covered buttons down the back!

When we were little, Mom sewed for the whole family—on that same Singer, as you can see from the picture of us (page 4) in our matching lederhosen-y outfits. (Von Trapp family, eat your heart out.) I'm the baby, and that's great-grandma Hallie. Later in the '70s, my mom and stepdad made a dollhouse—complete with resident dolls in handmade outfits. The dad doll even wore a tiny necktie. My mom sewed all their rugs and bed linens, and made curtains in tiny, tiny checks, florals, or lace for each little window. It was heaven. During my Barbie-loving years (which lasted quite a while), my mom made Barbie a full-on bridal gown

complete with floor-length tulle veil. There was no Ken or Barbie Dream House—
I didn't need 'em. I just wanted Barbie and her wardrobe.

I made clothes for my dolls as well, using
napkins and my dad's hankies, which I hand-
stitched into little dresses and vests. Hankies were
the perfect scale, and they were crisp and densely
woven so I could cut them up without too much
fraying. The minute I was old enough, my mom
had me stitching on the machine. I don't even
remember getting lessons. I'd just sit down and
noodle about or try to follow a simple pattern and
then go running to my mom when I got stuck.
I must have asked her to help me thread the
machine about 4,000 times—but she never lost
patience. A few times a year, we'd go to the store
and pick out fabric for a project, which was pretty

*Matching Easter outfits stitched by my mom
with love.*

much the highlight of the season. One of my first projects was a pair of knickers in purple
corduroy—which felt like the fanciest, coolest thing in my closet. (The knickers project in
this book is my little homage to those purple cords.)

In high school, I discovered vintage clothes. The patterned fabrics, the swing of the
skirts, the possible stories in all the dresses made me happy. Ventura, California, had plenty
of thrift stores, and I had plenty of energy to dig through them. I studied clothing details, like
pleats and pin tucks and gathers. My sewing smarts helped me alter and reconstruct those
vintage finds. I'd move hems, repair seams, take in waistlines (or bustlines, sigh). Then I'd
saunter off to school in my little '40s dress and Doc Marten shoes with ankle socks.

In college at Berkeley, I was still wearing vintage dresses, but I was ready to kick it
up a notch on the sophisticated grown-up scale. Designer clothes started to speak to me,
as did sexy shoes and richer fabrics. Plus, the Bay Area's inspiring fabric stores, like Stone
Mountain and Daughter in Berkeley and Britex in San Francisco, became my new meccas.
Sometimes, I'd stay on campus over holiday breaks and unwind with a sewing project.
My test-taking burnout would disappear upon crossing the Britex threshold. I'd pick out a
challenging pattern and some gorgeous jersey or gingham. The results? A navy blue Donna
Karan wrap dress one Thanksgiving. A baby-doll dress in ginger-y golds over spring break.
Of course, I made a cutting mistake on the back of the baby-doll dress, which meant I had
to tear out, remake, and reattach a whole new back piece. But now I definitely know how.

When my sister got married, I went to the Czech Republic and sewed her a wedding dress (her husband is Czech). It was the first time I measured and stitched using the metric system. But I did it! I made a simple slip dress in white eyelet and my sister cried and told me it was the best wedding gift possible.

Then came my career-girl-on-the-go years and my first apartment in San Francisco that I made feel like home by whipping up pillows, curtains, and duvet covers. I sewed for boyfriends, too. Such a good courtship maneuver—but only after the fifth date (and then only maybe). As a magazine fashion editor and stylist, I had to organize photo shoots and runway shows. When I needed just the right touch or accessory for a model, it was often easier to sew it myself—a little lavender knit shrug here, a red tweed skirt there. This gave me more control over the final look and saved me hours of searching.

During this era, I had an epiphany that carried through to all my designs and sewing ever after: I like clothes, not fashion. The idea of a new collection with new rules each season is ridiculous (I'm still the Cali girl who likes shorts in winter), and a lot of what comes down runways during Fashion Week is unwearable and unaffordable. I like real clothes that real people would wear in the real world. So, I hired models who were normal-looking and styled them into my version of pretty. It felt like I'd found my sewing "voice." I also started sewing and knitting hats, shawls, and little sweaters and selling them in boutiques. I realized something else: Working for myself was way more fun than working for other people.

So when I moved to New York City in 2001, I immediately started teaching sewing and knitting classes, along with doing some freelance fashion styling. I loved teaching so much that I started cooking up a dream plan to open my own studio—with lots of light and tables and sewing machines—where I could design projects all day and teach others to sew at night.

My dream became a scrappy, colorful reality in 2002, when I opened Make Workshop on the Lower East Side. It's in an old loft building abuzz with artists—photographers, jewelry makers, graphic designers—who all inspire me. My studio has big long tables with sewing machines, shelves full of books, fabric, and yarn, and a whole wall of inspiration board covered in art and swatches. I plugged in the boom box, and people started coming in to learn to sew. They share the tables and chatter (stitching and bitching) and help each other during class (mixed with the rumbling of machines, it's a great

Teaching a new student at Make Workshop— sewing isn't just for ladies.

Let's Get Stitching!
HOW TO START YOUR OWN SEWING CIRCLE

Think sewing is a solo activity? Au contraire, my dear seamsters. There's a very active sewing community out there, both online and in the real world, so there's no need to stitch (or bitch) alone. I host stitching circles at Make Workshop on a regular basis, and you're all invited! Can't make it to NYC?

Try looking for a group in your area at sewing.meetup.com. Or, if you're more of a ringleader type, start your own sewing posse. Here are some ideas to get you going:

✳ Come up with a gang name

Giving a group a name is highly motivating. Which sounds better: "Would you like to join my mumble-mumble sewing group?" or "Wanna be a STITCHINISTA?!!!" I rest my case.

✳ Blog it like it's hot

There's a reason everybody and their grandma has a blog. Go to blogger.com and put in the keyword *sewing* to see what all the fuss is about. I can spend hours and hours drooling over the amazing things people make. Why not join the fun? Create a simple page and post a few details about yourself and the projects you've made. I'd love to see what you can do, too!

✳ Play show and tell

There are many opportunities to sew-a-long. One of my favorites is Tie One On at www.angrychicken.typepad.com. The idea is genius: Every other month an apron-making theme, like Valentine's Day or Apron as Costume, is chosen and people are invited to send their creations. When you've finished your project, send a jpeg of it along with a link to your blog and it will be included in an online gallery for all to "ooh" and "ahh" over. How cool is that?

✳ Get the word out

E-mail friends, coworkers, and relatives to ask if they sew and/or if they'd like to learn; also ask them to forward your message to anybody else who might be interested. Keep track of potential members with a mailing list. Network whenever you're out and about. For example, see someone over on aisle 4 in the

sound). And there's definitely lots of light. One giant benefit of running Make is that when I read about someone cool who knows shoemaking or lingerie sewing or Japanese fabric dyeing, I can invite them to teach a course, and then my students and I learn even more. Make offers classes in jewelry making, yarn spinning, embroidery, quilting, and anything else that gets people excited. There are now as many as sixty workshops on the schedule, and the classes fill up as fast as I can post them on my website.

I really couldn't ask for much more, except to clone myself so I could teach more classes to the sew-curious everywhere. Until that scientific breakthrough, this book stands as my

Make Workshop's monthly stitching circle.

communities for help when you are stuck on a pattern, don't understand a particular technique, or are having trouble with your machine.

✳ Schedule a meeting of the minds

Once you have a few potential members, set a date to meet at a local café for a brainstorming session. How many people do you want to join? What will be the focus and the level of your group? And where and how often might you meet? Come up with some ideas for creating a logo for your group—a little branding goes a long way. Use the logo on your blog page and print it on flyers that you post to help recruit new members to your first official meeting.

fabric store picking out the same print you bought a few weeks ago? Don't be shy. Go over and ask them what they're making. Knitters also make for good marks. Next time you see someone knitting, ask her if she's ever thought about sewing, too. (There's even a blog devoted to this crossover demographic at www.scwlknit.blogspot.com.)

✳ Troll craft websites

Posting a message in a craft forum is another great way to get the word out. Sites like craftster.org and getcrafty.com have thousands of members. Chances are there is someone in your hood who loves to sew, too. You can also count on these online

✳ Look for sponsors

Many fabric stores would be happy to have you hold your meetings at their shop. It would get customers in the door, and makes for good PR. Churches and community rec centers are another possibility. Say the word "sewing" and I promise doors will open as if by magic.

attempt to get the word out: Sewing is fun, sewing is satisfying, sewing has made my life better in many ways (at least ten—see the next page). And sewing is growing as a pastime, which couldn't thrill me more. Knitting has come back to life big-time in the last five years, and now sewing is poised for its moment at the party. Actually, at Make I feel like I'm hosting the ideal party—where all these smart and stylish and interesting people come over and we sew! We get together to celebrate this anciently modern, usefully creative, super-accessible art form. And you know what machine I always have with me when I teach? My mother's Singer.

10 reasons why i sew

In the *Little House on the Prairie* days, Ma stitched quilts for the winter. The Great Depression made sewing a money-saving necessity. In the '50s, the Happy Homemaker sewed curtains and baby clothes because that was her job. But in the twenty-first century, sewing is no longer a required skill. Today, it's actually cheaper and faster to buy clothes from the Gap—especially if you count your valuable man-hours (or woman-hours). So why sew? Why do I wake up each morning excited to get to my machine and make something? Why do I spend each day spreading the crafty sewing gospel? Even though it's kind of like explaining why I love a clear blue sky, here is my boiled-down, subjective list of reasons why I sew.

1 i can go to the fabric store

When I go into a fabric store, I'm in an altered state. I love to walk around and look at the colors and prints and touch the velvets, velours, and voiles. I get to imagine all the possibilities. What to make next? What prints and textures do I want to spend the next few days with? Do I want to snuggle down with a soft fluffy mohair? Or maybe beat the winter blues with oversized pink florals? Am I feeling dotty? Every visit to the fabric store is like a good first date—filled with potential.

2 i can crack the code

I can look at a garment or a beautiful handbag and figure out how to make it myself. (This is easier than you think.) I can measure the sections and copy them, adding a seam allowance. I can take a shirt apart and use the pieces as a pattern.

Once you know the basics of sewing, clothes shopping is a whole new experience. Bloomingdale's becomes a research library with books on hangers. You can examine garments to get inspiration and ideas. You'll find yourself saying, "Oh, I can make that—but I'd rather do it in an elegant pinstripe." Which leads me to my next reason . . .

3 i can make what i really want, how i want

I know what looks good on me. I know what colors and fabrics I like. If I want a pencil skirt in silver brocade, I can make it. If I want that skirt in five different colors and different weights for different seasons (which I do), I can do that, too. And since I am somewhere between a size 4 and size 6, I can tailor my pencil skirt to fit just right, instead of having to pick the lesser of two ill-fitting evils in the store. It's crazy to think all the different bodies out there can fit into one of a half-dozen sizes. I find it empowering (and flattering) to make my clothes fit properly.

4 i can alter and repair clothes myself

I don't have to pay a tailor to hem my pants. I can shorten skirts and narrow jeans for free. I can buy vintage or thrift-store clothes and customize them to my heart's content. I just went to Anthropologie and rescued a perfectly cute lace dress with a broken zipper from the bargain bin. Ten bucks! Score! Alterations extend the life of clothes and give old clothes a new start. I think of it as my personal recycling program; clothes stay in my closet and out of the landfill.

5 i can relax and de-stress

I find machine sewing so pleasant and meditative. The feel of the fabric and the soft whir of the machine are soothing to me. I'm sure my blood pressure goes down every time I walk into the studio. Sewing keeps my brain focused but not taxed. It's impossible to think of my troubles—or anything else—while I am lining up notches to sew a dart. I guess it's why other people play golf or paint by numbers.

6 i can take pride in a practical skill

Sewing is so useful. It's like carpentry with fabric. And the satisfaction of doing a project from beginning to end satisfies me to the core. I'm proud that I can work with a machine and make a product. A wearable product.

7 i can express myself

Sure, it's practical, but sewing is also super-creative. I love the idea of making a one-of-a-kind piece of wearable art. I can play with color and texture and print. I can improvise and embellish. I think about draping, balance, and form like a sculptor does. I can get swept up in the process like a little modern-day Michelangelo (well, that's a bit self-inflated, but you know what I mean). And I don't need a gallery or museum to show off my work. I just put it on.

8 i can have fun sharing sewing with others

I love sewing with my students and with friends. Sewing goes nicely with chitchatting (think ye olde sewing circles and quilting bees). I've also been teaching my sister, niece, and nephew to sew, and this is pure quality time together. It's really easy to share a machine, since most of the sewing process involves preparing and cutting with little actual time spent on the machine. It helps to have other eyes and opinions in the room and to get instant feedback (aka praise) for my work. An added bonus of community sewing? The sharing of fabric scraps, scissors, and other supplies.

9 i'm part of a larger community

I don't have to be in the same room with a fellow seamstress to feel connected. The very act of sewing makes me feel closer to my mom and my great-grandma, the milliner. Then there are the sewing compatriots I never meet. Some are in cyberspace. I find them on Flickr and on sewing blogs like craftlog.org and chat rooms like craftster.org and getcrafty.com. Magazines (like *Lucky* and *Domino*) inspire me and give me ideas. I hope to open other Make Workshops around the country, but in the meantime, you can start your own sewing circle (see pages 6–7).

10 i can show others i love them

In an era when people think they have no time, it is a great gift to invest a few hours in making something by hand for someone else. It's extranurturing to sew a friend some custom-made cushions or a cozy quilt for her new apartment. (It puts the warm back in housewarming.) How often do people get such a treat? Try it and see. The happy reaction ("Oh my god, you *made* this?") makes the effort totally worthwhile. Sometimes, giddy recipients want to take the next step and learn how to sew for themselves. Then the sewing circle gets even larger.

CHAPTER 1 *gearing up*

*I*f you are reading this, chances are you already have the most important piece of equipment: the desire to sew. The fanciest machine and pins topped with emeralds will do you no good unless you have motivation, inspiration—a little Picasso mixed with Betsy Ross. A little Yves Saint Laurent mixed with Björk. Now that you are going to make clothes (and other things), you need to nurture and cultivate inspiration. Take notes. Tear out pictures. Open your eyes! I keep a little spiral notepad in my bag. When I see a person on the subway wearing something cool, I make a note before I forget ("trench coat in faux woodgrain fabric"). Sometimes, I draw an image or detail so I can use it later (like simple bunny shapes that become apron pockets). I look at patterns of wallpaper

make it build your own inspiration board

An inspiration board is like an ever-changing scrapbook for your wall, a place to gather visual fuel for your fire. To make one, buy a large piece of cork or Homasote (found at hardware stores) and staple fabric to it. Collect photos from magazines. Make color copies of your favorite book covers. Find the perfect leaf. Ask your mom for a picture of her in her favorite childhood outfit (or have her draw it!). Add portraits of your heroes (sewing or otherwise). Pin up fabric samples, scrumptious ribbon bits, measurements, shopping lists, and ideas for projects. On my board, I have a photo of my dog Rita, sketches of trees, coral red pompom trim, a picture of my twin niece and nephew laughing, swatches for projects in this book, and an

invitation to a friend's fashion show on this crazy gold-with-black-flocking stationery.

Be freethinking in your own choices. An inspiration board can hold anything that strikes you—pictures from Marc Jacobs's spring line, paint chips in happy colors, photos of an old Mexican graveyard, a handwritten note you found on the street, a vibrant feather, a page from a flower catalog, and a photocopy of your best friend's hand—rings and all. It's like a collage that keeps changing. In fact, you should make a point of adding and subtracting an item every week or so. I switch things on mine every time I finish a project—that's one of my rewards.

in restaurants. I visit clothing stores—whether it's Forever 21 or Prada—to see what shapes and details are out on the racks. My students are probably my biggest source of inspiration—the way they adapt a simple bag or embellish a skirt wows me. Sometimes ideas lurk in unlikely places (colors of Swiss chard—deep magenta veins on green leaves—good combo). So be alert and start keeping track. Because inspiration begets more inspiration.

one preparing your space

It's never too soon to start thinking about your work space. Whether you've inherited a sewing machine or you're getting one soon, start envisioning where you want to sew. Where is the magic going to happen? You know how athletes prepare for competition by picturing themselves running up the hill or swinging the golf club for a hole in one? It's helpful (and fun) to imagine yourself cutting and pinning, stitching and pressing. How can you keep tools within reach? You'll be sitting in one space for stretches of time; will you look out the window? Will you play music? Try on different mental versions of yourself in your sewing nook—it'll help you figure out your priorities.

Pick a Home Base

Take a look around your house or apartment. Is there a cozy out-of-the-way spot where your sewing machine can live? Can your work area be dedicated and available at all times? Or will you have to put things away between projects? Do you mind seeing your work area or do you want to hide it away? These are questions to start asking yourself. And there's no one right answer. My workspace is a closet—I call it the closet command center—and it holds everything I need for sewing, plus I can shut the door when not at work. If a closet isn't available, a rice-paper screen or rolling rattan blind hung from the ceiling are smart and inexpensive ways to cordon off a corner or hallway to use as a small sewing studio.

Get Organized

Think of a handyman and his tool bench. Think of a cook in the galley of a submarine. You want to get the greatest efficiency and ease out of your area. That means organizing your equipment and tools. Perhaps your equipment can be folded up or stashed away, or attached to the wall or the back of a door. Built-in shelving is fantastic—use shallow shelves for small storage jars, deeper ones for books and fabric. A small bookcase or filing cabinet works, too. Buy a pegboard, along with a pack of different-sized hooks, for hanging cutting and measuring tools so you can get at them easily. (Be sure to attach it to wall studs.) A thread rack and bobbin organizer keep thread neat and visible. Put pattern pieces into large manila envelopes with the original packaging stapled to the outside; then place in magazine racks or vertical files and onto shelves. (Keep your project-in-process in a clear, zip-top bag on the pegboard.) Smaller odds and ends like buttons, snaps, and seam binding can live in old recycled jars, boxes, cans, or baskets.

work space essentials

What you need for the special space you've picked out:

✳ Cutting table

A sturdy, fairly high table (at least 30 x 48 x 36 inches) accessible from at least two sides. A tabletop with adjustable legs from IKEA works well.

✳ Sewing table

A desklike table around 28 inches high. At least 6 inches of surface area on either side of the machine will give you room for your project, pincushion, and scissors while you're sewing.

✳ Comfortable chair with a strong back

When you're sitting in the chair, the sewing machine should feel a little higher than a keyboard at a computer. You can adjust once you start working (sit on a cushion or try a lower chair) so you feel comfortable.

✳ Ironing board and steam iron

The ironing board should be full-size, not one of those little tabletop numbers (see pressing tools on page 16).

✳ Lots of shadow-free light

You need a task light for your work and overall light for the sewing area. Natural light is wonderful for sewing (especially for matching thread to fabric and other color-related tasks), but it's not always available. If you aim area lights to bounce off the walls or ceiling, the light spreads nicely and makes fewer shadows.

table tip In a pinch you can use a big dining room table or the floor instead of a real cutting table. Either of these options will quickly take a toll on your body, so jack up a waist-high table with cans so it's at least 30 inches high. Your neck and back will thank you. If you are working on the floor, take breaks and stretch.

chair tip Some sewers like an office chair with wheels so they can roll from table to ironing board without standing up. If you're doing this on carpeting, get a hard plastic mat to keep wheels in motion.

two building a sewing kit

Head to your friendly neighborhood fabric store for a few basic supplies. Don't know where to go? Online searches, the tried-and-true yellow pages, and recommendations from crafty acquaintances will point you in the right direction. (Or see the list of retailers in the appendix, page 236.) Read through the list below before shopping. Fabric stores are typically jam-packed with merchandise, and you don't want to be overwhelmed by all that goodness. So start only with the essentials: needles, thread, measuring and marking tools. This requires an initial investment, but your sewing kit will be a constant and trustworthy companion for all patterns in the book and many projects to come.

> **scissor tip** If you can, buy dressmaker's shears and embroidery scissors as a set. The big shears often come with a bonus pair of little guys.

cut right: shears and scissors

Basically, you need four tools for cutting:

✳ **Dressmaker's shears**
These are special stainless steel bent-handled 7- or 8-inch scissors for fabric. And I mean fabric *only*. My all-time favorite brand is Gingher, the Rolls Royce of scissors, with a lifetime warranty. Dressmaker's shears are the most important tool in your sewing kit. You will use them every time you sew. So treat yourself to the best pair money can buy. And never use them to cut paper, stray tags, hair, pizza, or anything else.

✳ **Embroidery scissors**
These little cuties are for trimming off threads, clipping corners, and doing other intricate work.

✳ **Pinking shears**
These odd-looking scissors make zigzag cuts, which prevent (or slow down) fraying. Pinking shears help to finish seams.

✳ **Regular scissors**
These are for cutting paper (such as patterns) and anything else that comes your way. Most likely you have a pair of these kicking around the house somewhere. Having them in your studio will save you from inadvertently cutting something other than fabric with your dressmaker's shears, which would be very, very bad.

dressmaker's shears

embroidery scissors

pinking shears

regular scissors

measuring tools

✳ Sewing ruler

This transparent and bendable ruler helps you measure and mark fabric easily. Look for one that's 2 x 18 inches with markings down to $\frac{1}{8}$ inch (the standard unit of measurement in sewing). Since it's flexible, you can hold it on its side edge to draw curves—a big help when altering clothing or making changes to patterns.

✳ Cloth tape measure

This flexible tool is for measuring soft, curved areas, like your bust, waist, and hips. The standard length and width is 60 x $\frac{5}{8}$ inches, although there is a 120-inch

version for home decor projects. Make sure your tape measure doesn't stretch or fade. Measuring tools should be as accurate as possible.

✳ Sewing gauge

A sewing gauge (also called a seam gauge) has a moveable slider for marking hems, checking seam allowances, placing buttons, lining up trim, and more.

marking tools

✳ Tailor's chalk

Get two: white chalk for marking dark fabrics, and light blue chalk for fabrics and prints where white doesn't show. I prefer a clay chalk (vs. the kind that's waxy like a crayon) because it's easier to remove. Although not as precise as a pen, chalk works well for most tasks, is less expensive to replace, and won't disappear between sewing sessions.

✳ Disappearing-ink marker

To mark fabric easily and

with absolute precision, nothing works better than a disappearing-ink marker. Dual-marking pens have purple ink on one end that evaporates in the air (normally in forty-eight hours or less, so use it before you lose it) and blue on the other end that washes out (not a good choice for silk or fabric that is dry-clean-only). Brands vary, and humidity can play a critical role in how long the ink lasts. I've loyally used Dritz markers for years with good results.

> **pen tip** Do a test before using a disappearing-ink marker, especially when working with expensive fabric.

pins and needles and thread

✳ Straight pins

Pins temporarily join fabrics together before stitching. They come in several lengths and thicknesses. Thinner pins

are for finer fabrics and heavier pins are for thicker fabrics. Standard all-purpose or dressmaker's pins are just dandy for most projects (they're rustproof, too). Pins with colorful glass heads are easier to grab when they drop on the floor (which they inevitably do). Don't get too close to plastic pinheads when ironing—they melt!

> **pin tip** Use a magnetic tray or wand to pick up rogue pins—especially if you have kids or pets.

✳ Pincushion

Pincushions keep pins and needles safe and ready for action. When you sew, you're constantly grabbing pins and then, seconds later, putting them down. A traditional tomato-shaped cushion should ride shotgun every time you stitch. A wristband-style cushion keeps pins even closer. In my opinion, you can't have too many pincushions.

15

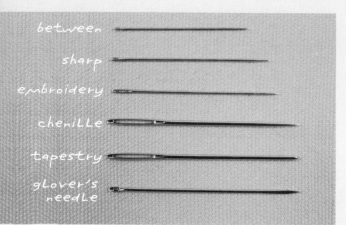

between

sharp

embroidery

chenille

tapestry

glover's
needle

✳ Hand-sewing needles

These needles come in assorted sizes and vary in eye shape, length, and point, according to their specific job (see chart, above). Like pins, thinner needles are for finer fabrics, smaller eyes for thinner thread. A multipurpose pack will give you more than enough variety.

✳ Thread

An all-purpose thread made from cotton-wrapped polyester—for ease and strength—works for almost every project. I'm generally not big on brands, but when it comes to thread, stick to Coats & Clark or Gutermann, and you'll know you're getting the good stuff! Pick up a couple of spools in your favorite colors, as well as navy blue, black, and white.

mama's little helpers

✳ Seam ripper

Meet your new best friend. True to its name, the pointy tip of a seam ripper picks up stitches gone awry, and the sharp, curved edge cuts them. Out comes your bad seam. (Trust me, it happens to the best of us.) The cutting edge also slices open buttonholes. Try to get a flat handle (instead of round) so your seam ripper isn't always rolling off the table.

✳ Magnetic seam guide

This tool works like training wheels; it provides a firm, straight edge for you to follow when you're sewing and creates a perfect seam line every time. Place the guide on the throat plate of your machine and adjust to any seam allowance. Although it can't be used on computerized machines, the seam guide is particularly helpful for correcting older machines that pull to the side or sew too fast.

pressing tools

✳ Steam iron

A steam iron that lets you control the amount of steam—from none to a heavy burst—is an absolute necessity. Some fabrics hate humidity, while others need a saunalike treatment before they obey. Spend extra for a higher-end model. Rowenta has an excellent reputation and makes a special line of sewing and craft irons.

✳ Ironing board

Use a firmly padded ironing surface every time you sew. Professional seamstresses cover their boards in flannel and muslin, but a standard ironing board with a cotton cover works for me. Once again, portable tabletop boards are a no-no. They're too small for ironing large swaths of fabric.

✳ Press cloth

It's a piece of protective fabric that you lay across your good fabric when pressing, shielding it from direct heat. It prevents shine and scorch marks. You can make a press cloth from clean muslin, T-shirt fabric, or men's handkerchiefs. Different projects call for different sizes, but store-bought press cloths are 24 x 14 inches.

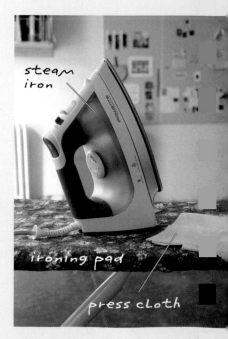

steam iron

ironing pad

press cloth

Good to Go: Mobile Sewing Box

Now that you've gathered the tools for your sewing kit, it's time to find them a good home. Sure, you could throw everything into some random plastic container and call it a day, but that's so boring! Pick something that matches your personality because it will be your constant companion while you sew. My tools live in what I call my mobile sewing box—it was auctioned on eBay as an "antique picnic basket." Made from enameled pink metal, it's girly yet practical. When I open the lid, I feel like I'm about to undertake some serious repairs, even if I'm simply fixing a torn seam or sewing on a button. A cute wicker basket or plastic craft bin could do the job too, as long as it has a handle and a lid. (Remember, you want things good to go.) Dividers or subcontainers help keep your bits and bobs tidy. And go big: Make sure your sewing box can hold that 18-inch ruler.

Pack your sewing suitcase.

don't be a dummy
INVEST IN A DRESS FORM

Sewing is usually a solo activity, but sometimes you need help—even if it's from a dummy. Getting the right fit is the hardest thing about sewing clothing. Taking things on and off in front of the mirror a hundred times is a pain. Having your very own dress form allows you to see clearly and quickly the changes you need to make. It's a huge help when you want to place pockets, mark a hem or lining, pin sleeves in position, adjust a pattern, and so on. The drawback is the cost. Adjustable home-sewing models start at $150, while fashion-industry-grade versions run around $500. You'll pay much less for a used one at a thrift store, flea market, or on eBay.

17

three getting a sewing machine

Your machine is your most important piece of sewing equipment, so take time to select one with care. A sturdy, well-built machine, with just enough bells and whistles for your needs and skill level, can bring you years of sewing pleasure.

Definitely do some test-driving before you buy. Using a machine—any decent machine—will familiarize you with the different components and help you decide what you want in your own. Do you yearn for a fancy new machine with computer chips, or are you fond of the old all-metal workhorses? Do you like a lot of different stitch patterns, or is zigzagging your idea of a wild time? Do you need it to go slow? Do you care about quiet? Pay attention to what bugs you and what feels satisfying.

Shopping for Your Dream Machine

Anyone who's Googled "sewing machine" knows there's a staggering array of makes and models out there ranging in price from $100 to more than $1,000. It can be a bit overwhelming. So which one to get? How much to spend? The good news is there is something for everyone. It just depends on your budget, your skill level, your sewing goals, and how many hours you plan on parking yourself at the machine.

If you're a beginner and just want to give sewing a try, go easier on your wallet. You can get a decent entry-level mechanical machine for $150. Spend a little more ($200 to $300) and you'll get a few perks that will make sewing more enjoyable and, frankly, easier. If you truly know deep down that you'll use the machine for a lifetime and can afford it, spend around $500. I did so recently and can't imagine I'll ever need to upgrade.

Remember that top-of-the-line is not necessarily the best buy. Resist the urge to get more machine than you need. Just like a toaster toasts and a blender blends, a sewing machine is an appliance that sews. So, don't get tricked by the up-sell. You'll probably never use more than five stitches. (For years, I worked on a vintage flat-bed Singer that could only do a straight stitch and zigzag, and I did just fine, thank you very much.)

Recommending a machine by brand name alone is tricky. Some people would take a bullet for their Bernina (these Swiss-made machines are considered the crème de la crème) but I'm not loyal to one manufacturer. For one thing, a

try before you buy
THREE GOOD WAYS

1. Take a sewing machine class at a fabric store or school—even a one-nighter can really help.
2. Have a crafty sewing friend show you some moves on her machine.
3. Borrow a machine for a week or two. Put the word out to family and friends, and you might be surprised how quickly a machine materializes. Many people feel guilty about not using theirs and are happy to dust it off for some action.

brand doesn't mean a lot anymore. Sewing machine companies change hands without changing names and they sometimes outsource production to different factories from year to year, with varying results. And just because a brand has an excellent reputation doesn't mean it's the right machine for you. It's much smarter to select a machine that meets your individual sewing needs and go by what real sewers who've used the machine have to say about it. So what kind of sewer are you? See below for your match.

♥ *playing matchmaker* (wo)man and machine

Sometimes you need to look within to decide what kind of machine is the right fit for you.

ASK YOURSELF:

Am I an independent gal (or guy) who sees sewing as a basic life skill and plans to stick to everyday jobs like hemming pants or sewing a simple A-line skirt? Do I see myself getting around to every pattern in this book? Do I want my finished projects to look like they came from a (really nice) store?

IF YES, THEN:

You need something as solid, straightforward, and plastic-free as you. Consider hooking up with a **MECHANICAL** sewing machine. These machines have all-rotary parts and discs inside called pattern cams that produce a variety of stitches. They cost about $100 to $400. The good ones have all-metal parts and at least twelve stitches, including those suitable for stretch knits, droppable feed dogs, and a one-step buttonhole.

ASK YOURSELF:

Do I have aspirations to be a future *Project Runway* contestant whose finished garments—even alterations—have an arty flair? Am I a home-decor diva who fantasizes about monogramming Egyptian cotton towels and is intrigued by upholstery techniques like piped seams and tufted cushions?

IF YES, THEN:

You need an **ELECTRONIC** sewing machine to keep up with your wildest sewing ambition. These machines have mechanical components with some circuits added. They create stitches with cams or even a computer. Electronic machines cost $400 to $800. The good ones have a drop-in bobbin, automatic needle threader, one-touch button for needle up/down, multiple needle positions, twenty-plus stitch patterns, decorative buttonholes, and speed control. It's enough to make you swoon.

mechanical

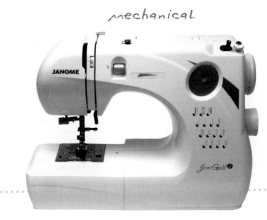

electronic

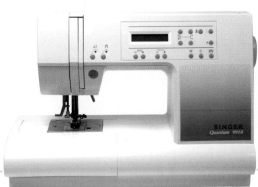

the lowdown: what to look for in a machine

You can make the projects in this book on just about any machine. As long as it sews seams and makes buttonholes, even grandma's old Kenmore will do. That said, here are qualities and features to look for when buying a new model:

✳ All-metal parts

A durable, high-quality machine has all-metal construction. (The exception is the plastic shell over the metal body.) Low-end machines (less than $150) are likely to use a plastic chassis and parts.

✳ Drop-in bobbin

A drop-in bobbin is a real sanity-saver and worth the extra $50 or so. A side-loading bobbin, found in many mechanical machines, takes more time and work to thread.

✳ One-step buttonhole

These days, even inexpensive models can do a one-step buttonhole, so there's no reason to get stuck with a machine that doesn't. (Watch out for the machines with a four-step make-it-yourself buttonhole. What a pain in the neck!)

✳ Adjustable speed control

Sewing too fast sabotages the quality of your stitching. If you prefer to work on a machine where you control the pace, spend the extra $100 for this feature.

✳ Droppable feed dogs

Feed dogs grip fabric from below and move it along in a straight line. If you have any interest in machine appliqué, embroidery, or quilting, you'll want a machine that allows you to sew fabric in any direction.

✳ Multiple needle positions

Being able to change the position of your needle makes hemming, topstitching, and inserting zippers much easier. Some machines will let you move the needle in small increments with a touch of a button, while others need you to physically scoot the needle to one of three positions (left, right, or center). Any flexibility is desirable.

take a field trip to the dealership

You can buy sewing machines at chain stores, such as Sears or Target. But if you're new to this hobby, it's better to shop at a sewing machine dealership. Sewing machine dealers are usually experts (at least within their brand) and sell higher-quality machines. You'll benefit from their knowledge, their desire to keep customers happy, and their willingness to introduce you to the world of sewing. You'll probably spend more, but you get a better warranty policy (see sidebar), and the in-person technical support is totally worth the extra expense. Plus, dealerships often give free lessons with purchase. (Check out the websites for sewing machine companies on page 237.)

When you visit the dealer, tell the salesperson the kind of sewing you plan to do and ask him or her to demonstrate some machines within your price range. Then, try them out yourself (ask first!). In general, see what feels good and seems solid and user-friendly. Some specific things to ask about, watch for, and do when you are at the dealership or trying a machine in a store are:

✻ *Does the machine sew quietly, or does it shimmy?*

✻ *Does the fabric feed straight through when you're not directing it, or does it pull to the side?*

✻ *How does the machine perform on different fabrics, like lightweight cotton, denim, and stretchy knit?* (Bring a few fabric swatches to try.)

✻ *How are the stitches forming?* Are the top and bottom threads even and loop-free? (Bring two different-colored spools of thread to see the top and bottom stitching better.)

✻ *Does it make a buttonhole easily?* If you don't know how, ask the salesperson to show you and notice if it's nicely finished or sloppy.

✻ *What accessories are included? Are there any extras like a carrying case?*

✻ *Can you return with questions if something goes wrong with your machine?* You'll want a "yes" to that or look elsewhere.

risky business
BEWARE THE WARRANTY-FREE MACHINE

The industry standard for a sewing machine warranty is twenty years mechanical, two years electrical, and one year labor. But when you shop at a discounter or online, the warranty may be as little as ninety days or voided altogether by the manufacturer. Before buying, ask questions about what to do if something goes wrong with your machine. Otherwise you might find yourself stuck with a lemon and spending more money in the long run.

preowned versus pristine

A used machine can be every bit as worthy and useful as a new machine. Models produced in the 1960s and earlier were built to last and cost so much less than a new machine. Look for a recently serviced used machine at a dealer or repair store with a limited warranty (it's worth the extra expense). Buying a secondhand machine at a garage sale or thrift store is more of a gamble, but sometimes it pays off. Just make sure whatever you buy runs, has its accessories (including the manual), looks cared for, and has no obvious damage.

shopping tip Don't be shy about making more than one trip to the dealer. Or try different dealers. It's actually fun—like shopping for a car.

Equipped and Ready

When you have all your sewing gear, you feel like a kid with a new pencil case on the first day of school. When you get your machine, you feel like a teenager with her first car (which is even better).

Even if you've been around the sewing block a few times, I'm sure I can show you something new, break your bad habits, and help you start good ones. Best of all, you get to make things—beautiful things you can wear into the world. (Did a car ever make anything? I think not.)

So turn the page and get ready for a driver's ed course on your sewing machine.

An orphan comes home:
a Dickens tale for the home ec nerd

There I was, taking out the trash from my tiny Brooklyn apartment. It was dark and late. I was tired from a long day in the sewing studio. Sitting forlorn on the curb, with its celery-green cover shining in the moonlight, a sewing machine appeared. I tried not to make any sudden movements: Maybe someone was just around the corner trying to flag a cab to carry it away. Maybe a rival seamstress was laying bait for me. But I couldn't walk away. No one appeared, so I grabbed the case by the handle and scurried upstairs to further assess. Off came the cover and—ta-da!— a 1960s all-metal Singer machine with a light-green enamel finish.

Surely, it wouldn't work, I thought. But just to be certain (and respectful), I spent a half hour cleaning it, removing dust and crud from the exposed parts. Then I plugged it in and—whir—the bobbin actually wound up! I threaded the top, grabbed a scrap of cotton, and found it stitched perfectly. I almost cried. Even though my apartment was the size of a teacup, I made room for my green machine. We were meant to be together. Now little greenie sits at the Make Workshop studio next to my mom's old Singer.

learn your machine parts

Start by studying the basic sewing machine diagram (left). Memorize these parts and locate them on your machine before moving on to the next section.

✳ **Accessory box and extension table** The box holds spare bobbins, presser feet, machine oil, etc. The table widens the sewing area around the throat plate but can be removed for sewing sleeves or anything narrow.

✳ **Bobbin** Metal or plastic spool that supplies the bottom (bobbin) thread.

✳ **Bobbin case** A cuplike case that holds the bobbin in place.

✳ **Bobbin winder** Transfers thread from a spool onto an empty bobbin, filling it quickly and evenly.

✳ **Bobbin-winding tension disk** This round metal disk is threaded to control the flow of the thread off the spool and onto the empty bobbin.

✳ **Flywheel** The big, round dial on the right end of your machine. Always turn it counterclockwise—or toward you—to move the needle up and down by hand. (Forcing it in the opposite direction can damage the machine.)

✳ **Foot pedal** Like the gas pedal of a car, the harder you press on it, the faster the machine will go (or sew).

✳ **Needle clamp and screw** Holds the needle in place with a small screw. You loosen this screw to release and replace a needle. Use the right-size needle for your fabric and replace it often.

✳ **Presser foot** Removable L-shaped part that presses down on the fabric, keeping it in place while you sew. There are many specialized feet for special sewing tasks. For the projects in this book, you'll only need an all-purpose zipper, invisible zipper, and buttonhole feet.

✳ **Presser foot lever** Raises and lowers the foot, and also engages the tension disks. Keep it down when sewing; lift it up when you're done.

✳ **Reverse stitch lever** Tells the machine to run backward, feeding the fabric toward you. You need this function to backstitch at the start and end of each seam in lieu of a knot.

✳ **Shuttle race** Located below the throat plate, where you insert the bobbin and bobbin case, and where the top thread comes down to catch the bobbin thread to form each lockstitch.

✳ **Shuttle race cover** Flap door that protects the bobbin thread area.

✳ **Stitch-length dial** Dial for setting and adjusting stitch length. The shorter the stitch, the stronger it holds (but is harder to undo if you make a mistake). For most projects, stitch length of 2mm to 3mm is fine.

✳ **Stitch selector** Dial for selecting and setting your stitch pattern (scallop, zigzag, etc.). New machines often have dozens of stitch patterns, which are fun, but you can get by with just a few.

✳ **Take-up lever** Small, metal arm that carries the top thread, pulling the right amount for each stitch during sewing.

✳ **Thread tension dial** Adjusts the thread tension disks, which control how much thread feeds down to the needle. The tension setting depends on the type and weight of fabric you're sewing. Heavier fabric requires more tension, but a setting of 3 to 5 works for most materials.

✳ **Throat plate** Horizontal metal plate with an opening for the needle to pass through. Fabric travels over this plate during sewing. It has engraved markings ⅛ inch apart—the standard unit of measurement in sewing—that serve as seam allowance guides.

Presser foot lever raises (left) and lowers (right) the presser foot.

presser foot Lever

25

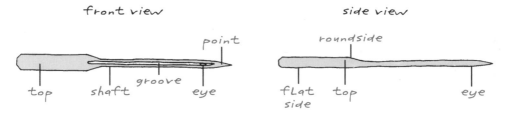

front view

point

top   shaft   groove   eye

side view

roundside

flat   top   eye
side

your leading lady: the needle

Take a moment to get to know the star of all the action. Familiar, yet a bit exotic, a sewing machine needle differs from a hand-sewing needle in that its eye is at the bottom, not the top. Look closer, and you'll see that it has one flat side and one rounded side. This helps you position the needle correctly in the needle clamp with the flat side against the flat side of the hole. (See page 44 for instructions on replacing a needle.)

Ranging from size 9 (fine) to 18 (heavy), your needle needs to match the weight and type of fabric you're sewing, or the machine won't stitch well. Sizes 11 and 14 are good for general sewing. An all-purpose, universal point will work just fine for the projects in this book. There are also special needles for knits, sheer fabrics, leather, and heavy-duty denim. Treat your machine needle with respect. Don't let it hit pins and don't use it for too long (it could bend or break). Keep replacements on hand and change needles when the stitches start to look less-than-fresh. Most new machines come with a starter pack. If you need to stock up, assortment packs cost less than $5.

needle tip You can tell if a needle is bent by laying it on a table with the flat side down. If it isn't flush, it's time for a new one.

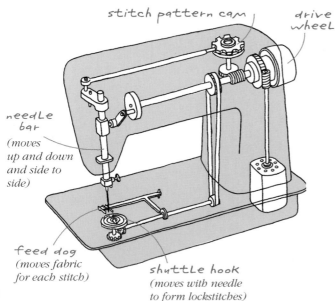

stitch pattern cam

drive wheel

needle bar
(moves up and down and side to side)

feed dog
(moves fabric for each stitch)

shuttle hook
(moves with needle to form lockstitches)

Parts at Play

A sewing machine is just that—a machine that sews. Mechanical parts like cams, belts, cranks, and gears are synchronized and driven by a motor that is controlled by a foot pedal, much like a car. In the diagram, left, all the marked components get into the action every time you sew. You turn them on or off, lift them up or down. Here's what's happening inside and out when you press the pedal to the metal.

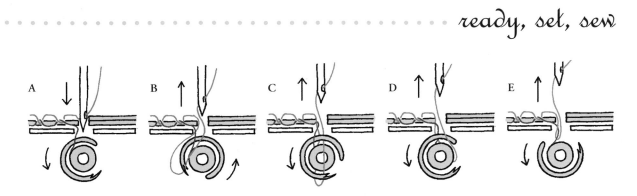

Fabric lies on top of a flat piece of metal—the *throat plate*—and the *presser foot* holds the fabric in place. At the start of each stitch, the needle—threaded with *top thread*—pierces the fabric and pokes down into the bobbin thread area, or *shuttle race* (A). The top thread forms a loop for the shuttle hook to catch (B) and then carries it under the *bobbin case* (C). As the loop slides off the hook, it goes around the *bobbin thread* (D). When the needle rises up, both top and bobbin threads are pulled up and set into the fabric as a *lockstitch* (E)—so called because the threads "lock" together in the hole that the needle has pierced.

How your machine makes a stitch, step by step.

watch it work It's one thing to read about how a sewing machine works; it's another thing to see it for yourself. When you are raising the bobbin thread, leave the shuttle race door open and watch the top thread come down, wrap around the bobbin case, and catch the bobbin thread. For an even better view, use two different colors for the bobbin and top thread. Make a few stitches by hand-turning the flywheel and pulling on the thread ends to feed them through the machine. You'll notice that the machine repeats the same loop-and-catch action over and over just like in the illustration above. It's pretty amazing!

know your manual, know your machine

Every machine has the same basic parts, but sometimes the parts (like the settings and dials) live in different locations and threading the machine may involve some unexpected turns. Most machines thread from right to left, but there's the occasional left-to-righty. You can clear up any confusion by reading your handy sewing machine manual in tandem with this chapter. It's customized for your machine, so consider it your bible on the parts, quirks, and perks of your particular model. Missing your manual? Go online to the manufacturer's website (see page 237) and look for manuals listed by make and model. If the manufacturer can't help you, try eBay. The last time I searched under "sewing machine manual," I found over 100 items. Surely, yours is among them.

just checking

Before moving on to the next section, make sure you know your parts. Look at your sewing machine, and with no book or manual, follow the top and bobbin thread along their paths and name every part they touch. Look at the dials, name their functions and what their settings mean. Don't cheat. Passing this test is required before you can move on to chapter 3, so start cramming!

birth of the sewing machine

For centuries, people tried to figure out how to sew automatically or mechanically. Can you blame them when sewing a shirt by hand took about fourteen hours?

In 1790, a British inventor built a machine for sewing leather and canvas. It pierced the material with an awl-like needle and made a chain stitch—a single thread catching one loop inside the next, repeating itself. But he just made a model or two.

In 1830, a Frenchman got a patent for a machine with a crochet hook–type needle that also sewed a chain stitch. He set up a workshop to make French army uniforms, but Parisian tailors attacked! ("Monsieur, stand down, or I shall hem you to death!") The tailors wanted to protect their trade, so they burned all the sewing machines (they were wooden), as well as his workshop.

Howe and his invention.

The first man to patent the type of sewing machine we use today was Elias Howe. Some historians argue that Howe's wife, Elizabeth Ames Howe, invented the machine and put the patent in his name. She would have had the motivation, since she was a seamstress and would have welcomed greater speed for greater profit. The Howe machine had top and bottom threads that linked together to form stitches. A breakthrough! To showcase this miracle, Howe set up a John Henry–type contest between his machine and five ladies sewing by hand in a Massachusetts public hall in 1845. The machine trounced the seamstresses, sewing five seams before they could sew one.

But it was German mechanic and cabinetmaker Isaac Singer who made the two-thread sewing machine a hit. Sure, he violated Howe's patent (and later paid up), but he added the foot pedal and about twenty other improvements. In the 1860s, Singer took his machines on the road and demonstrated them to groups of ladies (many of whom he seduced after the show—sewing groupies!). Singer let the housewives take a machine home and pay over time, making him a pioneer of the credit plan as well. Even though today's Singers (and Kenmores, Janomes, and Husqvarna-Vikings) have computer chips and forty-seven stitch options, the basic machine has remained the same for the last 150 years.

Early Singer machine and ad.

hands-on practice **two**

Like driving, you can operate a sewing machine pretty easily—maybe even the first time out. But you need practice, practice, practice to get comfortable. Hands-on time with your machine is crucial. Remember, you had to drive with your learner's permit for a while before you merged onto a six-lane freeway, right? Well, you have to do some time at the sewing table before you make your first project. Fortunately, much of the sewing process is just repetition. You thread the machine and wind the bobbin so many times that it becomes second nature, like looking in your rearview mirror or shifting gears when you drive. The first few seams you sew might not be super-neat or straight, but you'll get better at it quickly—and no one gets hurt.

make it no-thread stitching on paper

This is how they sewed the emperor's new clothes—on a machine with no thread. It's a good idea. No worries about tangles or tension. Although "stitching" on paper is different than sewing fabric on a threaded machine, you still get a feel for the speed of things, can practice your straight seams, and can get used to the routine of raising and lowering the presser foot and needle. Find a piece of lined notebook or legal paper. Select the straight stitch and a stitch length of 2.5mm to 3mm.

1. Place the paper under the needle about ½ inch down from the top edge.

2. Turn the flywheel toward you so the needle moves down and pierces the paper.

3. Drop the presser foot lever.

4. Step lightly on the foot pedal and the machine will start stitching forward; hold down the reverse lever to backstitch for a few inches.

5. Repeat until you feel comfortable and are able to sew right on top of a line (straight) in both directions.

Practice stitching on the straight and narrow.

> **paper tip** Down the road, try stitching on rice paper or cardstock with colorful thread. You can make greeting cards, place cards, invitations, and gift tags. Even just a zigzagged border amps up the style. Or write a love letter and stitch a big pink heart right over the text. (See pages 209–211 for Sew Very Pretty Cards.)

Winding Up for Real Action

Before you can sew a stitch, you need to thread your machine. And before you can thread your machine, you need to fill the bobbin. Here's how to take your spool of top thread and create another smaller spool of matching thread that works from below:

A

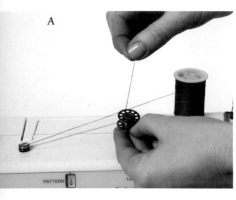

B

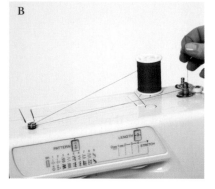

C

1. Put a spool of thread on the spool pin and draw the thread from the back and then around the bobbin thread guide (a small metal tension disk, used only for bobbin winding). Make sure to really get the thread snugly into the slot (it's a bit like flossing your teeth). Otherwise, the tension will be off and the bobbin won't fill evenly.

2. Take the empty bobbin (it's like a doughnut) and pick a small hole near the bobbin center. Poke the thread through this hole from underneath, so the thread comes out the top, as shown (A).

3. Place the bobbin on the bobbin winder, as shown (B). Push the bobbin winder to the right

against the bobbin stop. This is a crucial step. By moving the winder over, you're telling the machine to disengage the clutch from sewing mode. Hold the thread end tightly and press on the foot pedal. **Note:** If the machine starts to sew, you need to manually disengage the clutch to stop the needle from moving. Some models require this extra step. Consult your manual.

4. Allow the bobbin to spin around for a few seconds, stop to cut the extra thread at the top away (C), and continue pressing the foot pedal until the machine stops winding. It will stop when the bobbin is full.

5. Cut the thread, push the bobbin winder back to the left, and pull the bobbin off. Re-engage the clutch, if necessary.

bobbin tip I like to have six bobbins on hand loaded with my favorite thread colors. Spares are cheap, either from fabric stores or directly from the manufacturer. (Bring a bobbin with you to the store so you get the right kind.) Keep your backup bobbins in a safe little case so they don't unwind or tangle. I use an organizer especially created for this job.

load the bobbin

You've wound a bobbin, now put it in its place.

A
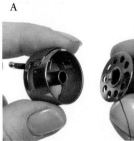

B
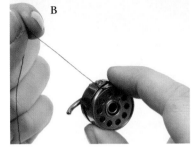

C

1. Remove the extension arm, open the shuttle race cover (the flap), and pull out the bobbin case.

2. Hold the bobbin case in your left hand between your thumb and index finger with the "arm" of the case pointing toward you, as shown (A). Hold the loaded bobbin in your right hand with the thread winding away from you, then drop the bobbin into the case.

3. Draw the thread through the diagonal cut in the bobbin case so the end comes out the window (B). On most bobbin cases, you can feel the thread click into place. Place the thread end so it's hanging away from you, to the left of the arm.

4. Lift up the hinged lever on the case. This locks the bobbin in place. (Let go, and the bobbin will fall out, which you'll learn right away!)

5. Place the bobbin and case back in the shuttle race by lining up the arm with the notch of the same shape and size (C). Push in and the bobbin case will lock into place. **Note:** If the bobbin case feels loose and jiggly, take it out and repeat all the steps.

6. Shut the shuttle race cover.

---

variation DROP-IN BOBBIN

If your machine has a drop-in bobbin, say a little prayer of thanks to the sewing gods, because your life will be easier. Drop-in bobbins lie flat and horizontal just under the throat plate of the machine and do not require a bobbin case. (Hooray!) To load this type of bobbin:

1. Slide back the metal plate or remove the plastic cover.

2. Hold the bobbin with the thread hanging straight down (A), so it looks like the letter *P*.

3. Drop the bobbin into the empty cylinder (as if you were dropping a doughnut on a plate). Tuck the thread under the cut or groove of the tension spring by pulling the thread to the left (B). (Make sure the thread is coming off the bobbin in a clockwise direction.)

A

B

S·E·W

Thread the Machine

Halfway done—woo-hoo!—but the bobbin thread needs a top thread to hook up with. Your machine's threading path might be a little different, so follow along with your manual.

1. Turn the flywheel to see where the take-up lever is. (It bobs up and down when you turn the wheel.) Keep turning until the take-up lever is at the top, which puts the needle in its highest position.

2. Lift the presser foot. (Now the tension disks are off, and the machine is ready for easy threading.)

3. Put a spool of thread on the pin so the thread draws from behind and comes out to the left. Lead the thread through (or around) the upper thread guide, which helps the thread turn the corner so it's running vertically.

4. Pull down (thread running parallel to the needle), go around the tension dial, and draw the thread back up in a U-turn toward the take-up lever.

5. Wrap the thread around the take-up lever from right to left (it will automatically go through the big eye, but check that it's really in there), and back down through the same slot you just came up.

6. Pull the thread through any guides or pins leading down toward the needle.

7. Thread the needle, from front to back (A). If it's difficult, cut the thread cleanly with sharp scissors and dampen the tip with your tongue.

8. Pull the thread into the cut of the presser foot and to the back, leaving a 10-inch tail. (Double-check your work by consulting your manual.)

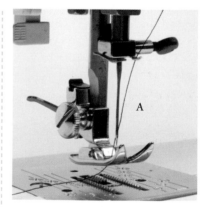

Thread goes through eye from front to back.

threading tip Many machines have marked-on numbers to guide you on the threading path. If yours doesn't, grab some masking tape and a felt-tip pen, and mark your own arrows and/or numbers.

bring up the bobbin thread

The final step is catching the bobbin thread and drawing it up through the hole in the throat plate. It's a little like going fishing.

A

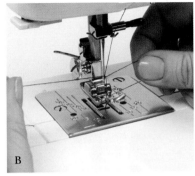

B

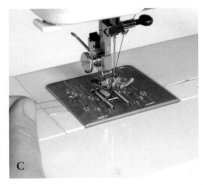

C

1. Hold the top thread tail with your left hand and turn the flywheel toward you one full rotation with your right hand, so the needle goes down into the shuttle race and then back up again to its highest position.

2. Take the top thread and pull it upward toward the ceiling. The bobbin thread (which

is caught) should follow up through the needle hole and form a loop as shown (A). (On some machines, you may have to jiggle the flywheel a bit.)

3. Pinch the loop in your fingers and pull it until the whole bobbin thread tail comes up through the needle hole (B).

4. Pull to make sure both threads are flowing freely and your machine is threaded properly (C). Then pull the threads to the back of the machine.

5. Cut both threads, leaving at least 10 inches. (This way the needle won't unthread when you start stitching.)

---

bobbin DOs and DON'Ts

DO use the same type and weight thread in the bobbin that you use on top.

DO make sure the bobbin is in good shape and the right size for your machine.

DON'T wind thread on top of a bobbin that has thread on it already. Leftovers could cause problems.

DON'T sew with a warped or cracked bobbin; the machine won't like it.

DON'T overfill the bobbin. Most machines stop winding when the bobbin is full. If yours doesn't, make sure you stop soon enough. The bobbin should fit into the case without being snug.

right way

wrong way

Sit in the Driver's Seat

Make sure you are comfortable. Correct posture improves your work and gives you a sense of control. So, sit squarely in front of your machine with both feet on the floor. Rather than leaning back, lean your upper body slightly forward. Place your left hand lightly on the material to guide it as it moves toward the back of the machine. You don't need to push the fabric; the feed dogs do this for you. Your right hand should be a few inches in front of the needle to steer the fabric and to keep the edge lined up with the seam allowance guide. The bulk of the work always hangs to the left of the machine, where there's room. Fabric on the right will block your seam allowance guide and squash up against the body of the sewing machine. That's no good.

Always assume the proper position.

> **rocking out** I've always wanted to start a rock band of seamstresses. I'd call us The Feed Dogs.

pinning for machine sewing

You'll quickly find that you spend more time preparing fabric pieces than actually sewing at the machine (the way carpenters spend more time planning, measuring, and sawing than actually nailing). This is normal. And the better you get at prepping things, the better your results. So practice your pinning with some fabric scraps.

1. Cut two pieces of fabric the same size and shape.

2. Place pieces on top of each other—with the right sides facing—and align the top, bottom, and sides.

3. Pin along one side, at right angles to the edge. Remember that the bulk of your work will be on the left side as you sew along the right edge, so make sure your pins will end up on top, not underneath. There's no exact rule for distance between pins, but about 2 inches apart is a good average. (Slippery fabrics like silk require more pins, and some stiffer fabrics may require less.) Place the heads of the pins near the edge of the material so you can easily grab them before the needle reaches them, and so the points won't stick you.

4. When you sew, remove each pin as soon as the front of the presser foot gets close to it. No matter how tempting it seems, don't sew over the pins in your fabric. You can get lucky and miss them, but at some point, you will hit a pin and end up breaking a needle. Start this good habit and spare your machine some trouble.

Start Your Engines: stitching your first seam

Almost everything you sew is assembled with seams. The most common is the straight seam, which is just one long line of stitches with a little backstitching at the beginning and end. Sound easy? It is. Here's how to make one:

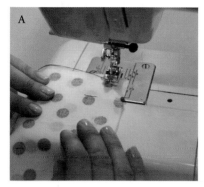
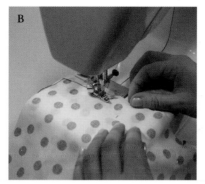
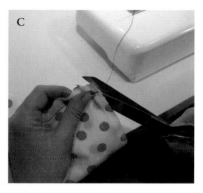

1. Set your stitch length (at the standard 2mm to 3mm) and select the straight stitch (that's probably where it's set already).

2. Raise the presser foot and place fabric under it, lining up the right edge of fabric with the ⅝-inch seam guide etched on the throat plate. This will create a ⅝-inch seam allowance (the distance between the raw edge and the stitching).

3. Turn the flywheel toward you until the needle goes into the fabric.

4. Drop the presser foot and you're ready to go (A). This is the most important thing to remember. If the presser foot isn't down, you could botch up the works.

5. Stitch forward three to four stitches (about ½-inch) by applying light pressure to the foot pedal. Then push the reverse lever and backstitch to the top edge of the fabric to secure the seam. (This is what machine sewers do instead of knotting the thread.) Release the reverse lever.

6. Press the foot pedal and sew straight ahead at an even and controlled pace, taking out the pins as you go (B). (Put those babies right into your pincushion! Pins lying on a table soon become pins on the floor.)

7. Backstitch again for about four stitches to secure the seam when you reach the far end of the fabric. Release the reverse lever.

8. Turn the flywheel toward you to raise the take-up lever and needle to the highest position. Lift the presser foot.

9. Pull the fabric out to the left, leaving a 10-inch thread tail, and clip the thread close to the fabric so it's completely trimmed away (C).

10. Use a warm steam iron to press open the seam allowance. Flip your work over and press the outside as well. (See pages 84–86 for more on finishing seams.)

how'd you do?

If that's your first seam ever, then welcome to the wonderful world of sewing. You're officially a sewing citizen. Now check your work. Does your seam look straight? Are the stitches even? Do they lie flat? Did the stitching start right at the top and finish at the bottom? How did you feel when you were doing it? Were you relaxed or nervous? Were your neck and shoulders tense or at ease? Practice some more stitching while keeping the fabric edge aligned with the seam guide. Sew slowly. Sew faster. Sew as many seams as it takes for you to feel as though you and your machine are a working team.

Turning a Corner: how to pivot

To stitch corners or curves, you will need to pivot the fabric. Pivoting allows you to stitch all four sides of a pillow cover, for example, with one continuous seam, rather than stitching them one at a time. This technique is a real timesaver because you don't have to keep taking the fabric off the machine, nor do you have to backstitch at each corner. Pivoting also makes stitching stronger because there are no breaks in the thread. Here's what to do:

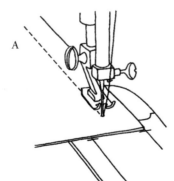

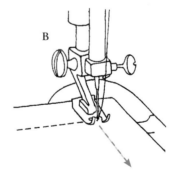

1. Repeat seam-stitching steps 1 through 6 (on page 35) on one side of your project or practice sample. But, stop at ⅝ inch from the bottom edge of the fabric.

2. Check to see if the needle is in the fabric. If it is not, turn the flywheel forward (toward you) until the needle is securely in the fabric as shown (A).

3. Lift up the presser foot and pivot the fabric one-quarter turn to the right. Again, the edge of the fabric should line up with the ⅝ inch mark on the seam guide.

4. Lower the presser foot (B) (don't forget!) and sew straight ahead until you reach the next corner. Pivot and repeat steps 1 through 3.

rip it
RIP IT REAL GOOD!

Everyone who sews has to rip out stitches sooner or later. You might as well do it right. A seam ripper allows you a second chance, and it's pretty fun to use. All that pent-up frustration—poof—gone! You can tear out seams as long as the fabric holds up. Although there's more than one way to use a seam ripper, the best—and safest—way is to slip the point under a stitch and cut the thread against the sharp edge. Continue to cut every two to three stitches, turn the fabric over, and pull the reverse thread out. Remove any loose threads and toss them. You can run the seam ripper between seams, but I don't recommend it because it's super-easy to cut a hole or tear in the fabric and ruin your project. After ripping out stitches, use a steam iron to close needle holes and restore the fabric back to its prestitched state.

wrong way

right way

Sewing a Curve

You need to be able to sew curved seams in your clothing so it fits the curves of your body. Let's practice. Draw an S-curve with a chalk marker on scrap fabric. Now, see if you can follow it on the machine, using what you've just learned about pivoting. Insert the fabric, lining up the presser foot with the drawn line, and stitch slowly and carefully. On gentle curves, simply turn the fabric while stitching. On sharper curves, stop the machine with the needle down, raise the foot, and adjust the line of the fabric, just as you did in step 3 when you were pivoting.

Don't be scared. Loosen up, have fun, and soon you'll be sewing in circles! And your circles and curves will come in handy when you're embellishing projects with machine embroidery.

curve tip Pssst! You'll get much better results if you move the needle up and down manually with the flywheel when things get tricky. It gives you more control than if you use the foot pedal alone.

three setting, adjusting, and maintaining

settings tip The more you stick to the middle of the road in the beginning—with easy fabrics and easy projects—the less you'll need to fiddle with the machine settings. In fact, you might not have to make any changes at all.

Whenever a new machine comes home with me, the first thing I do is play with the stitch patterns. I can't help it. So I wouldn't be surprised if you've tried a few already. (If so, nice initiative!) Consult your manual to learn how to select the different stitches on your machine. There might be a dial, button, or lever—and you may have to switch the presser foot for certain stitches.

Note: Keep the needle up and out of the fabric when selecting a new pattern.

Every stitch pattern has a special use; some make sewing jobs easier, while others are purely decorative. For right now, experiment with all of your different stitches on a piece of scrap fabric. Do at least one row of stitching using each pattern and learn to tell them apart. Don't worry about following a seam allowance, just play with the patterns in a purely artistic way. Imagine how they'd look on hems, pockets, or pillowcases. Try different thread colors and stitch lengths. A boring straight stitch can have impact in a contrasting color.

Meet the Stitches

Your manual will list all of the stitches your machine can sew. (Those manuals love to brag about their stitches.) Here are the most common stitch patterns:

✴ **Straight**
Use: Seams, topstitching
Note: A little contrasting color goes a long way in a straight stitch. Try making two or three parallel lines of straight stitch very close together.

✴ **Zigzag**
Use: Edging, machine appliqué, decoration
Note: I also like to use zigzag for machine hems. It looks pretty, and the side-to-side action keeps the fold nicely in place.

✴ **Overlocking**
Use: No-fray seam finishing
Note: Use close to the raw edges of a seam and then finish by cutting the extra fabric away. This is the same stitch pattern created by a serger (see page 20).

✴ **Satin**
Use: Buttonholes, machine appliqué, monograms
Note: This is a zigzag stitch set almost at zero stitch length (zigzags densely together). Satin stitch can cause gathering on a light-

weight fabric if it's too wide, so do a test on a swatch first.

✴ **Feather**
Use: Attaching insets or pieces of lace to other fabric
Note: Feather stitch can also connect two pieces of material that butt up against each other. Just feather stitch down the middle (where they touch) and the two become one. You can also do this with a wide zigzag stitch.

✴ **Honeycomb**
Use: Smocking, gathering, attaching elastic

Note: One of my all-time favorite stitches, the honeycomb is used these days in heirloom sewing. Though it has a functional purpose, it's also used as decoration for an old-timey vibe.

✴ **Blind hem**
Use: Creating a hem whose stitching is invisible from the outside
Note: Some machines come with a blind hem foot. See if you have one; it will make this stitch easier to sew.

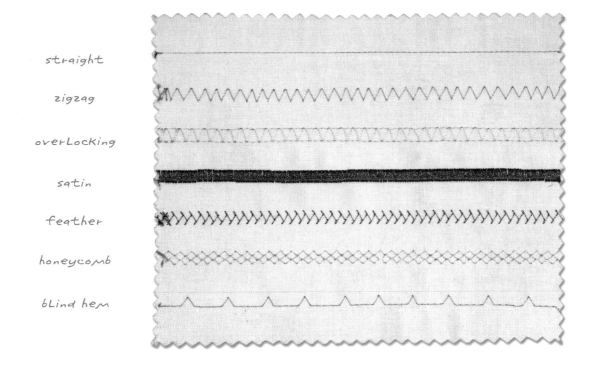

straight

zigzag

overlocking

satin

feather

honeycomb

blind hem

make it **stitch-sampler tea towel**

materials:

¾ yard cotton or linen at least 44 inches wide (for two towels)
Thread in a contrasting color

Using a ruler and disappearing marker or chalk, draw a rectangle 22 × 28 inches. Carefully measure and mark the length along the straight edge of the *selvage,* so the finished tea towel will be *on grain* (see page 49). Starting with the long sides, turn up the seam allowance by 1 inch, wrong sides together. Press. Tuck the raw edge under by half and press again. Repeat this step on the short ends. Pin as pressed, then edgestitch ⅛ inch on the wrong side of the fabric around all four sides near the folded edge of the hem, pivoting at the corners. Now comes the fun part: your own private stitching party! Try every pattern on your machine, rethreading it in all your favorite colors—this is really good practice—along the edges or free-form it on the front of the towel. Think of the fabric as your canvas, taking note of the purtiest stitching for future reference.

Making Adjustments

Your machine may sew automatically, but it's not automatically set to sew every kind of fabric and every type of project. A machine can't tell silk from denim or a slip from a slipcover. It relies on you to use the right needle and thread, to select the length and kind of stitch you'd like, and to set the appropriate tension. Knowing how and when to make these adjustments is key to learning how to use a machine.

stitch-length guide

The basic rule to remember is that shorter stitches are stronger, they use more thread, and they are harder to pull out if you want to undo anything. Longer stitches sew faster and are easier to take out, but they aren't as strong. So pick your stitch length based on your sewing goals. For, say, handles on a tote bag, you want super-sturdy seams—so you'd set a short stitch length. If you can't decide whether you want the handles on the outside or the inside of the bag, you might first use a long, loose (basting) stitch to attach the handles temporarily before committing to a shorter—and therefore more permanent—stitch.

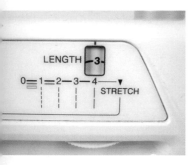

For an average stitch, set the stitch length to 2.5 or 3mm.

Stitch lengths are measured either in millimeters (mm) or stitches per inch (spi). Metric-based models have settings from 0 to 4, with higher-end models going up to 6. The higher the number, the longer the stitch. Machines using stitches per inch are just the opposite: The higher the number, the smaller (and finer) the stitching. Here are further guidelines on various stitch lengths and when to use them:

✳ **Zero stitch length**
Zero stitch length always sounds to me like something impossible and invisible, but it just means that the fabric doesn't move when set on "0," which allows the stitches to build right on top of each other in the same spot. Use zero stitch length when sewing on buttons.

✳ **Short stitches (1mm to 2mm or 60 to 13 spi)**
Use these when sewing lightweight fabric or wherever you want strong seams. Short stitches are the most durable and should be permanent.

✳ **Average length stitches (2.5mm to 3mm or 15 to 10 spi)**
These are good for sewing just about everything. Stitches this length are tough enough to stay put, and long enough so you can tear them out without wrecking the fabric.

✳ **Long stitches (4mm to 6mm or 6 to 4 spi)**
Because they are easy to remove, long stitches are useful for gathering, basting, and other temporary work. Decorative techniques like topstitching often require longer-stitch settings.

troubleshooting
DON'T SWEAT IT

The bad news: You are going to hit bumps in the sewing road. The good news: They are familiar, common, well-traveled bumps, and I can get you past them. So mark this page (heck, laminate it and hang it in your studio). Problems for beginners usually come from learning to use a sewing machine versus actual sewing machine dysfunction. That's also good news, because it means your machine's not broken! Here's your AAA guide to common mechanical difficulties.

Problem: You just wound a bobbin, and now the machine won't sew.

Solution: Re-engage the handwheel. If that doesn't work, check to see if the plug has fallen out of the back of the machine, and if it's turned on.

Problem: A mass of tangled thread has formed on the underside of the fabric, and the machine won't feed.

Solution: Did you remember to sew with the presser foot down? If yes, check to see if the thread has come out of the take-up lever. Then rethread.

Problem: The needle keeps unthreading.

Solution: Start sewing with the take-up lever at the highest position and give yourself plenty of extra thread, at least 10 inches.

Problem: The machine won't stitch properly and/or the thread keeps breaking.

Solution: Pull on the thread ends to make sure it's coming off the spool and the bobbin. If it's stuck, rethread the entire machine. As a last resort, change the needle.

Problem: The presser foot keeps falling off.

Solution: Check to see if you're inadvertently hitting the latch when you go to move the presser foot lever. If your machine has a foot that's attached with a screw instead, tighten it in place.

conquering tension

Tension is annoying in life but necessary in sewing. Understanding how it works will make you and your stitches much less uptight. In sewing, tension means how much the machine squeezes the thread as it passes through the machine.

The tension dial on your machine controls the squeeze on the top thread. Too much tension and the top thread feeds too slowly, making stitches tight and puckered. Too little squeeze and the top thread feeds too fast, making the stitches loose and weak. In the ideal stitch, both top and bottom threads feed equally into the fabric and link up smack in the middle of the fabric layers. Many new machines automatically adjust tension and pressure to suit the fabric, while older machines or those in need of a tune-up are more likely to cause a tension headache.

The number-one rule for adjusting the thread tension on your machine: If it ain't broke, don't fix it! The more adjustments you make, the greater the risk of throwing the machine—and the stitches it makes—quite literally for a loop.

tension tip Before you start a new project or work with a new fabric, test the thread tension. Take a scrap from the fabric you'll be using, fold it in half, and—after selecting the stitch length and any other settings you plan to use—sew across the edge as you would for a seam. Adjust tension, if necessary.

tension tip *Make sure the presser foot is down when adjusting the dial, so the tension disks will register the change.*

Most sewing works fine with a medium tension setting of 3 to 5. In fact, it's quite possible that you'll never move outside of this range. If you notice poor stitch quality (see below), first check to see if you're using the wrong needle for your fabric or a dull one and replace the needle. If the stitching is still off (the stitches are loose or the fabric puckers), then it means one of the threads is pulling harder than the other, and you need to adjust the tension dial, which is marked with numbers from 0 to 9. (The higher the number, the greater the tension—or squeeze—on the top thread.) Here's how to diagnose and adjust tension:

too tight

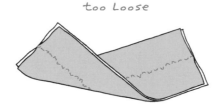
too loose

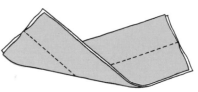
both even

✳ **Too much tension**
Links float toward the top of the fabric when there is too much pressure on the top thread. Set the tension control to a lesser number.

✳ **Too little tension**
Links move toward the bottom of the fabric when the top thread is too loose. Set the tension control to a greater number.

✳ **Correct tension**
When the tension is just right, the link between the upper and lower threads meets halfway between the fabric layers. Perfecto!

Zen and the Art of Sewing Machine Maintenance

Sewing machine problems—like car problems—often arise from poor maintenance or simple neglect. Take good care of your machine, and it will be good to you. Treat it poorly, and say hello to Breakdown City, USA. So, just as you check your car's tires and change the oil, you need to pamper and putter with your sewing machine. Show your machine you really care by doing the following:

keep it under cover

Nasty debris like lint, dust, and hair all find their way into machines and clog up the works. So keep your machine either in a hard carrying case or under a fabric cover—even when you are in the middle of a project and just walking away for the night. In a pinch, drape an old towel or small tablecloth over it. Coverage is coverage.

W·W·M·D?

I have a little confession to make, a small window into my sewing psyche. When I work, I imagine that the old pre–Camp Cupcake Martha ("mean" Martha) is right there with me, looking over my shoulder. I've even adopted a little mantra for this motivational mind game: WWMD? or What Would Martha Do?

The answer to this question remains the same: Martha would be neat, tidy, and quite the taskmaster. When you work, pretend she's with you, too, and she means business! Keep a trash bin near your machine and your ironing board (she always has one right at her knee when sewing on TV), and throw away threads as soon as you trim them. Put pins right into a pincushion as you remove them from fabric. Try to clean as you go, as much as possible. Then, always spend a few minutes at the end of a sewing session straightening up. You'll thank Martha as you sit down to a pleasant scene when you return for more sewing. Last, resist the urge to put the pedal to the metal. Sewing well takes time, as Martha knows, and if you pace yourself, you'll avoid annoying redos and sloppy results.

make it WWMD? (What Would Martha Do?) inspiration banner

Here are some directions to make a simple cross-stitch Martha-inspired banner to hang over your sewing machine. It's a good thing.

Materials
fabric 10-count Aida cloth (usually in packages of 12-inch x 18-inch pieces), **embroidery thread** (contrasting color), **pattern** printed on the page

Tools
Embroidery needle, frame (optional)

Instructions
Thread a needle with two strands of embroidery thread and a Rupp-alicious knot (see page 227). To center, turn cloth to wrong side and measure and mark 6¼ inches down from the top and 6½ inches over from left-hand edge. Start here by bringing the needle through from the back. Then, following the grid of the pattern (below), stitch an X on the fabric grid wherever you see one in a box here. Make cross stitches one at a time or work horizontally from left to right and then from right to left, crossing the stitches on your way back. Stitch each letter separately and secure the thread by tying a simple knot. It's super-simple and can be completed in a couple of hours while watching TV, traveling, or sitting in your favorite café. When you finish the lettering, measure and cut the cloth down to your desired dimensions, making sure that your motto is centered. Frame it.

Note: What makes this pattern easy is that the Aida cloth has a grid that's easy to follow.

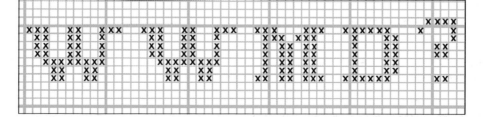

S·E·W

swap your needles often

When you sew on a machine, the needle travels through the fabric thousands of times per minute. Sew for several hours, and the needle gets worn down. Replace needles on a regular basis—say, each time you finish a project, or after you've been sewing for about eight hours. Here's how:

1. Turn the machine off and raise the needle to the highest position by turning the flywheel toward you.

2. Drop the presser foot and loosen the needle clamp screw by turning it toward you.

3. Pull out the old needle and throw it away.

4. Insert the new needle into the needle clamp with the flat side facing away from you.

5. Tighten the screw.

6. Rotate the flywheel to double-check that the needle is properly installed. If the point touches the throat plate, take the needle out and try again.

make it **the cover-up**

Make a simple machine cozy to keep your machine clean and dust-free. Keeping your machine covered will help it last longer. And a homemade cover is much nicer to look at than a plastic case. See pages 205–207 for instructions for making this Sewing Machine Cozy.

make a clean sweep

Clean your machine on a regular basis. First, unplug the machine. Wipe it down with a soft rag, such as a cut-up T-shirt, and brush out any lingering dust with the small brush that (hopefully) came with your machine (if you don't have a brush, buy a ¼-inch paintbrush). Polish the take-up lever, thread guides, and presser foot with a clean piece of cheesecloth. Compressed air—the same kind used to clean a computer keyboard—is great for dusting and de-linting hard-to-reach spots. Pay particular attention to the area around the needle, throat plate, and shuttle race, where dust, thread, and crud tend to collect.

add oil

Just like a car engine, a sewing machine motor needs oil to keep its parts running freely and to reduce friction and wear. Your manual tells you how often, how much, and where to oil your machine. After you've added oil (your machine should come with a small vial—like some magical Harry Potter–esque potion), run a scrap piece of absorbent fabric through the machine to soak up any excess. Some machines are self-lubricating, so it's really important that you find out what your machine needs. Ask the manufacturer or a sewing machine mechanic for guidance if you're unsure.

get a tune-up

Take your sewing machine to a professional mechanic for a yearly tune-up. (I have mine worked on every spring.) It's a good idea to bring in a used or vintage machine unless you know for a fact it's been recently serviced. When my mom gave me her machine, it had spent a few years in a garage near the beach. Not good. I took it to the mechanic, who opened it up and found wet rust galore. If I hadn't taken it in, the water would have evaporated and forever seized the motor. When I got the machine home, it sewed like a dream!

Maintain Yourself, Too— Take a Break!

Don't forget to take care of your own machinery— your neck, your back, and your eyes. Taking a time-out from machine sewing keeps you sane and helps your work. As with hand-sewing (or any fun, crafty project), it's pretty easy to get borderline obsessive and feel driven to finish at any cost. (Just ask Martha!) Spend twelve grueling hours hunched over a machine, and you literally might not be able to stand up straight the next day. If you catch yourself becoming boss and employee in your own personal sweatshop, stop. Go on strike. Do a few stretches— neck rolls, shoulder rolls, and forward bends where you just hang loose. Make some tea. Walk to the park. Look out the window. Call a friend. I promise the unfinished cushion cover or future tote bag will still be there when you return. Otherwise, you're sure to get tired, and when you're tired, you're so much more likely to make silly mistakes. Suffering for your work is one thing. Having your work suffer is another.

Pop Quiz

It's the moment of truth

Sharpen a No. 2 pencil and put away your manual. You must answer each question before moving on to the next chapter. (And no cheating!)

1. What type of stitch do the top thread and bobbin thread form?

2. What part on a sewing machine holds the fabric in place?
   a. Tension control   **c.** Presser foot
   b. Shuttle race   **d.** Spindle

3. When threading, does the thread go into the take-up lever or tension disks first?

4. True or false? Any sewing machine needle can sew on any fabric.

5. Which direction do you turn the flywheel?

6. What is the most common stitch length?

7. If the quality of the stitches on your machine deteriorates, what should you do first?
   a. Call 9-1-1   **c.** Start playing with the
   b. Switch to a different   tension control
      stitch pattern   **d.** Change the needle

8. What should you study before sewing on your machine?

9. What do you use to line up the raw edge of fabric while sewing?
   a. Seam guide   **c.** Seam allowance
   b. Edge of presser foot **d.** Tailor's chalk

10. True or false? A machine only needs to be serviced when it's not sewing well.

See page 241 for answers.

CHAPTER 3 *material matters*

*I*f a sewing pattern is like a recipe, then fabric is the main ingredient. You know how food fanatics—a.k.a. foodies—love to wax poetic about heirloom tomatoes, deep-sea scallops, and hand-rolled gnocchi? Well, I'm a material girl. I swoon over fabric. I love to examine the weave, feel the softness, play with the drape, and swag it over my arm. I feast upon textures— the sheer, the opaque, the matte, the shiny, the solid, the lacy.

If I'm in the worst mood in the world, all I have to do is step into a fabric store and my spirits brighten. (It's the best, cheapest antidepressant around.) While I'm taking in the sights and textures, I'm imagining all the possibilities. I touch a piece of gingham in pumpkin and cream and think, "This could be a blouse I'd wear while drinking iced tea on Savannah's patio." It's like the fabric starts telling stories—not of the past, but of the future. It's so much fun to walk around and decide which fabric tale I'm going to make come true. And for those minutes when I'm looking and touching, I'm not thinking about my troubles. I'm relaxed and happy and creative. Maybe it's how a painter or a gourmet cook feels wandering through a farmers market in the South of France. Inspired!

Of course, the joy of fabric goes well beyond the fabric store. I touch the goods in clothing shops, or read labels to see what material the designer used. Last year, Prada was using a lot of black cotton eyelet and lacy stuff. I had forgotten that eyelet (a light fabric with cut-out and embroidered holes) comes in colors other than white, and I made a navy eyelet camisole for about one-twentieth of the $300 Prada was asking. I check out the fabrics in people's homes: what they find cozy or soothing, what they choose to live with every single day. My friend did her summer house upholstery in red-and-white ticking (an old-fashioned striped mattress fabric), and now it has a 1920s feel.

Bolts of fabric make for some serious eye candy.

I want you to be able to explore a fabric store and find it a pleasure instead of an overwhelming forest of colored bolts. Knowing some basics about how fabrics are made and how each one functions makes the trip much more fun. You can pick out not just a beautiful fabric ('cause it's easy to fall for a chintz or a silk shantung) but the right material for your project—the best ingredient for your intended fashion dish, like the perfect tomato for your sauce.

fiber first one

Fibers are the raw ingredients of cloth. You twist fibers together to give them strength and to form thread. You weave (or knit) threads together to form cloth. Natural fibers are the most common and have been around the longest. Yarn is spun from sheep's fleece. Silk comes from the silk worm's cocoon. Cotton, linen, rayon, and hemp all start as plant fibers. Each fiber has a personality. Each one feels and wears differently. Wool is soft and warm. Silk is lustrous and hangs beautifully. Linen is absorbent and has an earthy quality, while cotton is cool and crisp.

sewing on celluloid

It always cracks me up to see sewing in the movies. It's never the stuff that takes all the time, like measuring and laying out and cutting. Instead, it's the star hunched over the sewing machine in earnest as it goes zip-zip-whir. Here are some of my favorite movies that feature sewing as a plot point. If you are feeling stuck, rent one of these sew-licious classics.

Real Women Have Curves, 2002

The Silence of the Lambs (ew!), 1991

Pretty in Pink, 1986

Sewing Woman, 1983

The Sound of Music, 1965

West Side Story, 1961

Rip, Sew, and Stitch (starring the
   Three Stooges!), 1953

Gone with the Wind, 1939

Bertha, Sewing Machine Girl, 1926

*America Ferrera
in* Real Women
Have Curves.

*Molly Ringwald
in her homemade
prom dress in*
Pretty in Pink.

Then there's acetate, nylon, and polyester—or as I like to call them, Franken-fibers. These are man-made or synthetic materials whose fibers are spun from plastic or chemicals. Scientists developed them to improve upon nature. They can be colorfast, wrinkle-free, and water-resistant. Synthetic materials work great for making car interiors, raincoats, or sports gear. But I rarely sew with them. There *are* some attractive hybrids that give you the best qualities of both natural and synthetic fabrics. Cotton-polyester, for example, has all the comfort of natural cotton, but fewer wrinkles.

So when you're getting dressed, it's often fiber content that steers your choice. Polyester means you can sleep that extra fifteen minutes before work instead of standing at the ironing board (thank you, permanent press!), while linen seems to wrinkle just by looking at it (but it's oh-so-breathable in August). You know that Lycra spandex is Sporty Spice and that silk is Posh. Wool is for a walk in the snowy woods. Cotton shrinks and fades but is super-comfy against your skin. You might have a nice vintage rayon blouse, but you wear it sparingly because the dry cleaning is a pain. That's all fiber stuff.

Think about fiber content and the fiber personalities when you shop for fabric. What does your future shirt or skirt need to do? Keep you warm? Keep you cool? Travel well? Pick the fiber that will do that best. Check the fiber content on the ends of the fabric bolts, where you'll also see a listing of the kind and quality of the material. And as you get more experience, you'll get better at deciphering fiber content by looking and touching.

Under Construction

The threads (made up of fibers) can come together in all kinds of ways to form whole cloth. Cotton, for example, might be *woven* into jeans-worthy denim or *knit* into stretchy T-shirt fabric. The method of construction affects how fabric behaves. It's another factor to consider when shopping for a specific project. Do you need good drape or tough stuff? Picture using T-shirt fabric to make a sexy, scoop neckline (would be good). Now picture making that scoop neckline in denim (not so good). Same fiber, different structure.

All fabrics fall into one of three construction categories: woven, knit, or nonwoven. And even within those categories, there's variety galore. There are loose weaves, tight weaves, weaves with thick threads, weaves with fine threads, and so on. It boggles and excites the mind!

weave-ology 101: warp and weft

Most of the projects in this book—most of the projects that you'll ever make—will start with woven fabric. If you think about how the fabric came to be, how it was set up on a loom, you'll understand better what it can do for you. Did you ever weave a potholder on a little metal square at camp? That's a loom. You stretched one set of loops vertically across the pegs, and then you wove another set over and under crossways to make the potholder. That is basically the same way machines weave fabric in factories.

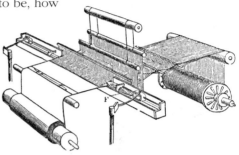

Drawing of an early loom.

Whether in a giant factory, a small workshop, or in Camp Lookout's craft corner, the vertical threads that stretch taut on the loom make up the warp of the fabric. The threads that come horizontally across the warp, interlacing over and under, make up the weft. The nice neat side edge of the fabric is called the selvage. When the warp threads and the weft threads meet at a perfect right angle, the fabric is said to be on grain. (Sometimes fabric stretches or distorts and the angle gets messed up, and then it's not on grain. I'll tell you how to fix this later.) You'll be paying tons of attention to the grain when you start laying out pattern pieces. All you need to know now is that grain means the direction of the threads when the fabric is woven.

weave-ology 102: weaving patterns

When weaving that potholder at Camp Lookout, you probably worked your loop (your weft) in a simple over one–under one–over one pattern. And then on the next row, you did the same—except starting with "under" instead of "over." Sound familiar? It's a classic plain weaving pattern, but there are about a million other ones. It's possible to create all kinds of textures and looks in woven fabric by varying the pattern of "overs" and "unders." Weavers have been experimenting with warp and weft patterns for centuries to find what's strongest, prettiest—or a combo of both.

A weaver makes hand-woven textiles on a loom.

When you are fabric shopping, it helps to think about weave for a couple of reasons. If the pattern is woven (versus printed), it won't fade, and it might look good on both sides. Some weaves are simpler but stronger, while some fancy weaves are less hardy. And they have other behavioral differences.

plain weave

twill weave

satin weave

warp

weft

Here are some of the greatest hits of weaving patterns and what they can do.

✳ Plain

This is the weave from the potholders. It creates a tiny checkerboard of threads. You'll see plain weave in silk shantung, some wool tweeds, and in broadcloth, which is the material for most men's dress shirts.

✳ Twill

The over-under sequence shifts to the side a bit with each new row, building up a pattern of diagonals. (Look at your jeans and see the diagonal ridges.) Denim and gabardine are well-known twills, which are good for hard-working garments like pants and jackets.

Herringbone is a fancy variation. The diagonal reverses, then reverses, then reverses, and so on to create Vs instead of just diagonals.

✳ Satin

Satin refers to a weave—not a fiber. It can be made from cotton, silk, or polyester. This is a weave with many "floats," or weft threads that skip over several warp threads before dipping under (or the reverse: warp threads that skip over weft threads). These floats help reflect more light, giving a shiny effect, but they also weaken the structure a bit. Damask and cotton sateen are good examples.

Weave patterns can create elaborate geometric shapes or even whole pictures, like a tapestry. But sometimes a really elaborate weave means sacrificing strength (so please don't make overalls out of a tapestry). When you see a pattern on fabric, look to see if the pattern is woven in or printed on top.

knowing knits

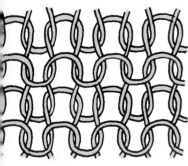
Knit fabric

Just like the hand-knitting that everyone seems to be doing these days, knit fabrics are made up of rows of interlocking loops of fiber. It's what gives knits stretch. The threads in the loops can slip, slide, and shift in a way woven threads can't. If you pull one knit loop, it gets bigger. And all the loops next to it will get smaller to give it slack. If you let go and then wiggle the fabric a little, the loops even out again. Commercially knit fabric is produced on industrial knitting machines, and with much smaller needles (which makes for a finer knit). But commercial knits can still have ribbing and patterns just like the sweaters grandma made. (Think of that wafflelike long-underwear fabric; that's a fancy commercial knit.)

Since knits are stretchy and super-comfortable, they make good T-shirts and sweats. But that very stretchiness makes them a pain when it comes to sewing. Knits curl when you cut them and can require a special sewing needle and technique when you're stitching. Knits may need less tailoring than woven fabrics—they naturally cling and conform to the body—but they're tricky. A word to the wise: If you're a beginner, skip the knits. Save bathing suits and yoga outfits for later on (if ever).

what's a nonwoven?

There are other ways to combine fibers and join threads besides weaving and knitting. Felts are my favorite nonwovens. Little fibers—usually wool—are smushed and compressed together so they tangle and become solid. Felt has no grain because the fibers go every which way. Felt can get wonky after many washings, so it's better for doll clothes, appliqué, or small craft projects. But I love how it feels. Lace is tatted with little shuttles or crocheted. Netting is knotted like loose macramé. Leather, suede, vinyl, and real fur aren't even made up of threads; they are more like flexible platters of material. Fake fur, Ultrasuede, and fleece are also considered nonwovens. Nonwovens are the weirdos. And sometimes, they are exciting for just that reason. I'd say save them for little accents, or save them for later.

Oilcloth is great for table and shelf coverings.

shopping for fabrics two

So now that you know a thing or two about fabric, it's time to go into the Temple of Textiles or what I like to call "The Happy Good Place." You can walk in, unintimidated, and watch all the possibilities (and aisles of delicious fabric) unfold before you. Don't be afraid to just absorb the environment. Look and touch. It's like getting comfortable with a language—just experience it without worrying what every little thing means. Start paying attention to what you are drawn to and how different fibers and weaves feel. How they drape, how they wrinkle, how they look next to your skin. Whether they are thin and sheer or have body and will hold their shape. Get acquainted. And then, start picturing the fabrics performing in the garment or accessory you have planned for them. You are quietly holding auditions—and *you* are the director.

The following fabrics are the ones I most like to sew with, the ones I like to spend quality time with, the ones I can count on. They are good for beginning sewers (unless otherwise noted).

cottons: the go-to fabrics

If you ever feel a little overwhelmed in a fabric store, just head over to the cottons. They are the tried-and-true basics. You know how they will wear and feel because you have been wearing them since you were in diapers. Many cottons are crisp and summery, but they will do you right year-round. And within the cotton family, there's great variety—even a few exotic cousins.

✳ Canvas

I'm a big fan of canvas. It's hardy and solid and takes a beating with no complaints. It's vaguely preppie—maybe because it reminds me of boats and sails. Canvas can be stiff and unwieldy in its heaviest form, so stick with lighter versions. A number of home-decor projects, especially shabby-chic slipcovers and curtains, as well as L.L. Bean–style tote bags and wrap skirts, are a good match for this über-durable material.

✳ Chintz

Think circa-1980s Laura Ashley. Think the Queen's tea parlor. Chintz has a fine, tight weave and features big prints of flowers and sometimes birds. Chintz has a noticeable glazed finish (which helps it wear well). It's lovely for pillows, slipcovers, and curtains.

✳ Corduroy

You can't blame me for sewing purple corduroy knickers back in fifth grade. Corduroy has a soft, plush nap and an enticing back-to-school vibe. From French, *corde du roi,* corduroy means "cloth of kings." The velvety stripes that give it texture are called *wales* and come in a variety of widths: Thick-waled corduroy works best for pants and skirts, while thin-waled corduroy sews nicely into shirts, dresses, and stuffed animals. Look for super-cute bright colors and even prints.

✳ Denim

The name is a mutated version of *de Nimes,* "from Nimes," France. Although indigo-dyed denim rules the racks, you can find it in all colors, prints, and blends—from sunny yellows and baby pinks to train conductor pinstripes and disco-worthy stretch metallics. Depending on the weight, denim is great for shirts, shorts, pants, jackets, skirts, upholstery, pillows, and more. And we all know how good it feels and how well it wears.

✳ Dotted swiss

Sheer cotton with small textured dots woven in, it's perfect for summer-weight blouses, dresses, nightgowns, and curtains. I love the sweet, old-fashioned quality of dotted swiss. I picture Doris Day wearing this fabric.

✳ Eyelet

This fabric is punctuated with sweet embroidered holes (little eyes, hence the name). The base fabric can be cotton batiste (a soft, fine fabric), plain weave lawn (a thin, sheer linen or cotton), broadcloth (another tightly woven plain-weave fabric), organdy (a sheer, stiffer fabric seen at a lot of weddings), piqué (with its slightly puckered texture), and even faux leather or suede. I like the classic white cotton eyelets best. I picture white eyelet

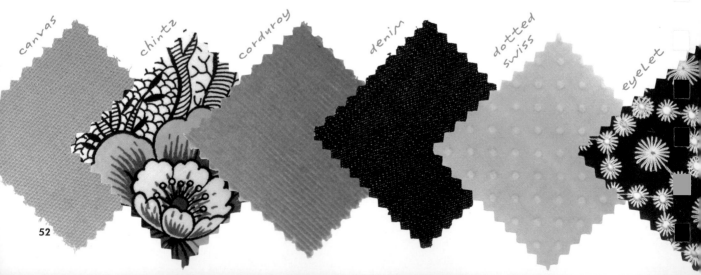

canvas   chintz   corduroy   denim   dotted swiss   eyelet

on a milkmaid working in a mountain valley. I've used white eyelet for a bunch of vintage-inspired summery tops, peasant skirts, shift dresses, and the aforementioned wedding dress.

✳ **Muslin**

Anyone who has watched *Project Runway* has seen muslin in action. It's the unbleached, plain-weave light-cotton fabric designers use to test patterns. Since it's cheap (a few dollars per yard), it's good for experimenting with a new pattern or to test-drive a technique. I also like it for making light, airy table napkins with machine-embroidered edges in colored thread. You'll find it near the interfacing.

✳ **Printed cottons**

Say hello to your new best friends. Also called "quilter cottons," these fabrics are some of the easiest and most satisfying to sew. Printed cottons are relatively cheap and take up a big chunk of the store, so you have a lot to choose from. Calico is a key member of this large extended family. It has busy, small floral patterns that are very *Little House on the Prairie* and great for tank tops, skirts, dresses, aprons, patchwork pillows, duvet covers, and more.

✳ **Quilted cottons**

Two layers of cotton fabric make a sandwich with a layer of batting (fluffy stuff) in the middle, and then it's all machine-stitched together. Quilted cottons are thick and cozy. I like them for jackets, robes, place mats, pillows, bags, and dog coats.

✳ **Shirting**

Plain- and twill-weave cotton materials like broadcloth, chambray (made with colored warp threads and white weft threads), gingham (little checks), and lawn all live under the shirting umbrella. Shirting fabrics come in solids, checks, and plaids. But unlike prints (which are, of course, printed), it's the actual weave and placement of colored threads on the loom that make the patterns. I like the crisp, clean look of shirting fabrics. But don't let the name fool you; these guys aren't just for shirts. Try sewing pajamas, boxer shorts, or skirts from shirting.

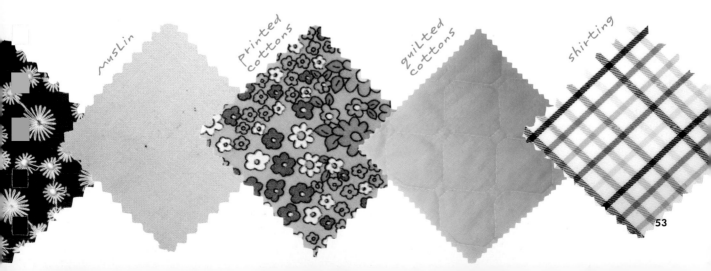

muslin

printed cottons

quilted cottons

shirting

❋ Ticking

Traditionally used to cover mattresses, ticking is heavier than most cottons and is a popular choice for home-decor projects with French country flair. It's easy to spot; look for lengthwise stripes—usually deep blues or reds—on a cream background. I like to play with the stripes, and once made some patchwork placemats with ticking where the stripes changed directions every square. Cute for aprons or bags, if you don't mind working with big stripes that you might have to align.

❋ Toile

Instantly recognizable with its eighteenth-century pastoral scenic pattern, toile means "cloth" in French. I love toile because it has scenes that tell stories—a maiden lounging in the grass while her lover plays the lute, or deer frolicking under a weeping willow. And the colors are usually rich and muted. Though I've seen toile in lighter cotton, it's usually upholstery weight. Because of the big-scale scenery, toile works best on bedding, pillows, slipcovers, and curtains. But it can also be fun for straight skirts and bags.

❋ Voile

From the French word for veil, voile is semitransparent and very lightweight. It's very girly, too—another wedding favorite. Voile is usually cotton, but sometimes it's rayon, silk, or wool. Since this soft, sheer fabric drapes and gathers well, it's a good match for feminine blouses, women's summer dresses, nightgowns, and curtains.

french influence

Why are so many fabric-related words derived from French? France has been the capital of textiles and fashion for hundreds of years. Local handcrafters became famous for their high-quality weaving in signature local styles. Check out the movie *Marie Antoinette* to see how important clothes were in the eighteenth-century French court. Jacqueline Kennedy was the first American First Lady to buy haute couture from Paris. Yves St. Laurent was one of her favorites.

woolens

Although the word may conjure up an image of heavy plaid blankets, this super-versatile fiber can range from cozy thick to medium-weight elegant to light and gauzy. I'm especially fond of woolens fit for strolling in the English countryside, like tweeds and herringbones, but they can be difficult to sew if too thick. Lightweight challis and menswear-style merinos are more manageable.

❋ Cashmere

Real cashmere comes from the hair of a Kashmir goat. Its luxurious softness makes you want to curl up by a fire with a glass of sherry. Maybe add a sugar daddy to that picture, because the real stuff costs $100 or more per yard. Cashmere is good for sewing

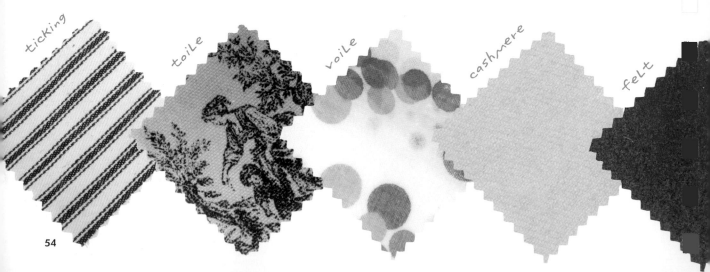

ticking   *toile*   *voile*   *cashmere*   *felt*

coats, jackets, sweaters, bathrobes, and more. If you fall in love with some nice woven cashmere, buy 1½ yards, carefully cut long rectangles about 9 inches wide, and fray the edges a bit for fancy no-sew scarves.

cashmere tip Unless it says "100% cashmere," most cashmere has some regular sheep's wool mixed in.

✳ Felt

A delightful nonwoven, high-quality wool, felt is ideal for appliqués. It doesn't fray much and comes in a nice range of colors. Except for its '50s heyday as a fabric for poodle skirts, wool felt is not very good for whole garments. **Note:** Wool felt is quite different from craft felt, which is acrylic and sold in precut squares.

✳ Flannel

I think cozy flannel evokes more memories than any other fabric: a robe on Christmas morning, a plaid shirt on a camping trip, a nightgown with tiny roses, toasty sheets. Basically, you want flannel on your skin when it's cold outside. Traditional flannel is a woolen, but there are cotton flannels, too. One side is brushed to give it that soft fuzz. A plain weave fabric, it's easy to sew (plus the soft fuzziness helps hold pieces in place when you stitch seams). Obviously, it's good for PJs and shirts, but also try making a flannel bag or stuffed animal.

✳ Gabardine

I associate gabardine with those gorgeous full trousers Katharine Hepburn wore in the '40s. It's got a certain heft, but it still flows. Tailored skirts, pants, trench coats, and suits are good projects for this sturdy twill weave. It usually comes in a wide spectrum of colors, from peacock blue to chocolate brown to highlighter yellow.

✳ Jersey

First made on the island of the same name, jersey is a stable but feminine knit. Jersey drapes beautifully, is comfortable to wear, and—for a knit (which I don't recommend to beginners)—is relatively easy to sew. Wrap tops, dresses, skirts, and pants all work well in this super-versatile material. Coco Chanel launched her career with wool jersey, really putting it on the fashion map.

linen, silk, and synthetics

Linen and silk come from natural fibers, and lots of synthetics act like they do. Others just do their own thing. I don't sew with the following fabrics as much as with cottons and woolens, but it's good to know how. A few of these fabrics are unfairly underrated and underused, so I'm delighted to sing their praises. They have their quirks and pitfalls, but see if the description sounds like something you are looking for.

✳ Faux suede

Faux suede is luxurious like real suede, only stain-resistant and washable. Also known as Ultrasuede, it's a nonwoven microfiber that comes in a few different weights and a rainbow of colors. Faux suede can be a challenge to sew and rather pricey (around $50 a

flannel   gabardine   jersey   faux suede

yard), so I like to use it for small-scale fashion accessories like clutch purses, belts, and embellishments. A little can go a long way.

✳ Fleece

Warm and cozy, fleece is a synthetic knit fabric with a deep soft *nap,* reminiscent of fleece on a sheep, and makes an excellent dog sweater! Make sure to stick to a high-quality version with a no-pill finish. Because it's a knit, it can be challenging to sew, so keep your projects simple at first.

✳ Lace

This fabric needs no introduction. Think of all those lace collars in the Renaissance, lace hankies, lace tablecloths, lace edges on cuffs. Both royalty and peasants adorned themselves with lace for centuries (and not just

the ladies!). Usually white or cream, lace also comes in colors. And black lace may be the sexiest fabric out there. (Picture Anita in *West Side Story* wearing black lace to mourn poor fallen Bernardo.) Threads become lace in a variety of ways—weaving, knitting, crocheting, or knotting—done by hand (expensive) or by machine. Lace can be the main material or the trim. Use it as an accent on lingerie, for straps on a camisole, or as an overlay on a pencil skirt. Foxy!

✳ Linen

Made from flax fibers, linen is about as old school as you get. It's been appreciated for its breathability as far back as ancient Egypt. The fabric is extra-crisp and can make you feel like an English baroness in colonial India.

I also picture linen on fancy Southern gentlemen whose suits have wilted in the heat—but still remain elegant. It does wrinkle like crazy, but I think if you accept this (rather than fight it), your relationship with linen will be happier. Some linens are as light and wispy as a handkerchief, while others are durable enough for Indiana Jones–style jackets and pants. Oh, and it's the preferred fabric of mummies everywhere.

✳ Silk

If lace is the sexiest fabric, then silk is a close second. (Imagine their powers when put together!) Most silk is collected from cultivated worms in Asia (I mean they are farmed; they don't read Shakespeare). Wild silk is a thicker, shorter fiber produced

by worms in their natural habitat. The classic lingerie-type silk is shiny, but silk can be matte or even rough and nubby. There's slinky charmeuse or relatively stable shantung, but I prefer light-weight habutai, which means "soft as down" in Japanese. Be careful when stitching any type of silk, as it's prone to slipping and pins can hurt it.

supporting roles: linings and facings

Sometimes you need to buy special fabrics to play backup, literally. It's good to be aware of these helpers.

✳ Lining fabrics

Silky or shiny and made from rayon or polyester, lining fabrics are relatively cheap and come dyed in dozens and dozens of colors, like brides-

fleece   *lace*   *linen*   *silk*

maids' shoes. Lining fabrics can be beautiful, durable, and even static-free. It's unfair that they have to play second fiddle to "real" fabrics, so feel free to consider them in the starring role for a blouse or camisole.

A lining neatly finishes the inside of a sewn item. It can make the fabric more opaque. Since slips aren't worn as much these days, linings are good for sheer skirts. Scratchy wool pants become comfortable, thanks to lining. Curtains might be lined with special heat- or light-resistant material to keep from fading. Let the lining be part of the fun. I like to use a contrasting lining, like the pink silk inside the herringbone wool Cape Mod (page 149). Just make sure your lining's as washable as the main fabric.

✳ Interfacing

Interfacing goes between layers of fabric to provide stability and form. It's usually white and looks a bit like flattened cotton candy. Interfacing gives oomph to collars, cuffs, plackets, buttonholes, some waistbands, pockets, and facings—anything that needs to hold its shape. You can also add interfacing to larger areas, such as the sides of a bag, to give support and add body. Interfacing can be heat-fusible (which means that you attach it with an iron) or sewn in. I prefer the fusible kind because it's easier and works on most fabrics, except textured ones like seersucker. A pattern will tell you how much interfacing to buy and what kind.

Lining

interfacing

Find Your Temple of Textiles

All fabric stores are not created equal. There are three basic types: the boutique store with expert salespeople and an array of everything from men's suiting to bridal fabrics; the all-in-one chain craft stores; and the discount fabric barns. I suggest putting in a little legwork and visiting them all. One shop might have vintage cotton prints, while another has the most interesting buttons. I'm fond of chain craft stores and discounters for their special offers, like marked-down patterns with purchase. But if you're a beginner, start with the upscale shops. The salespeople are more apt to spend time helping you. Many of these stores offer classes that give you quality time with an expert. Plus, you can enjoy the high-end selection of fabric and notions. It doesn't hurt to dream fancy!

cyberstores

If you don't have the time to shop or the stores in your area don't measure up (or don't exist), try the Internet. The obvious disadvantage is that you don't get to touch the fabrics, so stick to ordering reliable standbys like corduroys and cotton prints and maybe some wool twill. Find out what the site's return or satisfaction policy is before they cut anything for you. The upside is that you can find

S·E·W ··············

Fabrics are sorted by category and color.

some special fabrics on the Internet that stores might not carry. There are fabrics on eBay and there are websites specializing in vintage materials. (Personally, I adore www.ReproDepot.com.) But don't get lost out there: Navigating multiple websites can become more time-consuming than shopping in the real world! Find one or two favorite sites and stick with 'em. (See page 236 for a list of recommended sites.)

on terra firma, the lay of the land

The more fabric stores you visit, the better you'll get at navigating them. They tend to have the same basic floor plans, which helps.

Fabric bolts live in groups according to category: woolens, linens, cottons (within cottons there's shirting, prints, denim, corduroy, ticking, etc.). Then, within each category, fabrics are sorted by color. So, all the corduroys are together, arranged from light to dark. These groupings make shopping easier.

The fabric comes in widths from 34 inches to 64 inches. Some upholstery and home-decor fabrics are even wider. Depending on width, the fabric either wraps around a rectangular piece of cardboard or a long tube to form a bolt. You buy by the yard or fraction of a yard, with a ⅛-yard minimum.

Look for a printed label on the end of the bolt or a hangtag listing the fiber content and care instructions. If this information is missing, speak to a salesperson. Some stores sell remainder fabric or factory leftovers that are not labeled for the retail market, so be careful (or be willing to take a chance on fiber content in exchange for a bargain).

Notions like pins, thread, and scissors usually hang together on pegboards. Zippers, twill tape, bias tape, and rickrack come on rolls, individually in packages, or both. The interfacing is usually near or underneath the cutting table. Commercial pattern books sit on a shelf or on top of tables, while the actual patterns await in big filing cabinets nearby or behind the counter. Once you start to get a feel for the store's layout, you'll realize there's nothing intimidating about shopping for fabric. In fact, the whole ritual is a soothing pleasure!

Cotton prints labeled with hangtags and swatches (above); some great notions (below).

drape expectations

Drape is the term used to describe the way a fabric hangs. It's what makes some fabrics fall in graceful folds or puddle in a heap on the floor, as with lingerie-worthy charmeuse. How much or how little drape a particular fabric has is determined both by its fiber content and construction, and the amount of drape is always carefully matched to the style or cut of the garment by a patternmaker. (This is why it's critical that you stick to the list of fabrics recommended in a pattern!) The best way to explore drape is to pin fabric on a dress form. With a few yards and some pins, you can transform any raw material into inspiring faux garments, as demonstrated here. Many fashion designers work by draping fabric directly on a dress form exactly in this way, pinning, folding, and tucking it until the idea for a garment emerges. Sound like fun? Try it for yourself. Sign up for a draping class at a local community college or fashion school and learn to make your own patterns in 3-D.

Three diverse fabrics—silk, denim, and merino wool (left to right)—pinned to dress forms demonstrate the drape of each material and how it would look as a finished garment.

If you're a beginner, your first project probably will be a pattern in this book. But while you're at the fabric store, explore the world of commercial sewing patterns. There's nothing more inspiring for a beginning seamster than flipping through the glossy pages of a pattern catalog. (I did this for hours as a kid.) Page after enticing page of possibilities! Pattern companies—just like fancy ready-to-wear designers—issue new catalogs each season. It's kind of like Fashion Week without the runway. The newest patterns are in the front of the book, with the rest organized (and color-coded) by categories (formal wear, daytime sportswear, etc.). If you want to make pajamas, flip to the sleepwear section. The photos help you imagine the final garment, but pay closer attention to the line drawings—they give you a better idea of the actual cut and fit of the garment. If you're shopping in earnest, use Post-it notes to mark the pages, and jot down the pattern numbers in your sewing notebook for your final selection(s). Patterns often live under lock and key in large filing cabinets, so ask before "freeing" them.

McCall Pattern Co.

VOGUE PATTERNS

Nothing gets a sewer's heart racing like a new Vogue Patterns catalog.

Like a Virgin: How to Shop for Your First Project

1. start with a very easy pattern

If you want sewing to be fun—not frustrating—it's crucial to choose a simple project. I've designed the projects in this book with you, and your happiness, in mind. Simple can still be cute, especially if you pick a fabric you love. You can even add a monogram, make a matching bag, sew on cute pink trim—all bonuses within your beginner skill range. Better to do a simple project well than a difficult project crappily.

2. pick a preapproved fabric

A sewing pattern is like a recipe: It lists which fabrics work best and how much of them to buy, plus any other supplies you'll need. First-timers should always stick to this list. Easy patterns call for easy-to-sew fabrics. As a general rule, medium-weight woven fabrics like cotton prints, denim, or canvas are good for beginners. Slippery fabrics such as silks, satins, and sheers, as well as stretchy fabrics—not so good. Solid colors, small prints, overall prints, and narrow stripes are fine choices for beginners. Unlike plaids or big prints, they don't require any matching at the seams, which makes the layout and cutting process much easier. Napped or pile fabrics, like velvet, terrycloth, and corduroy, have special layout directions, so you'll want to skip them the first time out, as well. (For more information about shopping with commercial patterns, see page 61.)

3. examine the fabric carefully and read the label

Check out the goods. Do you like how the fabric feels when you touch it? When you unfold it from the bolt, are you happy with the look of the print and the color in a larger piece? Take note of the fiber content and care instructions. If the material sounds too high-maintenance, keep looking.

> **word tip** In fabric lingo, how a fabric feels to the touch is known as its "hand."

4. visualize the final project

This is the ultimate litmus test for me. If I'm able to "see" the project in a particular fabric and can't wait to get it home and onto my sewing machine, then I know I'm making the right choice. The fabric is really only as good as it serves the project. You may love a creamy silk charmeuse, but if you try to make it into a blazer, it'll all end in tears.

5. get a second opinion

Fabric is generally nonrefundable. Ask for input from a friend or your friendly store clerk before making the final cut.

the finance factor

You're spending valuable time and money sewing things. Saving a little lettuce per yard isn't worth it if the fabric is crummy or difficult to use. More expensive fibers tend to hang better, wear longer, and stitch up easily. That said, you may want to wait until you have the skills to pay the bills before buying the top-shelf stuff. The good news? Plenty of fabrics are delightful, sewable, and affordable. Cotton prints run $3 to $45 or more per yard. Go to a reputable store and buy one in the $8 to $12 range. I personally like to sew with a mix of high- and low-end materials—it keeps things interesting. Always inspect the goods before you buy, especially remnants (fabric-talk for leftovers). Look for rips, stains, misprints, discoloration, and fraying. If a material looks junky, it probably is. Walk away.

shop smart
USE YOUR PATTERN ENVELOPE AS A GUIDE

Whether working with this book or a commercial pattern, you have an expert-approved fabric shopping aid: the printed list of suggested fabrics on the commercial envelope or here, with each pattern. Make sure they make sense and sound good to you. (If not, pick another project.) Heed any special advice about what *not* to buy, as well ("Not recommended for plaids or large prints"). Next, figure out the yardage you need. Locate the style you want to make and the bolt width for the fabric you like. Match that measurement (say, 45-inch fabric width) with your size at the top. The number where the two columns meet is the amount to buy. Then, see if you need interfacing, and if so, how much. (Bring fabric and interfacing up to the counter for cutting at the same time.) Lastly, review the list of notions. You'll want to purchase them at the same time as your fabric for a good color match, and so you won't have to run out to the store mid-project.

don't shop 'til you drop

Those who spend too much time shopping are a bit like Goldilocks: You think if you try just one more store—despite the fact you've already been to twenty—you will find a fabric that's *juuuust* right. Perfection isn't necessary. A strong creative vision is good, but obsession is not. Your frustration could lead to creative block. Or, at the very least, if you overthink and overshop at this stage, you won't have time for the real action: sewing. Yes, you may have been daydreaming about a dotted swiss skirt in a certain shade of rubine. But when you think about it, wouldn't fuchsia be just as pretty? Remember we're talking about one skirt. You will make many, many more skirts. Learn to let go and just dig in.

thinking outside the bolt

There's no rule that says you have to stick to conventional fabrics and patterns from stores. I sew with offbeat materials like monogrammed handkerchiefs, embroidered tea towels, silk scarves, and loud Marimekko-esque printed pillowcases and sheets that I find at garage sales, flea markets, and thrift stores. These places also serve as graveyards for other people's would-be sewing projects, ones they stocked up for but never completed (or even started!). Vintage patterns, bags of ribbons, bias tape, buttons, and thread await a second chance (and cost a song). Old curtains, blankets, felted sweaters, and ball gowns also deserve a second chance. Refashion them into nifty new clothes and accessories—a move that is thrifty, eco-friendly, and on the cutting edge of fashion. Many top designers, as well as crafty up-and-comers, recycle. Since there is more and more competition for vintage materials, I recommend shopping for them in the real world, as opposed to eBay. There's a better chance you'll get what you want at a bargain. Plus, you can see and feel the goods for yourself before buying.

pushing your skills

If you're dying to work with advanced materials, buy a quarter yard and practice stitching seams and any other techniques you want to use on the fabric before buying the amount you'd need for a full-scale project. (You might also need a special needle, pins, thread, and presser foot. Ask for help in-store if you have questions.)

thinking in color **three**

Once you've decided upon the right fiber, the right fabric, maybe even the floral or dotted print, your next decision is: What color? I say go with your instincts. You know what looks good with your skin, what goes with your wardrobe or home decor, what makes you happy. If the color makes you feel so-so, say "so long." Whether you are sewing a skirt or a pillow, go ahead and mix and match patterns however you see fit. I find that unlikely pairings are the most intriguing. But let me offer some suggestions and a dab of color theory that might get you thinking and experimenting.

lessons from the color wheel

I'm all for instinct, but it helps to have a little science in your back pocket. Color theory explains the scientific relationships between colors in terms of light and pigments. There are principles behind different color combinations—what makes them harmonious or clashing. It's actually pretty cool. Once you know a little color theory, you start seeing it at work everywhere—on candy wrappers, bed linens, bowls of fruit—anywhere colors sit next to each other. A color wheel illustrates these relationships. You can buy one at an art or craft store for a few bucks. (Painters and quilters use them all the time.)

Some color wheels have handy windows so you can see how your fabric looks next to the different shades. So give the wheel a spin and see what works!

color choice
TIPS 'N' TRICKS

✳ Don't rely on your memory for coordinating fabrics. Bring a good-sized swatch of the fabric you want to match (a 4-inch square) to the store to try out combos.

✳ Step into daylight if at all possible. Fluorescent lights don't flatter anyone, or anything—including fabric. Ask a salesperson for permission first so you won't get arrested for shoplifting. Or bring the fabric to the nearest sunny window.

✳ Fabrics sometimes look better on the bolt than they do on your body. If you're making clothing, unwrap a few yards from the bolt and drape the fabric around your body in front of a mirror—all good stores will have one and encourage you to do this! Make sure the fabric is not too bright or busy and that the color is flattering.

✳ Apply your color wheel: Once you decide to make your cape bloodred, you've got some interesting color options for the lining, pockets, buttons, and thread. Do you want contrasts or monochrome? As you think about color and the overall design, you'll see more possibilities open up.

monochromatic

analogous

complementary

There are three color categories: primary, secondary, and tertiary. Primary colors are red, blue, and yellow. All other colors can be mixed from these three. Secondary colors are mixtures of two primary colors. Orange, green, and violet are secondary colors. Tertiary or intermediate colors are mixtures of a primary color plus a secondary color. Red-orange, blue-violet, and yellow-green are all intermediate colors.

The most common color harmonies (that is, combos that look good together) are monochromatic, analogous, and complementary. By knowing and understanding these combos, you can pick hues that make your sewing projects soothe or pop or just plain look great.

✴ Monochromatic

These colors are really one (mono) color, in lighter and darker forms. For example, red, pink (red + white), and dark red (red + black) are a monochromatic grouping. They're all variations on true red—just a little lighter or darker. This color scheme looks clean and elegant.

✴ Analogous

These colors are next to each other on the color wheel; for example, yellow, yellow-green, and green. Analogous colors are pleasant and cheery together.

✴ Complementary

These colors are opposite each other on the color wheel—like purple and yellow. They have the greatest possible contrast, so they pop and grab your attention.

open your eyes

Make a conscious effort to find interesting color combinations when you're out on the street or flipping through magazines. You might discover that lavender looks great with chocolate brown or that coral looks smart with navy blue. Remember that notebook I urged you to carry in your bag? Write observations like these in it. Pick up paint chips at the hardware store and arrange them on your inspiration board, or staple them to sheets of paper for reference and bring them the next time you're fabric shopping.

So Sayeth I

Ten Fabric Commandments

1. Only buy fabric you love.

2. Always choose the right fabric for your project.

3. Let the pattern be your challenge, not the material.

4. Skip high-maintenance fabrics in favor of those you can wash and wear, unless you have a crush on your dry cleaner.

5. Shop for fabric one project at a time. (Can't bear the thought? See commandment 8.)

6. Get as much fabric as you need the first time around—fabrics often sell out.

7. Pick a 60-inch fabric width over one that is only 45 inches because the wider the fabric, the less of it you will need.

8. Buy 3 yards of a fabric you just plain love but have no idea what to do with. This amount will keep your options open when you're ready to use it on a project.

9. Put unknown fabrics (like vintage or thrift store) to the test: Cut some off, jot down the measurements, then wash, dry, and measure again. If it shrinks, dry clean whatever you make from it.

10. Be kind to the things you make! Even machine-washable fabrics take a beating in the washer and dryer. Consider hand-washing.

four

sometimes a great notion

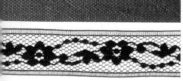

bias tape

elastic

grosgrain

piping

pompoms

rickrack

seam binding

Think you're all set once you have your fabric? *Au contraire.* You need notions. That is, everything that gets sewn on (or ironed to) your project besides the fabric. Notions are the icing on your sewing cake. Fabric stores carry much more than fabric. They sell lace, ribbon, ruffles, fringe, braid, beading, and other *trims* and *tapes.* Some of them are functional, some are decorative, many are both.

trims and tapes

Trims and tapes sell by the yard or in single packages from Wrights (a well-loved brand, in business since 1897). Before you get sucked into the trimmings section of the store, get familiar with the basic doodads you'll need for projects in this book.

✳ Bias tape

Bias tape is long, narrow strips of fabric used to give a neat finish to hems and seam allowances. It's cut on the *bias,* or at a 45-degree angle from the edge of the fabric, so that it is slightly stretchy. Bias tape is then pressed in half the long way so you can place it over the edge of a seam or over a raw fabric edge and stitch it into place. The stretch helps it curve around armholes or circular hems. Bias tape comes in single- and double-fold. I'm a big fan of extra-wide double-fold since it's easy to pin and sew in place.

✳ Elastic

You know elastic from your underwear and your sweatpants—it makes the waistband stretchy. Sometimes, there's elastic in sleeve cuffs, necklines, legbands. Most elastic gets covered by fabric. There's nonroll, cording, and clear tape for bathing suits and lingerie. Your pattern will tell you which width, type, and yardage to buy.

✳ Grosgrain ribbon

Although there's a giant array of gorgeous ribbons out there, I come back to grosgrain again and again. This '80s preppy classic dolls up just about everything from hems to handles to ties. Grosgrain has little ridges that run the short way across to give it texture and strength. It's cheap, durable, and comes in all kinds of colors, patterns, and widths.

✳ Piping

Made from a cord covered in fabric, piping runs along seams to define and decorate

edges. It actually looks like cake icing that squirts out of a little tube. You see it on pillows, couches, backpacks, and on Western-style shirts. Pretty!

✳ Pompoms

Maybe you had these on your ice skates as a kid. Pompoms are playful balls of wool, feathers, or other fluffy material. They punctuate hats and slippers. I find them hard to resist, and think they add a little sweetness to any project, from aprons to potholders to curtains.

✳ Rickrack

Rickrack transforms everything from pockets to hems to seams with its kitschy '50s vibe. It's a zigzag-shaped ribbon from ¼- to 1¼-inches wide and comes in almost any color—including metallics. You sew it on by hand, by machine, or attach it with fabric glue.

✳ Seam binding

Like bias tape, seam binding (or hem tape) is a long strip

of acetate fabric that finishes edges. Seam binding is not cut on the bias (can't hug curves), so only use it for binding straight lines, such as pant hems or wool blankets. Seam binding can also reinforce seams and keep knits or other kinds of stretch fabrics from losing their shape. Hug Snug is a good brand. One of my personal trimming secrets is to finish the edges of skirts with lace seam bindings—so girly and great!

twill tape

✳ Twill tape

This flat twill-woven ribbon can be cotton, linen, polyester, or wool. It comes in lots of colors and widths up to 1 inch. It's a little heftier (and softer to touch) than grosgrain ribbon or scam binding, a little more masculine looking. Use it to bind edges, reinforce seams or snaps, make casings, or for shoulder straps or ties.

needing closure

Sometimes you see them, sometimes you don't, but you touch them every day. You hook your bra, zip your zipper, button your coat,

Velcro-shut the flap on your bike bag. Some make a statement, others are purely functional. Closures are the finishing touches. Your pattern will suggest which closure to use. But when you pick one, consider what the weight of your fabric will bear and how much wear and tear that fastener will get. (See pages 95–100 to learn how to attach them.)

✳ Buttons

They are functional little sculptures that run the gamut from cheapo to bejeweled. Buttons can give your garment style and flavor. The buttons on the Canine Couture Coat (page 220) make Rita look like a movie star. I confess to having spent an hour in front of a button rack, holding each one up to my fabric.

Sew-through buttons have the holes on top (I'm a sucker for the ones made out of pearly shell). Shank buttons have a stem at the back. Self-covered have fabric over a little dome. You can make the self-covered kind with a kit that most sewing stores carry. It's a fun way to customize. (See pages 98–99 for sewing a button on by machine, and pages 231–232 for sewing by hand.)

Button crazy
BECOME A BUTTON-OPHILE

People are crazy for buttons. There are books, websites, and museums dedicated to the topic, as well as a worldwide National Button Society, founded in 1939. (Do they rumble with the National Zipper Society?) Look online and you'll discover a whole world of highbrow button enthusiasts, most of whom would consider the idea of actually sewing a button from their collection blasphemy. And who can blame them? We're talking buttons that came off royal waistcoats and such.

Now you don't have to go off the button deep end, but do watch for unique buttons; start collecting, and your projects will rejoice. Get a designated button bin with dividers and start grouping your buttons by color or size or material (shell, plastic, metal) or type (shank, sew through)—any system that makes sense to you. Widen your search by looking for buttons at flea markets, thrift stores, and garage sales, or look on eBay (if you dare). I bet if you just begin *thinking* about buttons, they'll start popping up everywhere. Years ago, a very kind landlady gave me her stockpile of vintage buttons, which I still use to this day. One final point: When a beautiful button comes into your life, use it *somewhere*. Buttons look much better on a beautifully sewn project than they do collecting dust in a bin. Leave collecting to the purists.

✳ Hooks and eyes

Hooks and eyes deliver what they promise: a little hook that catches on a separate little loop, or eye. Hooks and eyes connect adjoining fabric areas, like the top of a dress or the back of a bra. A straight eye is for lapped and heavy-duty jobs, such as a waistband. You usually sew on a hook and eye by hand, but there are no-sew versions that clamp into place.

✳ Snaps

Snaps are metal fasteners with a ball on one side and a socket on the other. They are the only fasteners that actually say their name—"snap"— when you close them. Snaps come in a variety of sizes. I love the look of the jumbo-sized ones, and use them whenever possible. Snaps only work when fabrics overlap, and there's not too much strain or pulling.

✳ Hook-and-loop tape (a.k.a. Velcro)

Anybody who has lived through the last few decades knows Velcro. One of the easiest and fastest of all closures to install, Velcro has its drawbacks—it loves to grab at things indiscriminately and picks up crud and threads. Do a test before sewing it in to make sure the type you're using is strong enough and won't damage the surrounding fabric.

✳ Zippers

Zippers are just rows of metal or plastic teeth that bite together or slide apart with the help of the zipper pull. The teeth attach to woven polyester tape—which is the part you sew. Zippers come in a few different weights. You want a heavyweight metal one for a denim jacket, for instance, and a light plastic one for a lacey clutch purse. I like invisible zippers because they're easy to sew. (See page 96 for how to put one in.)

invisible zipper

all-purpose zipper

fabric store treasure hunt

Here are ten things you should be able to identify by now. See if you can hunt them down in a fabric store and tap 'em with your finger for finder's credit (extra points for doing it in less than twenty minutes).

Wool gabardine in navy blue

Round pearly shank buttons, ½ inch in diameter

Red rickrack

Fusible interfacing

Cotton toile—with a person playing a musical instrument

Denim in a color other than blue

18-inch white invisible zipper

Loosely woven, nubby linen in green

Houndstooth tweed in black and white

Pink oxford shirting

What's Next?

If you've been playing along at home, you've got your sewing space, your sewing tools, and your sewing machine. Perhaps there's been some practice. Then you picked a project from this book and conquered the fabric store, choosing something delicious and delightful to sew with. You notioned up. If you were a cook, you'd be at the stage where you come home from the gourmet market, ready to start dinner. Well, that cook has to do a few more things before turning on the burners; she has to wash, prep, and cut up her ingredients. And so do you, dear seamsters. So turn the page for some schooling on prepping, layout, and cutting.

layout and cutting CHAPTER 4

Now you're ready to prepare your sewing ingredients for assembly. Layout and cutting are just as much a part of sewing as whipping up a seam on your machine. In some ways, these steps are even *more* important. You can unsew a seam, but you can't uncut fabric once your scissors have wielded their shiny jaws. In fact, from here on, sewing becomes more like construction. Measuring needs to be precise. There's an old carpenter's motto, "Measure twice, cut once," that I try to remember whenever I work with fabric. Following a pattern becomes much like following a blueprint: You need to know what all those markings mean, and you need to mark your cut pieces so they fit together just right.

Frankly, the layout-pin-and-cut stage can get tedious and might scare some could-be-great sewers into becoming nonsewers. But the good news is that these steps are not that hard. I mean, you've been using scissors your whole life, right? You just need to use them with more precision and patience. And because the designer (in this book, *moi*) has worked to figure out where the darts and buttons go and marked them on the pattern, you get the relatively easy task of reading and transferring those marks onto the fabric.

one things to know

Before your pattern touches fabric, there are some important things to decide (like your size) and some important things to understand (like how to decipher the diagrams and markings). If you are a beginner, you are probably planning a project from this book. Good move. Projects in this book look, feel, and behave like actual commercial patterns, except they don't come in the standard coded envelope, and they give much more detailed instruction. You should know how to read those commercial envelopes and instructions, though, because someday, you're going to run free and wild in the fabric store picking out whatever you want. If you know your size and can speak pattern-ese, then jump to Part Two of this chapter. If not, hang out here awhile.

the envelope, please!

The front of a pattern envelope is like the cover of a book—it tries to sell you on the project with a magazine-style photo or a fashion sketch. If you're unsure of what fabric or color to choose, you might use the cover as a guide. The front gives you the size, alternate designs, and the designer (if there is one). It also tells you the level of difficulty. Look for the words *fast* or *easy,* which mean the pattern maker has consciously designed for a beginner and has kept things simple (fewer pattern pieces, fewer markings).

The back has all the details you need to start the project. There's a lot of information, so let me break it down for you.

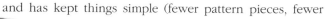

Commercial sewing patterns can be easy to sew and fashion-forward.

✳ Garment description
Gives more construction details. Read carefully: If it says "zipper" and you're still conquering a straight seam, keep looking (usually at top left, not shown here).

✳ Body measurement and size chart
Helps you determine which size to follow in the pattern.
Note: Sewing pattern sizes aren't the same sizes as ready-to-wear. You'll need to measure your body and go by this chart. (See page 73 for how to measure.)

✳ Number of pieces
Helps you figure out how complicated or easy the pattern is to sew. Easy patterns have fewer pieces.

17 PIECES

✳ Back views
Line drawings showing the back of garments, with important details such as seam lines, darts, and closures.

✳ Yardage block
Tells you the exact fabric yardage required for each style and size, based on various fabric widths and for materials with or without nap. Find your size and the bolt width, and see where they intersect on the chart. That's the amount of fabric you buy. Interfacing yardage is listed here, too.

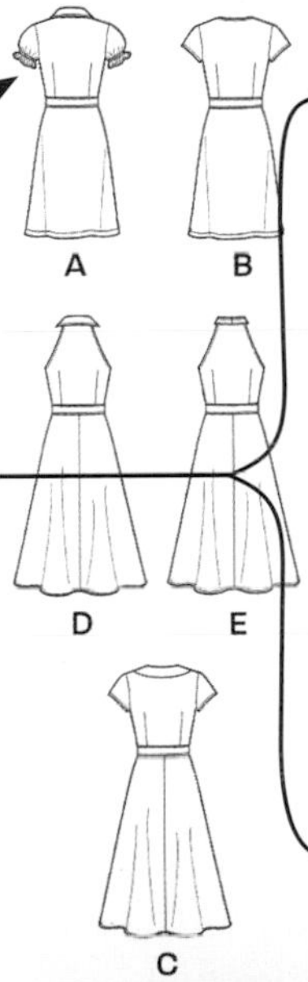

6674
SIZE A 10-22
FR. 38-50
EUR. 36-48

MISSES' SEVEN SIZES IN ONE

Sizes	10	12	14	16	18	20	22	
European Size	36	38	40	42	44	46	48	
Bust	32½	34	36	38	40	42	44	In
Waist	25	26½	28	30	32	34	37	"
Hips	34½	36	38	40	42	44	46	"
Back-neck to waist	16	16¼	16½	16¾	17	17¼	17⅜	"
A								
45"**	3¼	3⅜	3⅜	3⅜	3⅜	3⅜	3½	Yd
60"**	2½	2½	2½	2½	2½	2½	2⅝	"
Interfacing 1 yd. of 22" to 25" lightweight fusible								
B								
45"**	3	3	3	3	3	3⅛	3⅜	Yd
60"**	2⅜	2⅜	2⅜	2⅜	2⅜	2⅜	2⅜	"
C								
45"**	3½	3½	3½	3½	3⅝	3⅞	4	Yd
60"**	2⅜	2⅜	2½	2½	2½	2⅝	2¾	"
Contrast ⅞ yd. of 45"**; ¾ yd. of 60"**								
B,C Interfacing ⅞ yd. of 22" to 25" lightweight fusible								
D								
45"**	3⅝	3⅞	4	4	4	4⅛	4⅛	Yd
60"**	2¾	2¾	2⅞	2⅞	3	3	3	"
Interfacing ⅝ yd. of 22" to 25" lightweight fusible								
E								
45"**	3⅞	3⅞	4	4	4	4	4	Yd
60"**	2¾	2¾	2¾	2⅞	2⅞	2⅞	2⅞	"
Interfacing ⅜ yd. of 22" to 25" lightweight fusible								
GARMENT MEASUREMENTS								
A,B,C,D,E Bust	36	37½	39½	41½	43½	45½	47½	In
Finished back length from base of neck:								
A,B	38	38¼	38½	38¾	39	39¼	39½	In
C,D,E	45	45¼	45½	45¾	46	46¼	46½	"
A,B Width	49	50½	52½	54½	56½	58½	60½	"
C,D,E Width	77	78½	80½	82½	84½	86½	88½	"

SUGGESTED FABRICS: Cotton and Cotton Blends, Laundered Cottons, Chambray, Pique, Poplin, Seersucker, Crepe, Jerseys, Matte Jerseys, Lightweight Double Knit, Novelty Knit Fabrics, Linen and Linen Blends. Allow extra fabric for matching plaids or stripes.

REQUIREMENTS: All Views: One ½" button. A: One pkg. of ¼" wide elastic, one pkg. of ½" wide single fold bias tape. D,E: One pkg. of ⅞" wide single fold bias tape.

*without nap **with nap ***with or without nap

✳ Notions
Lists the number and types of zippers, buttons, ribbon, elastic, tape, etc. you need.

✳ Garment measurements
These numbers tell you the length and width of the finished project in the key places. You might adjust skirt length later when you hem.

✳ Suggested fabrics
Recommends material most suited for the style. If the pattern is rated easy, the suggested fabrics will be easy to sew with as well. Stick to this list, unless you are a real pro.

the sizing schism

WHY SO BIG?

Your size on the sewing pattern chart is at least a couple of sizes larger than what you're used to buying in a store. That's because clothing retailers indulge in vanity sizing. They attach a low number to a larger size in an attempt to appeal to your vanity (and to get into your pocketbook). Hence, a size 8 at The Gap will be equivalent to a size 12 or 14 at the fabric store. Since these numbers are arbitrary and basically meaningless, there's no reason to let them bother you.

anatomy of a pattern

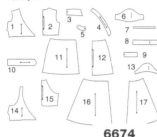

17 pieces given

6674   1/4

1-BODICE FRONT -A,B,C
2-BODICE BACK -A,B,C
3-COLLAR -A,D
4-FRONT FACING -A,B / FRONT BA
5-BACK FACING -A,B / BACK BAND
6-SLEEVE -A
7-SLEEVE ELASTIC GUIDE -A
8-MIDRIFF FRONT
9-MIDRIFF BACK
10-TIE END
11-SKIRT FRONT -A,B
12-SKIRT BACK -A,B
13-SLEEVE -B,C
14-BODICE FRONT -D,E
15-BODICE BACK -D,E
16-SKIRT FRONT -C,D,E
17-SKIRT BACK -C,D,E

U.S. & Canada Toll-Free
1-888-588-2700

Web Site
http://www.simplicity.com

E-mail
info@simplicity.com

Thank you for purchasing this New Look pattern.
We have made every effort to provide you with a high quality product.
Gracias por haber comprado este patrón de New Look.
Hemos hecho todos los esfuerzos para ofrecerle un producto de alta calidad.

Above, outline of each pattern piece; (right) back and front views of each style.

The pattern envelope contains two things: the actual paper pattern and the instructions for sewing the project. Printed on large sheets of tissue paper, each pattern piece has a name (like "top front"), a number (a five-piece pattern will have pieces 1 through 5), and sometimes a "view." To give you more bang for your pattern buck, the company might offer three versions of a skirt, and then each skirt version gets a different "view"—or layout configuration—in the directions. It might say "view A," "view B," or "skirt A," "skirt B." Circle or highlight "view A" (or whichever one you are doing) in all the directions and on all the pattern pieces to keep you on course. All these labels—name, number, and view—plus the distinctive shapes of the pattern pieces help you identify what's what on your layout diagram and on your sewing table.

The instructions are on newsprint. They include outline drawings of each style, outline drawings of each pattern piece (named and numbered), layout and cutting diagrams along with guides for each fabric width, a key to sewing terms and techniques, and step-by-step sewing instructions. Read through the instructions *before* cutting or sewing to plan and organize your time. Our ten S•E•W patterns include all the standard marks and details that you need, but the actual instructions are here in the body of the book (sparing you the newsprint dirty fingers).

using vintage patterns

Yes, the style is great, but vintage patterns have a few drawbacks. The instructions are not so user-friendly. Fabrics and body types have changed over the years, so the fit is likely to be off. If you like the retro look but want a more modern cut, Vogue Patterns has a line called Vintage Vogue that combines the best of old and new because they have revamped the sizing to fit modern body types and updated the supply list.

how to measure up

You'll need to know three body measurements when working with a garment pattern: bust, waistline, and hips. You may think you know these measurements, but you should double-check. One of the huge benefits of sewing is creating a custom fit, so make sure you're fitting the actual body you walk around in—not the one you imagine.

Record your measurements and compare your results to the size chart on the back of the pattern envelope. For the patterns in this book, see the size/measurement chart on page 104. Not all of us are a perfect top-to-bottom dress size. For a top or a jacket, pick the size that will accommodate your bust. For a skirt, dress, or pants, go by your hip size. (Clearly, this is not advanced physics.) Also, remember that woven fabrics don't stretch. Make a seersucker pullover top a size too small, and you may never be able to wear it. Sadly, I know this from first-hand experience. When in doubt, go with the larger size. You can always make a garment smaller if necessary. Here's how to take proper measurements:

✴ **Bust**

Place the tape measure under your arms, across the widest part of your back, and around the fullest part of your bustline. For high bust measurement, place the tape measure under your arms, across widest part of your back and above your full bustline.

✴ **Waistline**

Cut a piece of string or ribbon, tie it around your middle, and allow it to roll to your natural waistline—usually the place where you bend when you fold forward. You want to measure this exact location with a tape measure. This will be higher than where you might like to wear your pants and skirts. If you are making low-slung pants, for example, the pattern accounts for your waist and your hip measurements, and the waistband will fall somewhere in between. But you need to know what these measurements are first.

✴ **Hips**

Measure around the fullest part of your hips, or, put more bluntly, around the middle of your butt. This is usually about 7 to 9 inches below your waistline.

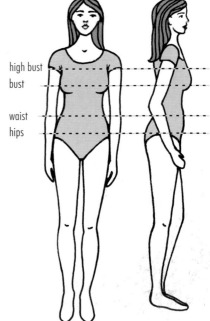

high bust
bust

waist
hips

two eight-step prep program

I love to divide and conquer, so welcome to my little eight-step program for laying out and cutting your fabric. And when you graduate, you get to sit down at your machine and sew, sew, sew (which is—I'm not gonna lie—the super-fun part). The eight steps to successful sewing prep are:

1. Prewash and iron the fabric.

2. Study the pattern and read the instructions thoroughly.

3. Prepare the pattern: Do a rough cut and press.

4. Lay it out: Fold your fabric and position the pattern pieces.

5. Pin the pattern to the fabric.

6. Check your work.

7. Cut it out!

8. Make your mark(s).

Start these steps when you have an hour or two to lay everything out and double-check your work. Make sure you're rested up and ready to pay close attention to detail. If you're not, then begin another day. (You'll thank me.)

going on grain
FABRIC TEST AND TAFFY PULL

Sometimes, when fabric is cut off the bolt, it's not done in a straight line so the ends aren't even and the fabric is "off-grain." Pull a thread that goes from selvage-to-selvage near the end to see where the true edge should be. Cut along the line left by the missing thread.

Other times, the fibers are a bit wonky or warped after washing. So do a quick check 'n' fix at this stage. When you fold the square or rectangular piece of fabric in half, the edges should line up on all four sides. If your rectangle is off kilter and it's more like folding a diamond, then get a friend and take the material by opposite corners and pull along the bias—gently at first, harder if necessary—until you achieve squareness. If one direction of bias-pulling doesn't work, try the other. And when I say, "Pull at the corners," I don't mean just the corners. You scoot around, grabbing hold of the fabric to the left and then the right of the corner, while your partner does the same thing. The fabric won't mind. It wants to be in alignment like it was in the first place—on the loom.

step 1 prewash and iron the fabric

If your fabric is machine-washable, trim the raw edges with pinking shears to keep raveling to a minimum. Then put it through the washer and dryer on the settings recommended on the fabric bolt label. Prewash the material by itself since the yardage is usually enough to take up the whole machine and certain colors, such as reds and darks, are likely to bleed the first time. Wash the fabric as you will wash the garment. Better the nice cotton gingham shrinks now, not later. Personally, I wash everything I make in cold water and then let it line dry. After all that work, I give my handmade clothes special, gentle care. But that's just me.

All fabric—there is no exception to this rule—*must* be absolutely wrinkle-free before placing the pattern on top. Set your iron to the right temperature for the fabric (marked on the dial) and press on the wrong side. If there's even a slight ripple or fold in the fabric, it will affect the size and shape of the piece. And that can mess up the outcome. Don't skip this step!

step 2 study the pattern

At first, a pattern may seem like a mysterious coded treasure map—not easy to follow, but definitely rewarding in the end! See the cheat sheet at the end of this chapter to decode pattern symbols. Read through the pattern instructions a few times before digging in. Mentally execute the steps. If there are terms or techniques that you don't know, highlight them and look them up before you get to that point and have to halt everything. If you're highlighting way too much, you might want to reconsider making this project now. You can always tackle that pattern later, and begin with something easier. Learning to read a sewing pattern is a skill you'll hone over time. The more you sew, the clearer patterns will become.

step 3 prepare the pattern

Your pattern (or blueprint) helps you cut out nice crisp pieces from your big swath of fabric. The neater the paper, the neater the cut piece of fabric, and the better it will fit together with other pieces.

Note: Some of the projects in this book are so simple that you don't need a paper pattern. Instead, you measure and draw on the fabric itself with a ruler and chalk or a disappearing-ink marker. (See pages 103–104 for instructions on how to make your own pattern.) For commercial patterns, be sure to prep them as follows.

✳ **Circle the layout**

Find the cutting layout for the style (or view) you're making and for the fabric width and type you're using (for example, view 1B, 60-inch width, normal non-napped fabric). Circle this layout and embrace it as yours.

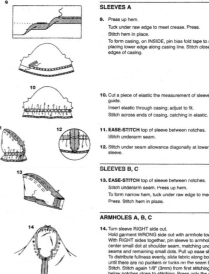

SLEEVES A

9. Press up hem.
   Tuck under raw edge to meet crease. Press.
   Stitch hem in place.
   To form casing, on INSIDE, pin bias fold tape to sleeve placing lower edge along casing line. Stitch close to both edges of casing.

10. Cut a piece of elastic the measurement of sleeve elastic guide.
    Insert elastic through casing; adjust to fit.
    Stitch across ends of casing, catching in elastic.

11. EASE-STITCH top of sleeve between notches.
    Stitch underarm seam.

12. Stitch under seam allowance diagonally at lower edge of sleeve.

SLEEVES B, C

13. EASE-STITCH top of sleeve between notches.
    Stitch underarm seam, tuck under raw edge to meet crease.
    Press. Stitch hem in place.

ARMHOLES A, B, C

14. Turn sleeve RIGHT side out.
    Hold garment WRONG side out with armhole toward you.
    With RIGHT sides together, pin sleeve to armhole with center small dot at shoulder seam, matching underarm seams and remaining small dots. Pull up ease stitches to fit. To distribute fullness evenly, slide fabric along bobbin threads until there are no puckers or tucks on the seam line. Baste. Stitch. Stitch again 1/8" (3mm) from first stitching. Trim seam below notches close to stitching. Press only the seam allowance, shrinking out fullness.

Step-by-step instructions.

Cutting Layouts

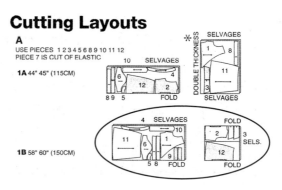

A
USE PIECES 1 2 3 4 5 6 8 9 10 11 12
PIECE 7 IS CUT OF ELASTIC

1A 44" 45" (115CM)

1B 58" 60" (150CM)

✳ **Find your pattern pieces**

Be gentle with the pattern tissue—this is fragile stuff! As you open up each pattern piece, check it off the list on the cutting layout (see page 75). Separate the pieces by cutting the empty space around them, but don't cut on the actual cutting lines yet (and yes, you should use your regular scissors, not your dressmaker's shears).

✳ **Put the rest away**

Fold the leftovers and put them away in a manila envelope with the pattern envelope attached to the front. I've spent many hours of my life—I'm a slow learner!—trying and failing to get the pattern back into the envelope. Don't bother. Put the envelope where it will be easy to find. Your working pattern will need to go in there when you're done with it as well. I usually punch a hole at the top of the envelope and hang it from the pegboard above my sewing machine.

✳ **Iron the pattern pieces flat**

Press the pattern pieces on a lukewarm setting with no steam in order to remove wrinkles. Just like fabric, the paper pattern must be flat and smooth.

✳ **Connect the dotted line**

Have you ever bought shoe insoles that have several foot outlines, one for each size? Pattern pieces are like that, too. Since multisized sewing patterns show six sizes at once, it can be tough to keep track of *your* size. Using a felt-tip marker and a flexible sewing ruler, draw along the cutting line for your size before placing the pattern on your fabric.

step 4   fold the fabric and position the pattern pieces

✳ **Telling right from wrong**

You'll hear a lot about the "right" and "wrong" sides of the fabric. This is not a value judgment. It's just a way of describing which side will show when you wear the piece. The right side is the outside; the wrong side is the inside. Usually it's super-easy to determine which side is the right side just by looking. Napped fabrics, such as corduroy or velvet, make the choice obvious. Prints are also hard to mess up. Some fabrics—like most solid cottons—are completely reversible. So if you really can't tell the difference, pick a side and go with it. When there is no visible difference between sides, make one the wrong side and mark it with chalk to avoid confusion. By marking a wrong side, you'll know which side is meant when, for example, the instructions say, "pin seams, wrong sides together." Sometimes, though, you might like the wrong side more than the right—if so, go for it!

biased opinion

SKIP BIAS-CUTTING AT FIRST

For most of the projects in this book, the pattern pieces are all lined up on the fold or the grainline. There are some projects, like the Power Tie, page 212, that line up and cut on the bias of the fabric—or on a 45-degree angle from the selvage. Bias-cut garments have a pretty drape and flow, but first-time seamsters should stick to the grainline.

✳ Folding in half

Unless your cutting diagram tells you something else, fold the fabric selvage to selvage with right sides together. This way, you make your marks on what will be the inside, or wrong side, of the fabric—which is where you'll need them when it's time to sew.

Align the fold of the fabric with the straight edge of the table and make sure the selvages are absolutely even where they meet. Smooth out any wrinkles by running your hand along the surface of the fabric, and check each end—this is important—to see if the fabric underneath lines up with what's on top. (Since the fabric cutter doesn't always make a neat line, cut ends don't always match up.) If the fabric is shorter underneath, flip the whole fabric piece over so you know that you're pinning through both layers.

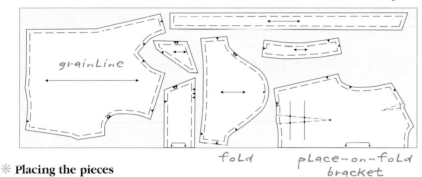

selvages

grainline

fold

place-on-fold bracket

✳ Placing the pieces

There are grainline arrows on each pattern piece, and you line them up with the grain of the fabric (the lengthwise threads of woven fabric). These lengthwise threads want to hang straight down when worn. If you cut with the pattern and the grain going in the same direction, the garment will hang charmingly. Pattern makers have this in mind when they plan the arrangement of pieces on the fabric. If you ignore the grain, you risk ruining your project because fabric cut off-grain often twists.

> **layout tip** Don't allow the fabric to hang off the edge of the table. Support it with a chair or roll it up so the weight of the extra fabric doesn't pull and distort things.

Start by placing the largest piece(s) on the fold and then work down in size from there. Don't worry about pinning at this point. Just follow the layout diagram and place the pieces where they belong. Lay them printed side up or down as the instructions indicate. The pattern makers have worked everything out for maximum efficiency, minimum fabric waste. Stick to the plan—it's there to help you.

---

know when to fold it

Many garment pieces are completely symmetrical. That is, they have identical right and left sides, but in mirror-image. Look at the back of a finished skirt or jacket, and you'll see what I mean. So, many pattern pieces are only half the width of the garment piece, but by laying them on the fold of your fabric when you cut them out, they're doubled. It's like folding a piece of paper in half and cutting out a lopsided arc to make a heart. You end up with a neat symmetrical piece. Working with half-sized pattern pieces means less labor on your part (half the cutting), and less pattern bulk to store later (half the paper). Pieces *not* lined up on the fold will become two identical garment sections that are mirror-images of one another (and again, half the cutting). See how smart sewing is?

corduroy, checks, and plaids, oh my! WORKING WITH DIRECTIONAL FABRICS

At some point you may be working with some special-needs fabrics. Consider the following layout scenarios before breaking out your scissors. And remember, avoid these materials if you're a beginner.

Napped fabrics, such as corduroy, velvet, and suede, have a texture that's like the fur of a cat. When you pet these fabrics (or a cat), one direction feels smooth, the other rough or weird. Napped fabrics also reflect light differently depending on the direction of the "fur." All this means is that you need extra yardage and extra planning when sewing with napped fabrics. In sewing, you want the smooth direction running from the top down to the bottom of the garment. Keep this in mind when you lay out your pattern pieces. Also, make sure the nap direction on the front and back pieces are the same so they will go together. Sometimes, there's a separate layout view (and bigger yardage requirement) for napped fabrics.

Plaids, large checks, and stripes can be challenging. But don't get mad, get even. If you're making a skirt, for example, find the side seam notches on the front and back pattern pieces. Where the notches line up, the side seams on the skirt will line up, right? (See pages 80–81 for more on notches.) Pick a nice centrally located horizontal line in the plaid or striped fabric. Arrange the pattern pieces so the side seam notches all line up on that same horizontal line. It's like a parlor trick!

Be sure to line up notches, if you want stripes to line up.

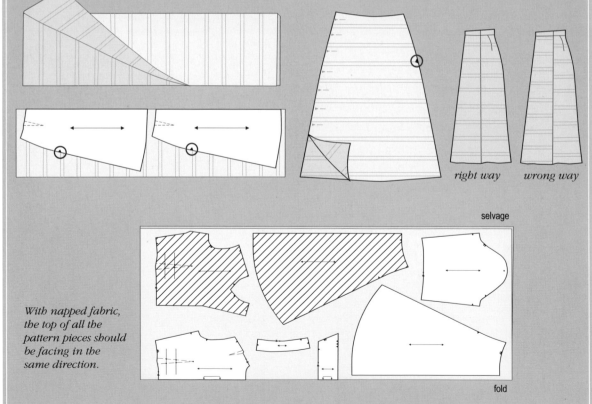

right way   *wrong way*

selvage

With napped fabric, the top of all the pattern pieces should be facing in the same direction.

fold

step 5 pin the pattern to the fabric

You've laid your pattern pieces out according to the diagram, the grainline, and any special directional needs like nap or stripes. Now you carefully pin the pattern pieces through both layers of the fabric, keeping everything neat and flat. Insert pins parallel to the edge of the pattern about every 3 to 4 inches or a palm's width apart. You might want a few more pins if the fabric is slippery or soft. Keep pins about ⅛ inch away from the cutting line so they don't get clipped by the scissors.

Pin the pattern pieces that are on the fold first. Work along the edge that's touching the fold, and then go around the remaining three sides. Or, I sometimes get better results after pinning along the foldline ('cause you have to), then pinning down the center of the piece, working my way out to the corners. Don't let the pattern tissue or the fabric underneath it wrinkle when you're inserting pins. If it does, take out the pins, smooth the pattern and fabric with your hand, and try again.

The pieces that aren't along the fold are a bit trickier to pin. Instead of using the folded edge as your guide, use your ruler to make sure the grainline arrows are parallel to the selvage or fold. Measure from one end of the grainline arrow to the fold or selvage, and then measure the other end of the grainline arrow to the same fold or selvage, as shown. The distance should be the same. (If not, adjust.) This means you are cutting on-grain. Pin both ends of the grainline arrows first so the pattern doesn't shift. Then pin diagonally at the corners, and finally pin the edges, smoothing the pattern as you go.

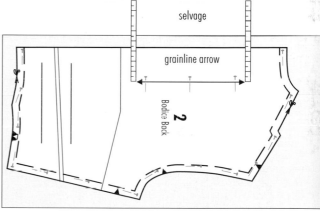

You may be surprised to discover that something as seemingly straightforward as pinning paper to cloth takes some practice. Luckily, it won't take much.

step 6 check your work

After you've finished pinning, take a break. Go outside, get some fresh air. Cutting is a crucial step, so don't start it in haste. Remember the carpenter's motto, "Measure twice, cut once." Measure your grainline distances again. Compare your layout to the cutting guide on the pattern. Did you account for every piece? Note where you'll be cutting one piece and where you'll be cutting two or more. Do you feel super-confident about the job you've done? Good. Let's go to the cutting edge.

step 7 cut it out!

Keep one hand resting on the pattern so you don't accidentally move it as you work. With your dressmaker's shears, cut directly on the cutting line, using long, smooth strokes for straight lines and shorter ones around curves. Slide the scissors gently across the cutting table so you don't have to lift the fabric. *You* should move, not your fabric.

When you come across notches or diamond-shaped marks along the edge, cut through them (the bottom half of the diamond-shape will remain). After you have cut around the pattern, go back and make a small snip or slit with the tip of your scissors down the center of each notch, ¼ inch below the cutting line. Be careful not to cut too far, as you don't want to cut into the seam allowance. These marks indicate where you need to match up one cut piece to another, like the center of each side seam on a skirt.

Note: In my experience, nothing good comes of trying to neaten up a jagged edge. It's worse than cutting your own hair badly and then trying to even things out. For now, just do the best you can the first time around and leave it at that.

❋ **Save your leftovers**

It may be tempting to toss the leftover fabric into the trash bin, but don't! There's always the possibility that you forgot a small part of a waistband or only have one shoulder strap instead of two. Scraps also come in handy for testing stitch patterns and thread tension, practicing buttonholes, making covered buttons, and more. I recommend storing all leftovers in a designated bin.

step 8 make your mark(s)

The last step in the layout and cutting process is marking, or transferring some of the symbols printed on the pattern to the fabric. You usually do this with chalk, or with a tracing wheel and dressmaker's carbon, on the wrong side of the fabric. Pattern instructions include a key for each symbol, and the more basic the pattern, the fewer marks you'll make. (See the facing page for decoding the symbols.) Every mark you transfer is a reference point that will help you later, so go for accuracy—not speed or beauty.

After notches, the most common marks are dots. Like notches, dots can also tell you where one pattern piece lines up with another, such as the top of a sleeve with the center of the shoulder seam. Here's how to transfer dots using pins and chalk, which is my preferred method.

W·W·M·D?

Martha likes her tools, and she doesn't mess around with them. I know for a fact that Martha uses a fancy labeling machine (called a P-Touch) to label all her dressmaker's shears "for fabric only." If you live with loved ones or roommates, you'd be wise to copy the Big M by keeping your shears in a glass jar with a round of felt at the bottom to cushion the point. I'm sure Martha also keeps her shears in shape by having them professionally sharpened and oiled at least once a year. (Many sewing machine and fabric stores offer this service for $5 or less.) You know what Martha *wouldn't* do? Cut through pins or drop the shears on the floor. That's not a good thing.

cheat sheet
PATTERN SYMBOLS AND MARKINGS

The following is a quick reference for all the symbols and markings you might find on a commercial pattern. Learn the symbols, names, and meanings, and you'll have fewer headaches down the road.

✳ Cutting lines

Multisized patterns have different cutting lines for each size.

✳ Place-on-fold bracket

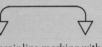

A grainline marking with arrows pointing to the edge of the pattern. Place on the fold of the fabric.

✳ Grainline

Double-ended arrow that should be parallel to the selvage or fold.

✳ Seam line

A long, broken line indicates where the stitching will take place, usually ⅝ inch in from the cutting line. Multisized patterns often do not include seam line markings.

✳ Notches

Diamond-shaped symbols used for accurately matching seams. Pieces to be joined will have corresponding notches. Tops of darts have notches, too.

✳ Dots

Come in a variety of sizes and shapes, including solid dots and squares. They indicate the position of darts, zippers, pockets, and seam openings, and mark the beginning and end of gathers.

✳ Darts

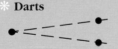

Dashed lines and dots mark darts. The dashed lines show where the stitching will be, and the dot tells you when to stop stitching! (See page 88 for instructions.)

✳ Adjustment lines

Double lines specify the place to lengthen or shorten a pattern. These help you make your alterations before laying the pattern on the fabric. If you want to make your pattern piece bigger or smaller, cut at these lines and spread the pattern evenly apart to lengthen (tape paper into the gap), or overlap evenly to shorten. This is not a move for beginners.

✳ Hemline

The hem allowance is printed on the cutting line ("1 inch," "2½ inches," etc.). Turn up the hem by the specified amount or adjust on an as-needed basis.

✳ Button and button-hole placement marks

Solid horizontal lines indicate buttonholes, and will be the same size as the buttons listed on the back of the pattern envelope. An "X" is the button symbol and shows the placement.

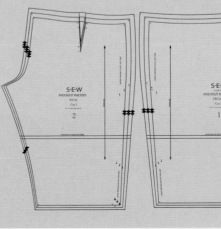

To transfer marks onto your fabric:

1. Push a pin through the dot in the pattern paper and the fabric below (A).

2. Lift the paper pattern piece gently, leaving the head of the pin in the fabric (B).

3. Rub chalk against the pin where it pokes into the fabric. (You mark the location of buttons and buttonholes exactly the same way.)

4. Turn fabric and mark on the underside (C).

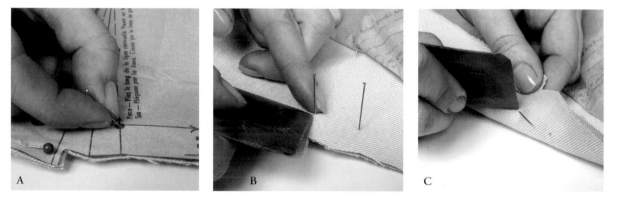

Keep 'em pinned

Don't completely remove the tissue just yet! You need it to identify each cut piece of fabric and to prevent mix-ups. Stack the still-pinned pattern pieces in a neat and tidy fashion or arrange them on a hanger to prevent wrinkling. Remove the paper as you start to actually sew and remember to put it back into your manila envelope.

Looks like we made it . . . well, *almost*

This is the stage in the game when you should go back and cut your lining and/or interfacing, if you have any. Refer to the cutting layout for instructions. And don't forget to make your marks!

Hallelujah!

At this point, you should stop and throw a small party for yourself, because you have gotten through the persnickety, sloggy prep work. You may have forgotten that you actually have a magical machine that will help turn this stack of carefully washed, pressed, pinned, cut, and marked fabric into something wonderful to wear or decorate your digs with. So enjoy the moment, pat yourself on the back. But then put your toolbelt back on and rev up the machine, because you are about to start construction.

the sewing playbook

*I*f you've been following along, you've picked a pattern that matches your mad skillz (or lack thereof), bought a fabric so perfect that, yes, you might actually want to marry it (or at the very least take it out on a date), and cut it into pieces so artfully that you have fantasies of signing up for med school and becoming a surgeon. This is the long-awaited stage when you actually start to sew. All the planning and preparation become action and production. It's the Big Day.

The playbook will take you through the basic techniques that will transform flat pieces of fabric into something dynamic and 3-D that fits the curves of your body. Seams are the hammer and nails of sewing; they're literally what hold a garment together. And because you are classy (and hate fraying), you want to know how to finish seams so they last. You'll learn tricks for making curved seams on places such as waistbands, armholes, and necklines. We'll spend time on techniques like darts, easing, and gathers that give garments their shape—they put the D in 3-D. And when you get to the end of your project, you'll need some closure—in the form of buttons, snaps, or hooks. I even share my secret weapon of sewing: the invisible zipper.

If you are still a sewing newbie, read through this chapter for a heads-up on what awaits you in Sewingville, USA. Maybe get in some more practice. But, if you are a more experienced sewer, or simply cannot wait another moment before you put needle to fabric, then skip ahead to the pattern section and refer back here if you get stuck.

one "seam-ingly" beautiful

Sewing a seam is the most basic and essential task. You will sew more straight seams than all your darts, zippers, pockets, and gathers combined. So it pays to sew seams right. And you aren't done with a seam until you press and finish it. When sewing a seam for a garment, remember these tips:

❋ **Go slow**

If you don't rush, you have more control. Your seams stay ruler-straight or gently curved (as needed).

❋ **Don't pull your fabric**

Let the machine (really, the feed dogs) do the pulling for you. Your hands just steer and guide.

❋ **Watch your seam allowances**

Use the marks on the throat plate to keep your seam allowances on track and consistent. You generally sew clothes with a ⅝-inch seam allowance. Home decor and accessories get a ½-inch seam allowance. Check and see what your pattern requires. The pattern was designed and sized with an exact seam allowance in mind, so please respect it for the best fit possible.

pressing matters

You need to press every seam you make, every time you sew. Always. This locks in the stitches, evens out the tension, and keeps your work neat and crisp as you go. (Don't forget to use a press cloth if your fabric needs one. How to tell? See facing page.) To press a seam:

1. Place your garment on the ironing board, wrong side up.

2. Press along the stitching on one side of the seam and then the other.

3. Then open up the seam allowance and press it flat (left).

For curved seams, you might need to iron on a rounded form called a tailor's ham (right). Plus, it's always fun to use something called a tailor's ham.

finishing school

It's a sad fact that woven fabrics start to fall apart the minute you cut them. To keep fraying in check and to protect seams from wear, you need to finish the raw edges of the seam allowance. The good news is these finishes can make your projects pretty inside and out. Here are three basic ways to finish a seam:

✳ Pinked

This finish gets points for being fast and dirty, but it only works well on tight weaves like shirting, denim, and canvas. Do a test on a scrap of your project fabric to see if it's in the pink. If yes, simply take your pinking shears and cut ¼ inch off each raw edge of the seam allowance. If the fabric is lightweight, you can even pink through both allowances together. If your fabric is thicker, press the seam open and flat, and then pink one side at a time.

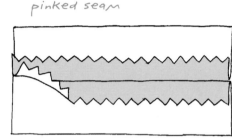

pinked seam

✳ Zigzagged-and-trimmed

I most often use the zigzagged-and-trimmed technique because, unlike pinking, it tames even the most fray-prone materials. To do it, select the zigzag stitch on your machine. Work along the edges of the seam allowance only, and zigzag a line ¼ inch in from the edge of each side. Next, trim away ⅛ inch from each edge, taking care not to cut into the zigzag stitching (or anywhere else on your project). This finish also works well on knits.

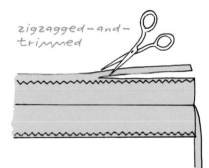

zigzagged-and-trimmed

✳ French seam

Leave it to the French to come up with such an elegant finish. In a French seam the raw edges of the seam allowances are enclosed within the seam itself, and the outside appears as a neat fold.

 **W·W·M·D?**

When zipping along on the machine, sewing seams by the mile, I'm tempted to bag the pressing step and just keep sewing. But guess whose voice I hear urging me to stop? The Iron Lady's. Not only would Martha press all her seams, but she'd do it just right. So I try to meet her high standards. Martha would test a scrap piece of fabric to see how it responds to ironing. I know she's big on using a press cloth, too. So I'd place a press cloth (see facing page) on the right side of fabrics like woolens, silks, and rayon to prevent those ugly shine marks. Then she would gently press the iron down on the fabric, moving it very little and always in the direction of the grain, not sliding it back and forth as you do when ironing out a wrinkle. It's a good thing to lift the iron up to move to another section.

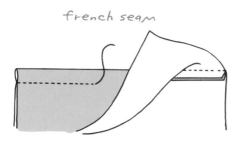

french seam

French seams are de rigueur with sheer fabrics where the seam allowances are visible, but they do take more work. (**Note:** This seam finish is for straight seams only.) Here's how:

1. Pin fabric with the *wrong* sides together.

2. Stitch ¼ inch from edge on right side of fabric if you're using a ½-inch seam allowance. For projects with a ⅝-inch seam allowance, stitch ⅜ inch in from the edge.

3. Trim seam allowance to ⅛ inch.

4. Fold the fabric *right* sides together with the seam line exactly on the fold. Press flat.

5. Stitch ¼ inch from the fold. Check the right side to make sure there are no raveled threads messing up your handiwork.

6. Press enclosed seam to one side. Voilà!

trimming seams

As you're stitching merrily long, your pattern will often tell you to trim your seams (thus reducing annoying bulk forever!). The instructions will spell out when, where, and how much to cut off, but the most common techniques are:

trimming

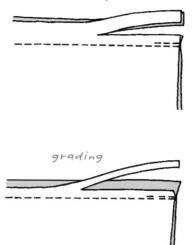

grading

✳ **Trimming**

When the full width of the seam allowance is going to get in the way, directions will ask you to *trim* the excess. You might see this direction when you're sewing a French seam or before putting in a lining.

✳ **Grading**

This only happens to straight seams. Sometimes, if the seam allowance ends up encased somewhere—like the inside of the Breezy Easy Wrap Skirt waistband—you need to *grade* the excess fabric. That means you trim away the seam allowances to different widths on each side of the stitching so there's not a ridge where the raw edges meet. The seam allowance that lies closer to your body should be wider; the one that's away from the body should be narrower.

clipping and notching

Curved seams do not lie flat, so you have to help them. To reduce fullness on *inward* curves (like the cinched waist of a dress), you *clip* them. Using the tips of your dressmaker's scissors, snip into the seam allowance without cutting into the stitching. (Be careful!) This lets the seam allowance spread out around the curve.

On *outward* curves (like around the hip of a dress), cut notches or small V-shaped wedges into the seam allowance. This lets the seam allowance scrunch together a bit without getting too bulky.

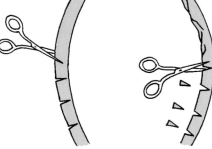

clipping   notching

squaring off

Perfectly square corners require special trimming on the inside or the seam allowance will bunch up, making it more of a rounded nub than the crisp corner you want. When sewing a pillow, for example, you square off the corners by cutting off the point. Then trim the seam allowances at each point at a 45-degree angle, as shown, and taper them on either side. (Just don't get too close to the stitching.) The more elongated the point, the more you trim the seam allowance—so when you turn the point right-side out, the corners are sharp.

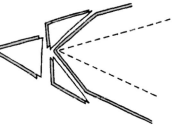

trimming a corner

shaping up two

Because we are not paper dolls, our clothes need darts, gathers, pleats, and tucks to give them shape. Bust, waist, hips—sometimes even elbows—need special treatment so garments fit right and flatter. Without shaping techniques, we'd all be wearing togas and muumuus. Here are a few basic ones:

staystitching

Staystitching is often your first step in sewing a garment that needs shaping. Sewing patterns will tell you when and where to staystitch, but it happens most often on curves and angles such as necklines and armholes. Staystitching is simple: It's just a line of straight stitches ½ inch in from the edge and through a single layer of fabric, which "stays" the fabric, or stops the garment from stretching while you work. When staystitching a neckline, start at each outer edge and stitch in toward the middle (no wonky stretching this way).

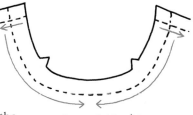

staystitching

making darts

Darts draw fabric closer to the body. Dart-making is often the first step in sewing fitted garments. First-timers should definitely practice on a piece of scrap fabric before stitching on the real thing. Good darts are straight, smooth, and free from puckers. While some experienced sewers show off their chops by eyeballing the stitch line, I prefer to draw lines onto the fabric with chalk or a disappearing-ink marker. This way, I know I'll hit my mark. Here's how to make killer darts:

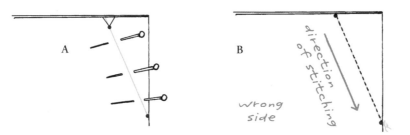

1. Lay the fabric piece on a table, wrong side up.

2. Fold the dart in half, right side to right side, lining up the dots. Use your ruler and chalk or disappearing-ink marker to draw a line from the center of the notch down to the dot. Pin with the pinheads toward the folded edge (A).

3. Stitch a straight line from the notches down to the dot (B), using a short stitch length so it won't pop out the first time you wear it.

Note: Instead of backstitching at the dot, leave long tails of thread and tie off in a knot. (Backstitching here would keep the dart from lying flat.)

4. Press the dart to one side, usually toward the middle, but check your pattern.

easestitching

Sometimes, you have to sew together two garment pieces of unequal length—a sleeve into a slightly smaller armhole, for example. This situation calls for *easing* or *easestitching*. Here's how: Line up any notches. Use pins ever-so-gently to gather the longer piece until it's the same length as the smaller one. Distribute the extra bulk evenly across the section, pinning as you go. The goal of easing is to hide any extra little tucks from the long side, so sew slowly and carefully.

If the size difference between the two pieces is great, let your machine help you. Switch setting to the longest stitch length and sew a line ½ inch in from the edge of the longer piece. Pull the thread tails to gather the longer section evenly. Then pin it to the shorter piece and sew the seam with a regular stitch length.

gathering

Gathering is much the same as easestitching, except you sew a much longer piece to a much shorter piece, distributing the extra bulk evenly in little soft folds that show. Gathers give a soft rounded shape and looser fit. You may want them for a waistline, yoke, cuffs, or sleeves. I'm a huge fan of gathers as a design element. I like their '70s peasant vibe. Here's how to host a gathering:

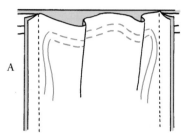

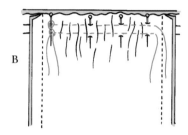

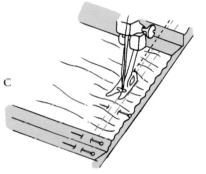

1. Set your machine to the widest stitch length possible and a loose upper thread tension.

2. On the longer piece of fabric make two lines of parallel stitching about ¼ inch apart. One line should run along the seam line, the other within the seam allowance (A). Leave 10-inch tails at each end.

3. Secure a pin at one end of the stitching, as shown (B), and wind the thread around it in a figure eight.

4. Pull the threads at the opposite end as gently as possible until the gathered section is the

same length as the straight section. (Patterns usually mark the beginning and end of gathered sections.)

5. Distribute the gathers as evenly as possible and pin the gathered piece to the straight section—right sides together, as shown (B). Use lots of pins.

6. With the machine set back to normal length, stitch slowly with the gathered side face up so your seam line falls just outside the gathering stitch line (C). Hold the fabric taut on both sides of the presser foot. Make sure the underside stays flat.

7. Trim seam allowances and press according to pattern directions (D). Do not press across the top of gathers or you'll flatten 'em!

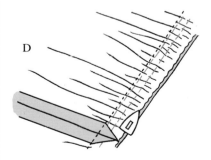

other ways to shape

Pleats, tucks, and smocking are other ways to shape a flat piece of fabric. But they are a little more advanced, and you don't need 'em to make any of the awesome S•E•W projects. But start watching for pretty shaping details on clothes you see and touch. And by all means, add those techniques to your repertoire down the sewing road.

using interfacing

Interfacing is like the hairspray of sewing, helping the garment hold its shape. The most likely spots are facings—separate pieces of fabric for finishing edges, such as necklines, collars, and cuffs. Interfacings can either be sew-in or fusible, depending on the delicacy of your fabric. We use only fusible interfacing for the patterns in the book because it is so easy to iron it on to the back of the fabric. It is cut with the same pattern piece you used to cut the fabric. Although applying fusible interfacing is straightforward, let me walk you through it the first time:

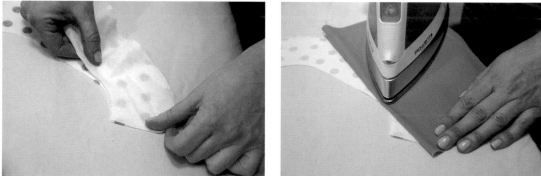

1. Set a dry iron to the temperature appropriate for your fabric.

2. Place the fabric piece wrong side up on an ironing board and lay the adhesive side of the interfacing (which is bumpy or shiny) face down on the fabric so the cut edges line up perfectly. If the interfacing is too big, trim it down to fit. If it's too small, cut a new piece.

3. Place a press cloth on top of the interfacing and fabric and press until the two pieces are fused together. Place the iron firmly across the whole piece. Don't slide it around.

4. Let the interfacing cool, and then check to see if it fused all over. If not, iron again until there are no loose spots.

Tailoring and Fitting

No one is a perfect size 6, 12, or 18. We all have variations and bumps that make us delightfully unique. When you make your own clothes, you can adjust them to really fit your figure—big bonus! Here are a few techniques and tricks to help you shape your garment to fit *your* shape.

"cheating" the paper pattern

You can make simple changes to the paper pattern with the stroke of a felt-tip pen. In a multisize pattern, where there are several size lines around the edge, you can use those size lines to your advantage. If you are somewhere between an 8 and a 10, then make a new size line halfway between the two. If your hips are a 12, while your waist is a 10, then trace your pen along the size 12 line around the hips of the skirt or pants and taper the line to meet the size 10 line at the waistline.

sewing up, narrowing down

It's much easier to make garments smaller than bigger. Better to err on the side of sewing your garment large and making adjustments later. Sew for the fullest part of your body. For example, if you have a big bustline, then baste the side seams of your shirt and try it on inside out. It's much easier if you can get someone to help you pin-baste a better fit while you're wearing it. But if you're alone, pinch where it needs narrowing, take it off, pin-baste (with pins inserted the long way and in the direction the stitches will go), and try it on again. The line of pins should fall where you want the seam to be. (Here's where a dress form comes in handy.) Make chalk marks at every pin. Holding your flexible ruler on its edge, connect the chalk marks. Baste and sew.

If you have big hips and a smallish waist, you can cut and sew for your hip width and take in the side seams at the waistline—trying the pants on, pinning, basting, and sewing. (Make sure to narrow the waistband as well, if you have one.) You can also adjust darts to be shallower or deeper. If it hits in a funny place, mark a new place for the dart point. Put a pin where you want the dart to end, open up the old dart, and make a new triangle. You can even add darts where there were none, though it's much easier to make adjustments to seams that already exist.

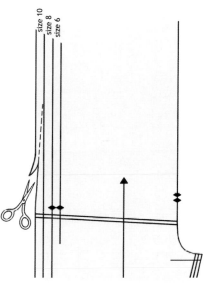

Cut the pattern to fit your size. You're the boss!

make it

narrow a store-bought skirt

A good way to practice fitting is on clothes you already have. And you can get into the groove of doing your own alterations. Try taking a skirt you own and making it narrower—more pencil-like. To do this, you'll need dressmaker's carbon paper and a tracing wheel. Here's how:

1. Put the skirt on inside out.

2. Starting a few inches below the waist, pinch the extra skirt bulk—you only have to do this for one side—and pin. Pins should run the long way, parallel to the seam line (A).

3. Take off the skirt. Mark with chalk at every pin (B).

4. Take the pins out and connect the chalk marks by holding your flexible ruler on its edge and using it as guide to connect the dots (C).

5. Fold the skirt in half (still inside out) the long way. Stick dressmaker's carbon paper facedown under your chalk line and trace over it with a tracing wheel to make the exact same line on the other side of the skirt (D).

6. Sew along both lines with a basting stitch.

7. Try on the skirt. Repin and rebaste the skirt until you are happy with the fit.

8. Sew with a standard stitch length. (The key is to blend the new side seam with the old one. They should merge subtly—ahem, seamlessly—like a car merging onto a gently curving highway.)

9. Cut away the excess seam allowance, press, and finish the seams.

A

B

C

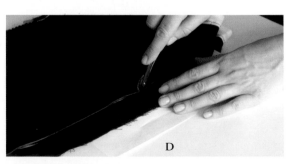

D

fit check

Even if your figure is pretty true to size you should check the fit along the way. Pin-baste your major seams; don't bother with cuffs and collars and such. Put on the garment right-side out, as that's how you'll wear it. Pin shut any closures and see how things hang. Check to see if any seams pull. Look for any major bulges. If there are problems, mark with pins (again, get a friend to help if you can). Take the garment off and repin where needed, and try it on again. Repeat this until you are satisfied.

Check also where the darts fall. Do they hit your hips and bust where they should? This is your last chance to redo them. Check to see that your grainlines look vertical or horizontal, not slanty. Since the S•E•W patterns are pretty basic and not super-fitted, there shouldn't be many adjustments to make. But checking the fit is a good habit to get into.

Always double-check the fit before stitching seams.

getting closure: hems, zippers & buttons

I have to confess: For years, I only used patterns if they were zipper- and buttonhole-free. Perhaps this fear of closure had to do with the scary 1950s buttonhole attachment on my mom's machine. It wasn't until I started Make Workshop that I overcame my phobia and started making projects with proper closures. What changed? I discovered two things: the invisible zipper and a one-step buttonhole. They can make your sewing life easier, too. And hems—well, they aren't nearly so scary, but they are just as essential to finishing a piece (unless you're going for the funky, frayed look of a raw edge).

machine hemming

In addition to seam allowances, the bottom edges of your projects—the hems—need finishing. Patterns often ask for a turned-and-stitched hem, which just means you fold the hem allowance to the inside so the raw edge is hidden, and then edgestitch in place. Edgestitching is just what it sounds like: stitching on top as close to the edge as possible, about ⅛ inch from the fold or seam. In the fashion biz, this is called a sportswear finish. It does have a sporty, casual look, and it only takes a few steps, which is great when you're at the finish line. You can dress up a machine-sewn hem by adding an attractive seam binding, which comes in woven or lace form. These directions are for a ½-inch or double-turned hem, but you can follow the same steps for a wider hem allowance.

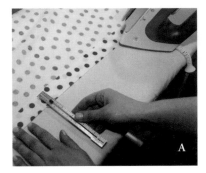

1. Measure and trim your garment to your desired hem length, plus 1 inch.

2. Using your sewing gauge as a guide, turn the hem allowance up by 1 inch, wrong side to wrong side (A). Press.

3. Tuck the raw edge under by one half and press again on the hem foldline (B).

4. Pin the hem in place.

5. Edgestitch ⅛ inch from the hem foldline (C). Press again to set the stitching.

---

topstitching vs edgestitching
WHAT'S THE BIG DIFF?

Seams are commonly finished either with an edgestitch or a topstitch. *Edgestitching* is used to keep a seam allowance from rolling, to keep an edge flat, or to strengthen a seam. To do it, stitch ⅛ inch from the finished edge.

Topstitching, on the other hand, can be practical or purely decorative and is typically stitched ¼ inch in from an edge. While it does reduce seam bulk and add strength, it's also a cool embellishment, especially when done with multiple lines of stitching.

fusible webbing

Fusible webbing can bond two layers of fabric together. Made from polyamide, it's like double-sided tape for sewing. The most common brands are Stitch Witchery and Steam-A-Seam. To work with it, you simply tear off a strip the length of your hem (or do it in sections), tuck the webbing underneath the fabric, and iron. The heat melts the webbing and fuses the two pieces of fabric together.

Use it to put up hems or to hold patches, trims, or appliqués in place before you sew. Then simply stitch on top of it. **Warning:** Don't let the fusible web make direct contact with your iron because it will melt and stick to the plate! Should this happen, set your iron on the highest setting and iron a scrap of terry cloth for ten seconds.

centered zipper

To install a regular, standard zipper (as opposed to an invisible zipper, page 96) that's centered on the garment, you sew parallel lines of visible stitching along each side of the zipper teeth. Have the zipper foot on your machine handy and follow these steps:

A
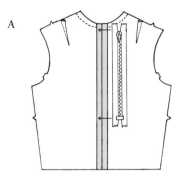

B

C
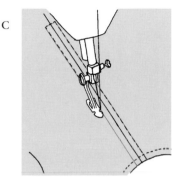

1. Sew the center back seam up to the notch point indicated on your fabric (and as illustrated by your pattern instructions). This is where the zipper will end.

2. Set your machine to the longest stitch length and baste the rest of the seam closed where the zipper will be.

3. Finish the seam allowances along the entire center back seam. Press the seam allowances open.

4. Place the closed zipper face down on the pressed-open seam allowance per your pattern instructions (A). Check that the center of the zipper is lined up with your basted seam.

5. Hand-baste (B), machine-baste, or apply a fabric glue stick

to the seam allowance to hold the zipper in place while you sew. (Press with your fingers and let dry a bit before sewing.)

6. Turn the fabric over to the right side and using a ruler and chalk or disappearing-ink marker, draw two stitching lines on either side of the zipper, ¼ inch from the center seam.

7. Put the zipper foot on your machine and stitch along the lines you've drawn (C), backstitching at the beginning and end.

8. Stitch a short horizontal line at the bottom. You can pivot or do it as three separate seams, just be careful not to hit the stopper, which would break your needle!

9. Remove all basting with your seam ripper.

get shorty
HOW TO SHORTEN A ZIPPER

Zipper lengths are not sacred. You can take a longer zipper and cut it down for your needs. Just mark your desired zipper length with a disappearing-ink marker. With the machine set at a zero stitch length, zigzag across the teeth at that spot to form a mound of stitching that will serve as your new bottom stop. Cut off the excess zipper, and you're done!

invisible zipper

There's no visible stitching on a garment with an invisible zipper (hence the name)—only the zipper pull shows at the top. The actual zipper is like a regular zipper, except the line of teeth coil inward a bit. And it requires an invisible zipper foot with a roller to flatten it out as you stitch. (You can get an invisible zipper foot that will fit any sewing machine at most fabric stores for around $5.) Invisible zippers are applied to an open seam, and to seam allowances only. They can be used wherever conventional zippers are. You can follow the sewing instructions on the invisible zipper package or follow mine, but definitely practice your moves before inserting a zipper in a project. To prepare: Press the teeth and tape flat with a dry, warm iron to make the teeth stand away from the zipper tape. Put the invisible zipper foot on the machine.

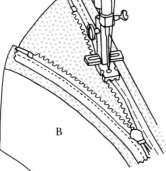

A

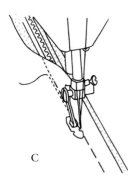

B

C

1. First, fold the raw edges of your fabric pieces back to the wrong side at the correct seam allowance and press. Or mark your seam allowance with a disappearing-ink marker.

2. Unzip the zipper and position it facedown on the right side of one of your fabric pieces, lining up the teeth of the zipper with the future seam line (which is the crease or line you drew in step 1). Pin or hand-baste into place.

3. Place the pinned or basted zipper under the invisible zipper foot, as shown. Starting at the top of the zipper, stitch along the tape as close as possible to the teeth without stitching on top of them (A). Sew all the way down to the slide. (It won't be possible to sew past the zipper pull.) Backstitch to reinforce.

4. Pin and baste the other side of

the zipper along the seam line of the remaining side, right sides together, as shown (B). Zip up the zipper to check placement, but then unzip to stitch.

5. Sew as you did the first side.

6. Close the zipper. Now you have to finish sewing the seam of the garment. Pin and baste the seam together below the zipper with right sides together. (Keep the free ends of the zipper tape away from the seam allowance.)

7. Put the regular zipper foot in place. Drop the needle into the fabric where you just stopped sewing. Backstitch and continue sewing to the end of the seam line (C). Press seam open.

8. Leave the zipper foot attached and sew the free ends of the zipper tape to their respective seam allowances.

make it
zipperific pencil case

1. With chalk and ruler on scrap fabric draw and cut out two pieces 9 x 4½ inches.

2. With right sides together and leaving a ½-inch seam allowance, baste together the two pieces on one long side (A). Press the seam open (B).

3. Center an 8-inch zipper facedown on the seam allowances and baste it in place (C). Sew on the zipper using steps 6–9 of the centered zipper directions (page 95).

4. Pull the zipper tab open by an inch. *This is very important!*

5. With the zipper at the top, pin right sides together and sew around the other three sides using the regular foot (D).

6. Clip corners. Remove basting from zipper and turn your pencil case right side out.

This looks cute with two different pieces of fabric. You can also embellish with appliqué or embroidery.

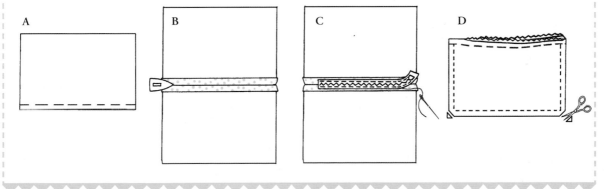

A   B   C   D

button tip Your buttonhole should be ⅛ inch bigger than your button. Very fat, round buttons may need ¼ inch extra. If in doubt, try making a buttonhole on scrap fabric. It's good practice anyway.

buttonholes

The buttonhole markings should have been made during the layout and cutting stage. But if they weren't, look at your pattern and transfer the markings using the pins and chalk method (pages 80–82). Buttonholes should be ½ inch away from the finished edge. Use your stitch gauge or stick down some ½-inch tape to make sure you keep that distance from the edge. See pages 231–232 in the Hand-Sewing Appendix for help on how to sew on buttons.

one-step buttonhole

I've got my fingers crossed that you followed my advice and got a machine with a one-step buttonhole attachment. What makes them so great? You simply put the button in the buttonhole tray and the machine stitches a buttonhole to fit—it's like magic! (If not, no worries, I'll teach you other ways to sew buttonholes.) Always practice on a piece of your project fabric whenever you need to make a buttonhole. It's much safer to work out the kinks on something other than your practically completed project. Here's how:

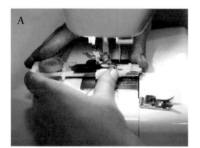

1. Select the buttonhole stitch and set the stitch length to zero.

2. Remove the presser foot and attach the buttonhole presser foot.

3. Drop the presser foot, hit the latch, and the shank should snap into place. Pull the buttonhole lever straight down as far as it will go.

4. Place the button into the sliding tray (A).

5. Center the foot on the fabric, at the end of your buttonhole mark. There's usually a metal arrow in the center front that works as a guide.

6. Start stitching and the buttonholer will automatically sew all four sides without your needing to turn the fabric (B). The machine "feels" the button it's holding and stitches the entire buttonhole in the perfect size in

one operation. Stop when the stitching begins to overlap.

7. Lift up the presser foot, pull the fabric off the machine, and cut the thread ends away.

8. Slice the buttonhole open carefully with your seam ripper (C) and strengthen the cut edge with a liquid fray-preventer, such as Fray Check by Dritz (or in a pinch, use clear nail polish).

zigzag buttonhole

If you don't have the one-step buttonhole function, you can make a buttonhole by using the zigzag stitch on your machine. Here's how:

1. Mark the buttonhole length on the project with a chalk line.

2. Set your machine for the zigzag stitch at a short stitch length. Stitch along the left side of the line and when you get to the bottom, pivot 180 degrees and stitch back up the opposite side (A).

3. Bar-tack the top and bottom by resetting your machine to a zero stitch length and sewing in place a half-dozen times at each end of the buttonhole (B).

4. Lift up the presser foot, pull the fabric off the machine, and cut the thread ends.

5. Slice the buttonhole carefully with your seam ripper (C) and strengthen the cut edge with liquid fray-preventer.

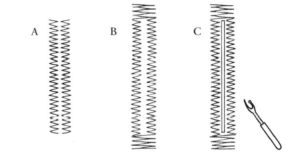

hooks and eyes

Hooks and eyes often fasten the tops of waistbands and necklines. Hooks are pretty much little hooks, but eyes can either be straight or round. A straight eye is good for overlapped edges, and a round eye is better for edges that line up flush. These old-fashioned but super-useful fasteners come in several sizes and styles, including a heavy-duty version. **Note:** If the waistband is wide, you might need two sets of hooks and eyes, or a single skirt/pants hook. Sew by hand, using doubled thread (for extra strength) in a color that blends with your fabric.

For edges that overlap:

1. Lay the hook on the wrong side of the garment ⅛ inch in from the edge. Sew in place through the holes and across the end to hold it flat. The stitches should not show on the right side.

2. Close the opening and align the overlap. On the underlap, mark the position for the eye—where the bend of the hook hits—with pins.

3. Sew the eye to the underlap.

99

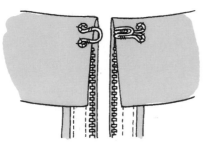

For edges that meet:

1. Repeat steps 1 and 2 from overlap directions.

2. Close the placket (opening) to align the edges. Mark the position for the eye with pins. Let the round eye extend slightly beyond the garment's edge.

3. Sew short stitches through the holes. Make a few stitches along the sides of the loop to hold it flat.

hook-and-eye tip
Use a piece of tape to keep the hook or eye in place until you're ready to stitch.

snap to it

Snaps come in two parts: a ball and a socket in several weights. Use snaps only on overlapping edges where there will be little strain—otherwise they'll pop open when you least expect it. As with hooks and eyes, take care to stitch them neatly in place, with no threads blocking the snap or socket. To install them:

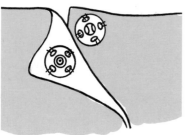

1. Sew the ball of the snap to the wrong side of the overlap about ⅛ inch from the edge. Make several stitches through one of the holes, then run the thread under the snap to the next hole and repeat. Stitches should not show on the outside of the garment.

2. Rub chalk on the ball and close the overlap. The chalk will mark the place for the socket.

3. Sew the socket in place in the same way you sewed the ball in step 1.

Fly! Be Free!

Them's the basics. You can take your imaginary tassle and move it to the other side of your imaginary mortarboard. As much as I adore talking about sewing (ask my students), the best way to learn is to do it, sew it, try it. You can always refer back to something here later. So stop reading and stitch to it!

CHAPTER 6 *get stitchin'*

Sure, I teach you machine parts and terms and techniques (see whole first half of this book), but what makes this a workshop—what puts the "W" in S•E•W—is that I walk you through each project as if you were sitting in my workshop, getting a personal tutorial. I even give you the paper patterns to do it. But first here are a few pointers about the level of projects, the sizing, materials, and instructions.

In making my own pattern, I use a hip curve on professional pattern paper.

Designed with You in Mind

I custom made these patterns for you, my dear beginning sewer (or revisiting sewer), keeping the designs simple and super-doable, but also hip and fashionable. These are things you might see in your favorite boutique. Nothing dowdy or home ec-ish. I took couture or designer sportswear looks and boiled them down to the pure essentials, so a beginner could actually make them. Simple is often best anyway. The projects are all things that would excite me if I saw them in a book, the sorts of clothes that I wear—capes, knickers, and a pretty party dress. And I designed things to give to friends and loved ones, like a tie for Father's Day or an elephant or patchwork throw for a newborn baby. This was my favorite part of writing this book: actually inventing and sewing the projects. Shopping for fabric, wrestling with it, and shaping it in my studio, using my tools and my imagination together—that was pure pleasure. It's why I sew. I wish you that same pleasure.

Match Projects to Your "Skillz"

Patterns range from easy-as-pie to slightly more challenging, and each one is labeled with a spool of thread from 1 (very easy) to 3 (advanced beginner). In addition, each one lists the techniques needed to complete the project so you can tell if it matches your skills (or as we say here on the Lower East Side, "skillz"). The projects are really a series of manageable building blocks, allowing you to add on skillz and techniques as you go. But most of the easy patterns (🧵) are in the later part of the book, in the accessories or home sections. Feel free to jump around from easy to hard, or just pick whatever strikes your fancy. Make every pattern in the book and you'll have a strong foundation of sewing techniques you can apply to commercial patterns. Or use this knowledge to create your own designs. Be brave. Sewing (like lots of things) can feel scary the first time out, but then it becomes easy and even a bit thrilling.

Using Paper Patterns

There are two types of paper patterns in this book: the ten that we include in the attached box and the simple ones that I teach you to measure and cut yourself—thus introducing you to the wonderful world of pattern making. Actually, some projects are so simple you just measure and cut directly on the fabric. But most involve a paper pattern that you can use over and over again.

how to make your own patterns

For the most part, you draw simple rectangles and on some projects you connect the dots to form curves, like the neckline of the Canine Couture Coat, page 222, or along the bottom of the Hobo Bag, page 174. To make your own pattern, I recommend buying real pattern paper (available online or at certain fabric stores). This paper has a 1-inch grid that makes measuring and drawing straight lines—something I find hard to do—a cinch. (Regular Kraft paper or poster board will also work, but without that groovy grid, your patterns won't be as exact. Plus, you'll feel like a pro if you use professional paper!) In addition to your regular sewing ruler, it's good to have a hip curve and a French curve (which give you more curvy options). You'll use these plastic tracing tools for altering patterns and projects down the road, so it's worth buying one of each.

Follow the measuring and marking directions in the project instructions under "Make the Pattern." Then, cut out your masterpiece and pin it to the fabric just like any regular sewing pattern.

my motto

Make things with love and what you make will be loveable. (Corny, but I mean it!)

🧵 Very easy

🧵 🧵 Easy to intermediate beginner

🧵 🧵 🧵 Advanced beginner

Accuracy is the most important thing when it comes to creating your own patterns. Do NOT do sloppy work, unless you're prepared for sloppy results—a real heartbreaker! Give yourself time to do it when you won't feel rushed or under pressure. There is an art to pattern cutting. Curves should be subtle. No sharp angles or extreme shapes.

Draw your pattern with a sharp pencil and have a good eraser handy. Clearly label each pattern piece as you create it, so you'll be able to ID it months later when you go back to make the project again. I use a light turquoise permanent marker on my patterns for labeling and for drawing grain lines and other markings. If you're going to share patterns, you might also want to rubber stamp your contact info on them. Then store and label your patterns in a ziplock bag for safekeeping and happy sewing.

Tools of the trade.

How to Read These Instructions

One of the biggest complaints I hear from my sewing students is that commercial patterns don't provide enough info. The instructions here have more detail so you get a lot more guidance, and there is less guesswork. But they still follow standard pattern procedures, so you're also getting training for that day when you use a store-bought pattern. Here's what you can expect in the instructions for each project and what it means to you.

✳Sizing

First, you get the finished measurements of each project, unless it's clothing, in which case you have a choice of three sizes—small, medium, or large—and all patterns are very forgiving, not super-fitted. Each size is graded up three inches from the one preceding it. The best way to ascertain your size is to take your measurements (see page 73), then find them on the size chart for the patterns in this book (below).

Size/Measurement Chart			
	Small	**Medium**	**Large**
Bust	32–34"	35–37"	38–40"
Waist	26–28"	29–31"	32–34"
Hips	34–36"	37–39"	40–42"

If you are between sizes, go with the larger size. If your measurements fall outside of either end of the spectrum, add or subtract the difference between your measurements and the sizing measurements to the pattern. For example, if you have 46-inch hips and want to make the wrap skirt, add four inches to our large pattern size. For patterns on the fold, divide this measurement by half. If you want better results, test your patterns in muslin first. Although you may not be able to make something fit perfectly the first time, you'll get there. And you can often make adjustments after the fact. (See page 232.)

✳ Materials

Next comes a list of all materials you will need for the project, including notions like buttons, bias tape, and thread. Here you'll learn if the pattern is included in the box attached to the book or if you need to make your own. And, of course, suggestions for kinds of fabric to use and the exact yardage to buy (broken down by fabric width). If what's on the model isn't your cup of tea, no prob! I show you lots of fabric swatches that the project would also look good in for inspiration. Enjoy!

✳ Tools

Make sure you have all the basic tools we covered in the sewing kit section of chapter 1 (see page 14). Have your kit at the ready for each project. If the pattern calls for any additional, special tools like a French curve, I list that here.

✳ Techniques

For each pattern, there's a list of techniques used and a reference to the page where this technique was taught so you can refer back. You might want to quickly review these techniques before starting the pattern.

✳ Seam allowances

For fashion projects, I stick to the standard seam allowance of ⅝ inch; for home decor and accessories, I use ½ inch. Sometimes I broke the rules, where a ½-inch seam allowance made the pattern easier to make. So pay attention to the given seam allowance.

✳ Cutting layout

Our cutting layout diagrams have been designed to make as little work as possible and to keep wasted yardage to a minimum. Although folding fabric selvage to selvage with right sides together is the most common scenario, a few patterns call for a single layer of fabric with the right side faceup (e.g., Foxy Boxers and Power Tie), or with the selvages folded towards the center (e.g., Tender is the Nightie and Tunic), or with a partial fold (Breezy Easy Wrap Skirt). Another quirk: Most pattern pieces are cut with the printed side up, but a few need to be flipped over and cut out printed side down. You can tell a printed-side-down pattern by the hatch marks on the pattern piece.

Layout Key

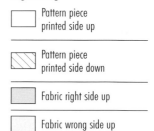

Pattern piece printed side up

Pattern piece printed side down

Fabric right side up

Fabric wrong side up

Illustration Color Key

[·.·.·] Right side fabric

[ ] Wrong side fabric

[ ] Lining

✳ Instructions

Last, but by no means least, are the actual step-by-step sewing instructions. Each project is broken down into smaller tasks (e.g., "Sew darts," "Sew side seams," "Attach waistband," etc.) and then those tasks are broken down into a few numbered steps that have illustrations. *Please note that in the illustrations, white means the wrong side; yellow polka dots means the right side; and lining is shown in pink.* I've tried to foresee any potential problems that come up for students and deal with them so you don't get lost or stumped. And when you cut the final thread and press your first finished hem, there's also an implied last step: A loud "ta-da!"

Ready to Dig In?

Enough with the theoretical situations; let's dig in for real. Begin by gathering your sewing kit and supplies and keep them nearby so you don't have to stop

No-Frills, No-Nonsense Secrets

As you get ready to assemble your assemblage, don't forget what you've learned so far. Like driving a car, you have to think about a lot of things at once—but pretty soon, it will all become second nature. Some final reminders and pointers:

follow instructions

If this is the first time you've sewn, follow the instructions exactly. I'm all for breaking rules—but you've got to know the rules first.

keep right sides together

You almost always sew with right sides together. If you haven't already, mark the wrong sides of each fabric piece with an X in chalk so you know which side is which at a glance.

match notches

Remember when you cut notches? They tell you where to sew pieces to one another. If the notches aren't lining up per your pattern instructions, then Houston, we have a problem. Go back to your pattern and figure out what went wrong.

pin before stitching

A student recently complained that having to pin her fabric before stitching felt like having to eat her vegetables as a kid—an annoying obligation. She's right! Sometimes pinning is a drag, but it's good for you, and you *have* to do it. It takes some practice to figure out how far apart you need to place the pins and how close to the edge. (See page 79 for a refresher on pinning.)

cut your project on a table, not on your lap!

Always, and I mean *always,* cut your project when it's flat on a table (the same is true for measuring). I once got the bright idea to

to, say, get more pins. Set up your ironing board and iron (and press cloth, just in case) because you'll need them a lot. Make sure your machine is ready to sew (it's clean, has a sharp needle, operates smoothly) and you have good light. Wind up a few bobbins in a color that matches your project. Check that you have all the pattern pieces that are called for in the layout—for example, the skirt front, back, waistband, etc. Pick your stitch settings. This might mean taking a scrap of your project fabric (You did save some bits when you were cutting, right?) and sewing a little sample until you find the right stitch length, tension, etc. (See page 40 for a refresher.)

If you haven't studied your pattern and sewing instructions, do it now. They are your bible and guide for the next few hours (or days). Follow them as you would follow directions for building a bookshelf or a recipe for cooking potato-leek soup. Just think "divide and conquer," because that's what sewing really is—working on sections, then slowly combining them into one lovely piece.

to Sewing Success

neaten up the seams on a dress that I'd just spent about 60 hours sewing. Instead of prettying up the edges, I cut a huge hole in the back. (Did I mention that I'd been sewing all day and that the dress was wadded up on my lap?) Luckily, I had leftover fabric, so I tore out the back and replaced it with a new one.

go with the grain Stitch your projects with the grain—the lengthwise or crosswise threads of the fabric. Your biggest seams should run parallel to the fabric threads. This will stop the fabric from changing shape or dimension when you wear it. It's called directional sewing. As a general rule, if you stitch from the widest part of

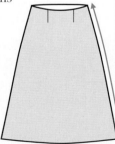

the garment to the narrowest, you'll be stitching with the grain. (See pages 49 and 77 for more on grain.)

accept imperfection Often my students will sew a dart or a seam, not like it, and tear it out. I say, take a deep breath and see if you can live with it. Ripping out and resewing usually hurts the fabric, and the redo ends up looking even worse. If you fall into the perfection trap, your work can slow down and become frustrating. And then sewing stops feeling fun. Small mistakes are no big deal if you learn from them. This is not to say that I encourage lazy or shoddy sewing. I do not. A punk rock look (which I do appreciate sometimes) is no excuse for sloppy work. I mean, you want everything to hold together for years, right?

cuddle-up cardigan

level

materials

Fabric Double knits (wool or cotton) or sweatshirt fleece

Thread in color to match

Snap

1 package Wright's bias tape in color to match (for facing)

Embroidery floss (to match) or ¼ yard narrow ribbon

Pattern (make your own; pattern paper needed)

yardage

45" fabric
S = 2⅝ yards
M–L = 2¾ yards

60" fabric
S = 2⅝ yards
M–L = 2¾ yards

tools

Yardstick

techniques

Edgestitch (page 93), topstitch (page 94), hems (pages 93–94), snaps (page 100)

seam allowance

⅝" unless otherwise indicated

Simple to make. Chic to wear. While other people are throwing on a hoodie, you can don this kimono-style wrap cardigan that you whipped up yourself. The construction is quite simple—just rectangles sewn together in a few crucial spots. There's a hidden snap closure and a belt for extra coziness. It's a wrap for the beach or a Thursday night pizza party. If you want to get fancier, make it in a soft but stable wool. Then put it on and start smoking a pipe and writing a novel. Inspiration guaranteed.

Make the Pattern

1. On pattern paper, draw a line S (M, L) 32 (32¼, 33¼)" long. Label the left end A. Mark B 11" to the right of A. Mark the end of the line C. Draw a vertical line straight up from A 8¾ (9¼, 9¾)" long for A1. Draw a vertical line straight up from B 14 (14¾, 15½)" long for B1. Draw a vertical line straight up from C 14 (14¾, 15½)" long for C1. Connect A1 to B1 to C1. Label this piece "Cardigan front, cut 2."

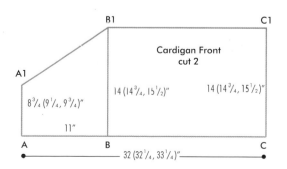

Cardigan Front
cut 2

B1   C1

A1

8³/₄ (9¹/₄, 9³/₄)"

14 (14³/₄, 15¹/₂)"   14 (14³/₄, 15¹/₂)"

11"

A   B   C

← 32 (32¹/₄, 33¹/₄)" →

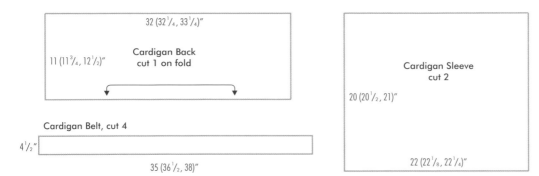

32 (32¼, 33¼)"

Cardigan Back
cut 1 on fold

11 (11¾, 12½)"

Cardigan Sleeve
cut 2

20 (20½, 21)"

22 (22⅛, 22¼)"

Cardigan Belt, cut 4

4½"

35 (36½, 38)"

2. Draw a rectangle S (M, L) 32 (32¼, 33¼)" long x 11 (11¾, 12½)" wide. Label this piece "Cardigan back, cut 1 on fold."

3. Draw a rectangle 22 (22⅛, 22¼)" long x 20 (20½, 21)" wide. Label this piece "Cardigan sleeve, cut 2."

4. Draw a rectangle 35 (36½, 38)" long x 4½" wide. Label this piece "Cardigan belt, cut 4."

5. Cut out the pattern pieces as drawn in steps 1 through 4.

Lay Out Pattern and Cut Fabric

1. Fold fabric selvage to selvage with right sides together, and smooth out on table.

2. Position the pattern pieces as shown, and pin them in place.

3. Cut out cardigan front, back, belt, and sleeve pieces.

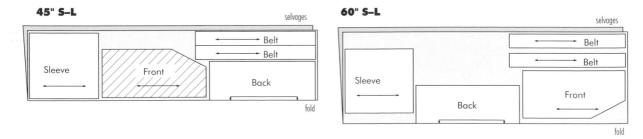

45" S–L

selvages

Belt

Belt

Sleeve

Front

Back

fold

60" S–L

selvages

Belt

Belt

Sleeve

Back

Front

fold

Sewing Instructions

Sew shoulder seams

1. Layer one front piece on top of the back piece with right sides together, lining up the straight edge of the front with the straight edge of the back. Pin together from shoulder to neck opening.

2. Sew along the pinned area, backstitching at beginning and end.

3. Press seam open. Turn right side out and press again.

4. Repeat steps 1 through 3 with other front piece.

5. Fold over and press the raw edge along the top back (the neck area) to the wrong side. Pin in place.

6. On right side, topstitch ¼" along shoulder seams and neck area on both sides of the seam allowance. (There will be short seams on the two front pieces and one long seam along the back, as shown.)

7. Trim seam allowances carefully.

Sew sleeves to cardigan

8. Mark the center of the short side of one sleeve with chalk. Line this mark up with the shoulder seam, right sides together. Pin in place.

9. Sew sleeve to the body of the cardigan, backstitching at beginning and end. Press seam towards the sleeve. Turn sleeve right side out and press again.

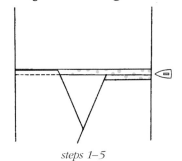

steps 1–5

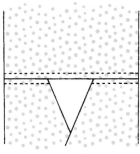

step 6

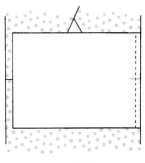

steps 8–9

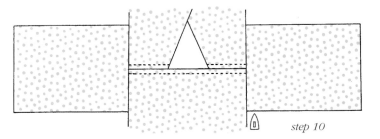

step 10

10. Repeat steps 8 and 9 on the other sleeve.

11. Fold one sleeve in half the long way, right sides together. Pin along the long raw edge.

12. Stitch the sleeve seam, backstitching at beginning and end. Press seam open. Turn right side out and press again.

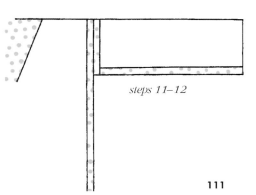

steps 11–12

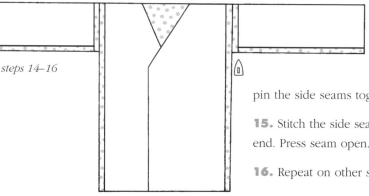

steps 14–16

13. Repeat steps 11 and 12 on other sleeve.

Sew side seams

14. With right sides together, pin the side seams together.

15. Stitch the side seam, backstitching at beginning and end. Press seam open. Turn to right side and press again.

16. Repeat on other side seam.

Finish neckline and center front

17. Trim points of cardigan fronts so they're slightly curved. This will make bias tape application easier.

18. Unfold bias tape and pin to right side of the front and neck edges, aligning the raw edges. Stitch along the first fold, ¼" from the edge of the garment. Turn the bias tape completely to the wrong side of the cardigan. Keeping the opposite raw edge of the tape turned under, pin in place. Edgestitch the folded edge of the tape in place.

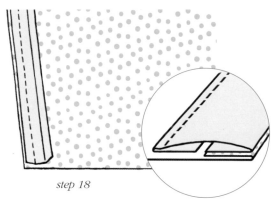

step 18

steps 19–22

Finish hems

19. Turn cardigan inside out.

20. Fold the raw edge of sleeve cuffs toward the wrong side ¼". Press. Fold over again 1"—or desired length—on each sleeve. Pin in place.

21. Edgestitch on one cuff and then topstitch for two lines of stitching. (It's cuter this way!) Press on both sides.

22. Repeat step 21 on the other sleeve cuff.

23. Follow steps 19 through 21 to finish the bottom hem.

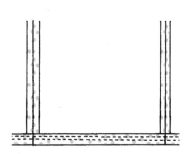

steps 19–23

steps 24–25

step 26

Make belt and loops

24. Layer two belt pieces, wrong sides together. Pin along one short end, leaving a ⅝" seam allowance. Stitch. Press seam open and flat. Repeat on remaining two belt pieces.

25. Layer the sewn belt pieces wrong sides together. Pin. Stitch long sides. Press seams open and flat. Turn right side out (see page 132). Press.

26. Turn the raw edges of each end to the inside of the belt and press. Edgestitch around all four sides, pivoting at corners. Then topstitch so you have two lines of stitching as you did on sleeve and bottom hems.

27. Using a disappearing-ink marker, measure up 14" from bottom hem at side seams and make marks for belt loop placement. Tie belt around you and adjust position, if needed.

28. Using your marks, make belt loops by stitching a 3" loop out of embroidery thread. Or, cut two pieces of ribbon 4½" long. Press each end to the wrong side ¼". Pin one ribbon to the belt loop markings at side seam. Stitch in place.

Stitch a snap at neckline for closure

29. Try cardigan on. Pin front together ½" below point of overlap.

30. Mark pin with chalk or disappearing-ink marker.

31. Remove the cardigan and hand-stitch snap in place.

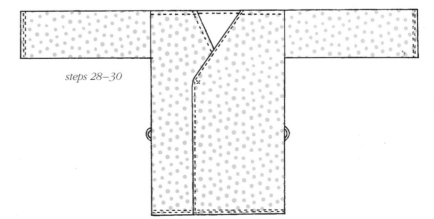

steps 28–30

breezy easy wrap skirt

rap yourself up like a very special present, complete with a bow (though you are welcome to make a square knot and leave the pretty ties to dangle). This '70s-inspired wrap skirt is easy to make, easy to wear. It fits and flatters basically every body type—just one of the reasons I love it so! The pattern lets you practice your darts (and I don't mean the kind you play at a pub over beer), so that even a complete novice can score a fashion bull's-eye. If you're new to sewing, make a few of these skirts before trying the more advanced pencil skirt. Your repeat wraps will feel totally fresh if you work with different fabrics. I've made mine in spring-worthy gingham and another in back-to-the-books corduroy. And they're both super-cute. You can embellish with patch pockets or appliqué. Sew rickrack all along the edges. Embroider cherries or a bicycle onto the front. Then wrap yourself to go!

Lay Out Pattern and Cut Fabric

For 45" fabric:

1. Lay a single layer of fabric right side up and smooth out on table. Fold up one selvage lengthwise. Measure the folded fabric from the fold to the selvage to make sure it's folded back evenly, with a wide enough fold to accommodate pattern piece 4.

2. Position pattern pieces, as shown on page 116. **Note:** Cut out the skirt back twice, with the pattern piece printed side up AND printed side down.

level 🧵 🧵

materials

Fabric Cotton, cotton blend, challis, gingham, chambray, canvas, denim, or corduroy

Thread in color to match

Pattern (enclosed in box)

yardage

45" fabric	60" fabric
S–L=2½ yards	S=1⅝ yards
	M–L=1¾ yards

techniques

Darts (page 88), edgestitch (page 93), hems (pages 93–94), grading seams (page 86), notches (page 87), slipstitch (page 230), zigzagged-and-trimmed seam finish (page 85)

seam allowance

⅝" unless otherwise indicated

pattern pieces

1. Skirt front (cut 1 on fold)
2. Skirt back (cut 2)
3. Front waistband (cut 1)
4. Back waistband/ties (cut 2)

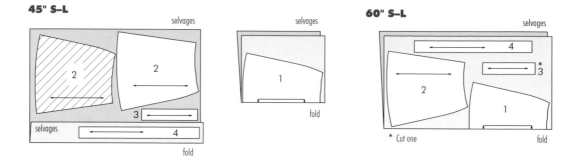

45" S–L
selvages
2
2
3
4
selvages
fold

selvages
1
fold

60" S–L
selvages
4
2
*3
1
* Cut one
fold

3. Cut out wrap skirt pieces, transferring all necessary markings.

4. Fold remaining fabric selvage to selvage, with right sides together, and smooth out on table. Position piece 1 on the fold. Repeat step 3.

For 60" fabric:

1. Fold fabric selvage to selvage with right sides together.

2. Position the pattern pieces as shown, checking the grainlines against the folded edge or selvage, and pin them in place.

3. Cut out wrap skirt pieces, transferring all necessary markings.

Note: *You only need one center waistband. Pin and cut it out after you've cut the rest of the pattern pieces.*

Sewing Instructions

Note: *This skirt can be worn with the wraps in the front (my personal preference, so I can keep an eye on things) or reversed with the wraps in the back. Tie it in the center front or back or at your hip (as shown in photographs on pages 115 and 118).*

steps 1–2

Make darts

1. Sew the two darts in the skirt front, as marked. Press darts toward each other, and the center of skirt.

2. Take one skirt back piece and sew the dart as marked. Press the fold toward the center back of the skirt.

3. Repeat with other back piece.

side seams tip It's more important that the skirt pieces line up at the top than at the bottom. If one pattern piece is slightly longer, you can cut it away when you finish the bottom hem.

Hem the skirt backs

4. Place skirt back on table with wrong side up. Fold the raw edge of one back piece toward the wrong side ½". Press. Fold again ½" to make a ½"-wide finished hem. Press again and pin in place.

5. Edgestitch along the inside folded edge. Press on both sides.

6. Repeat steps 4 and 5 with the other back piece.

Sew side seams

7. Layer the skirt front and one skirt back at the side seam with right sides together and aligning notches. (This will be the side seam.) Pin in place.

8. Stitch side seam, backstitching at beginning and end.

9. Press seam open. Turn to right side and press again.

10. Finish seam with pinking shears or zigzagged-and-trimmed finish.

11. Repeat steps 7 through 10 with other back piece.

Stitch center waistband to waistband sides/ties

12. With right sides together and matching notches on the short ends, layer one back waistband/tie piece on the front waistband at the right side seam. Pin in place.

13. Stitch right waistband seam, backstitching at beginning and end.

14. With right sides together and matching notches and pull-through dots, layer the other back waistband/tie piece on the front waistband at the left side seam. Pin in place. (Make sure your waistbands have four dots along the short ends. If not, pull out your pattern and use pins and chalk to transfer these dots onto the fabric pieces before pinning together.)

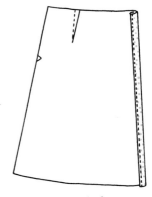

steps 4–6

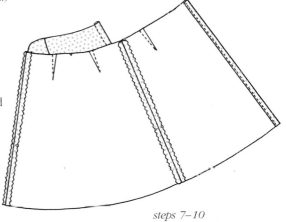

steps 7–10

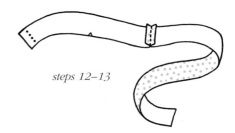

steps 12–13

S·E·W

steps 15–17

important tip So many of my students accidentally stitch too small of an opening that I want to warn you: If you think the tie isn't going to fit through the hole, you need to remove some of the stitching now. Then reinforce the remaining stitches by going back and forth a few times.

Note: Since this skirt has a pull-through waistband, you need to create an opening for the tie on the left-hand side of the skirt—like an eye for thick thread.

15. Sew from top edge down to the first dot, and then backstitch up and down again to reinforce seam.

16. Lift needle and presser foot, and skip space along the same seam line to sew between the two center dots. Stitch backward and forward to reinforce.

17. Finish seam by sewing and then backstitching from the fourth dot to the far edge of the waistband. (The gaps you create will become the hole for threading the tie.) Press seam open.

18. Fold the waistband in half lengthwise and double-check the size of the opening.

Attach waistband to skirt

19. Pin waistband to skirt with right sides together, aligning seams of the waistband with side seams of the skirt. Pin at these two points, then keep pinning from center of waistband out toward the edges of the skirt, evenly distributing the fabric. As you pin, make sure side seams remain flat and open, and darts lie the way you pressed them.

Note: The top of the skirt is curved and the waistband is straight, so you may have to pull fabric gently to line them up.

20. Sew waistband to skirt, backstitching at beginning and end.

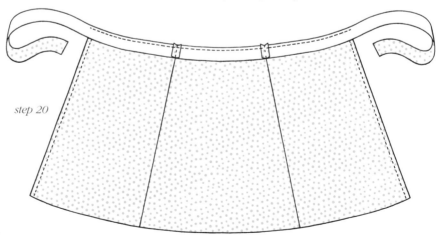

step 20

21. Press seam toward waistband, ironing on both sides. To reduce bulk, grade the seam, cutting away excess seam allowance.

Finish waistband and topstitch ties

22. Press the top and bottom edges and both short ends of the waistband/tie to the wrong side ⅝".

23. Fold waistband in half lengthwise with wrong sides together and double-check pull-through opening. It's likely that the seam allowance—where waistband meets skirt—and/or the fold on the top of the waistband blocks the opening. If so, clip a notch into the seam allowance in both the bottom and top of waistband to unblock the hole. Be careful not to cut beyond the seam allowance.

24. Fold waistband/tie in half again lengthwise, press, and pin into place. The folded-over edge should just barely cover the stitching along waistband.

25. Edgestitch the entire waistband/tie together from one end of the tie, through the waistband back and front sections and finishing at the opposite end of the tie. (Stitch as close to the folded edge as you comfortably can.) Press.

26. Slipstitch around the hole of the opening.

27. Turn skirt inside out and fold the raw edge of bottom hem toward the wrong side ¼". Press. Fold again 1" and press again. Pin in place.

28. Edgestitch along the entire hem.
Press on both sides.

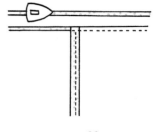

step 22

steps 24–25

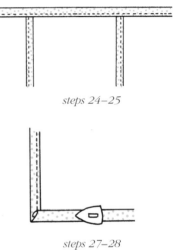

steps 27–28

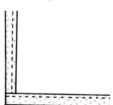

Add pocket (optional)

29. If you'd like to add a fun, contrasting patch pocket as shown here, see patch pocket instructions, page 167.

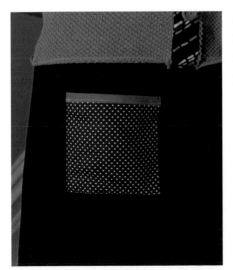

wear anywhere yoga pants

level

materials

Fabric Light- to medium-weight cotton, linen, shantung, or silk

Thread in color to match

Twill tape or grosgrain ribbon (⅜" wide x 2 yards long)

Tapestry needle (or safety pin)

½" button (needed only if using one-step buttonhole)

Pattern (enclosed in box)

yardage

45"	60"
S–L=2⅝ yards	S=1⅜ yards
	M=1¾ yards
	L=2⅜ yards

techniques

Zigzagged-and-trimmed seam finish (page 85), buttonholes (pages 98–99), edgestitch (page 93), topstitch (page 94), hems (pages 93–94)

seam allowance

⅝" unless otherwise indicated

pattern pieces

1. Pants front (cut 2)
2. Pants back (cut 2)

Your chakras will vibrate with delight (and magically align) when you wear your stylin' yoga pants to class. Not a yogi? Wear 'em while you read the Sunday paper and sip coffee. These low-slung, wide-legged, super-comfy cotton pants are great for lounging, beach walking, errand running. Or use a more sophisticated fabric—like laundered silk, silk shantung, or crepe de chine—and sashay over to your next cocktail party. A word to the wise: Select your fabric carefully, or you might end up looking like you're running around in your PJs. Or, if you want to embrace the PJ-ness, sew them in cozy flannel.

Lay Out Pattern and Cut Fabric

1. Fold fabric selvage to selvage with right sides together, and smooth out on table.

2. Position the pattern pieces as shown. Pin in place.

3. Cut out pants pieces, transferring all necessary markings.

45" S–L

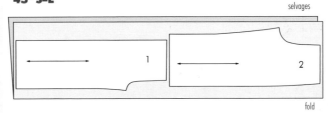

(Layouts continued on next page.)

60" S

selvages

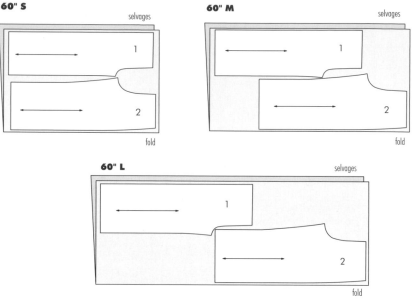

fold

60" M

selvages

fold

60" L

selvages

fold

steps 1–2

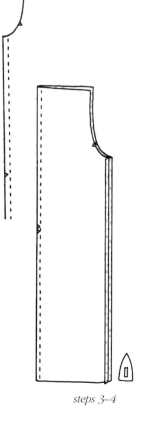

steps 3–4

tip Hand-baste the top of the inseams together so the center seam won't shift out of alignment while you're stitching.

Sewing Instructions

Sew the inner and side leg seams

1. Layer one back piece and the front piece that mirrors it with right sides together matching single notches. Pin in place along inner leg seam.

2. Stitch the inner leg seam, backstitching at beginning and end. Press seam. (I used a zigzagged-and-trimmed seam finish to make my yoga pants extra neat.)

3. Pin the side leg seam with right sides together matching double notches.

4. Stitch the side leg seam, backstitching at beginning and end. Press seam.

5. Repeat steps 1 through 4 on remaining front and back pieces for opposite leg.

Sew the center seam

6. Turn one leg to the outside. Slip the turned leg into the other leg with right sides together, matching the inner and side leg seams and curved edges. Pin in place.

7. Stitch the center seam, backstitching at beginning and end. Press seam open.

8. Finish seams.

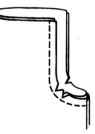

steps 6–8

Make the buttonholes for the ribbon

9. Make two buttonholes where you marked them, on the top front of the pants. If you're using a one-step buttonhole (page 98), put a ½" button into the buttonholer foot. The buttonhole will be ⅛" larger, or ⅝". If not using a one-step buttonhole, plan for a ⅝" finished hole.

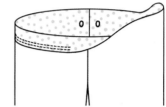

step 9

Sew waistband casing

10. Turn pants inside out. Fold the top raw edge toward the wrong side ¼". Press. Fold again 1¼" and press. Pin in place.

11. Edgestitch along the folded edge of the waistband. Press.

12. Stitch a second time, topstitching ⅛" away from the first line of stitching. Press on both sides.

steps 10–12

13. Fold the raw edges of each bottom leg hem toward the wrong side ¼". Press. Fold again 1½" (or desired length, see page 235). Press again. Pin in place.

14. Repeat steps 11 and 12, creating two lines of topstitching on each pant leg, just as at the waist.

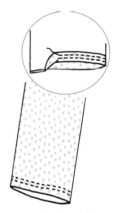

steps 13–14

Insert ribbon into the waistband

15. Thread the tapestry needle with the ribbon or twill tape and insert into one of the buttonholes in the waistband.

16. Use your fingers to wiggle the needle through the waistband and out the buttonhole at the other side.

17. Try the pants on again, tie the ribbon into a bow, and cut the ribbon ends to desired lengths with pinking shears.

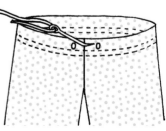

steps 15–16

tunic (or not tunic) . . .

T hat is the question. Whether 'tis nobler to don a garment that hath a long and flattering shape—or to suffer the slings and arrows of unpleasant fashion. To leave the arms free and unencumbered and say "nay" to all buttons and zippers (they are but a sea of troubles). Perchance you dream of a tunic you weareth over jeans when you are feeling the moon's pull, or to the water's shore to cover thy bare bod when the sun shines bright. If this be beauty and the style you seek, then get thee to a sewing machine and sayeth, "Aye, tunic!" before you shuffle off this mortal coil.

Lay Out Pattern and Cut Fabric

1. Fold fabric selvage to selvage with right sides together and smooth out on table.

2. Lay out and pin pattern pieces as shown, keeping grainlines straight.

3. Cut out tunic pattern pieces as shown, transferring all the necessary markings.

4. Pin and cut front and back neck pattern pieces in interfacing.

level

materials

Fabric Cottons/blends, linen/blends, or wool

Interfacing (lightweight fusible)

Pattern (enclosed in box)

yardage

Fabric

45"	60"
S=2¼ yards	S=2¼ yards
M=2⅜ yards	M=2⅜ yards
L=2½ yards	L=2½ yards

Interfacing S–L ⅞ yards

techniques

Staystitch (page 87), darts (page 88), interfacing (page 90), zigzagged-and-trimmed seam finish (page 85), pivoting (page 36), trimming seams (page 86), clipping curves (page 87), hand-basting (page 229), topstitch (page 94), hems (pages 93–94), edgestitch (page 93)

seam allowance

⅝" unless otherwise indicated

pattern pieces

1. Front (cut 1 on fold)
2. Back (cut 1 on fold)
3. Front neck facing (cut 1 in tunic fabric, 1 in interfacing)
4. Back neck facing (cut 1 in tunic fabric, 1 in interfacing)
5. Front armhole facing (cut 2 in tunic fabric, 2 in interfacing)
6. Back armhole facing (cut 2 in tunic fabric, 2 in interfacing)

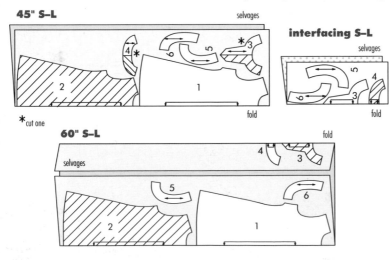

45" S–L selvages

interfacing S–L selvages

*cut one

fold

fold

60" S–L fold

selvages

S·E·W ....

Sewing Instructions

Staystitch front and back neckline edges

1. Using a ½" seam allowance, stitch along the front and back neck edges in the direction shown.

Make darts on tunic front

2. Mark, pin, and then stitch the two darts on the tunic front. Press darts toward the bottom hem.

Sew shoulder seams

3. Pin front to back at shoulder seams. Stitch. Press open.

Note: *Staystitching will not appear in the following illustrations.*

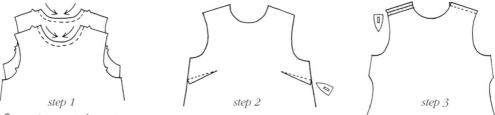

step 1

front and back

step 2

step 3

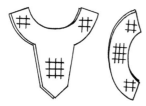

step 4

Apply interfacing to neck facings, stitch facings together, and finish edge

4. Apply interfacing to the wrong side of the front and back neck facings following manufacturer's instructions.

5. With right sides together, pin the front facing to the back facing at the shoulder seams. Stitch. Press.

6. Finish raw outside edge of neck facing with a zigzagged-and-trimmed seam finish.

7. Turn ¼" of the zigzagged edge to the wrong side of the facing, clipping at the inner corners to allow fabric to spread. Press.

steps 5–7

Stitch neck facing in place

8. With right sides together, pin facing to front and neck edge, matching dots. Sew along stitching line of front facing around neck seam, pivoting at corner dots, as shown. Start stitching at the back neck so stitching is continuous through dots.

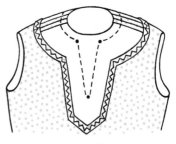

step 8

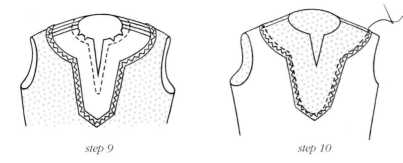

| *step 9* | *step 10* | *step 11* |

9. Cut the neckline open between the stitching lines sewn in step 8 to the bottom point, being careful not to cut through the thread. Trim seam allowances of neckline and clip curves.

10. Turn facing to the inside. Press. Neatly hand-baste facing in place with a thread in a contrasting color, close to the pressed edge.

11. Turn tunic right side out, and topstitch as basted. Remove basting, and press.

Sew side seams

12. Layer tunic front and back, right sides together. Pin one side seam. Stitch. Press.

13. Repeat step 12 on opposite side seam.

Finish armholes with facings

14. With right sides together, stitch ends of front and back armhole facings at top and bottom (shoulder seam and side seam). Repeat with other armhole facings.

15. Staystitch ¼" from outer edge of each armhole facing. Press ¼" to the wrong side of each facing.

16. On outside of tunic and working one side at a time, pin right side of facing to right side of armhole edge, matching notches. Stitch. Trim seam and clip curves. Press.

17. Turn facing to inside and press. Turn tunic inside out and edgestitch along the inner edge of facing(s). Press again.

Press and stitch hem

18. Try on the tunic, and hem to your desired length (a 1¼" hem allowance has been given).

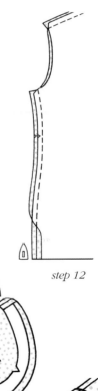

step 12

step 14-15

step 16

127

level

materials

Fabric Cotton or cotton blends, sateen, silk and silk types, or soft lightweight linen and linen blends

Thread in color to match

Lace (⅝" wide x 2¼ [2½, 2¾] yards long)

Pattern (Make your own; pattern paper needed)

yardage

45"	60"
S=2 yards	S–L=1¼ yards
M–L=2¼ yards	

tools

Hip curve (optional)
Yardstick
Loop turner

techniques

Zigzagged-and-trimmed seam finish (page 85), topstitch (page 94), trims and tapes (pages 66–67), edgestitch (page 93), slipstitch (page 230)

seam allowance

⅝" unless otherwise indicated

I'm on a campaign to bring back the nightie. No more sleeping in big T-shirts. It's not sexy! Remember Elizabeth Taylor in *Cat on a Hot Tin Roof*? Picture any lady (fictional or real) before 1965, and she's sleeping in a slinky little gown. This very easy nightgown project will have you feeling ladylike and pretty in no time. (I swear pretty sleepwear is good for your self-esteem.) It's constructed like a simple slip with silky material and come-hither lace detailing. Want a cute camisole instead? It's the same exact pattern, except shorter! I've made one in peek-a-boo eyelet, but you could try a sweet cotton print or a summery linen.

Make the Pattern

1. On pattern paper, draw a horizontal line S (M, L) 9⅝ (10⅜, 11⅛)" long. Label the left-hand end A. Mark B 4⅞ (5, 5⅜)" to the right of A. Label the right-hand end C. Draw a vertical line straight up from A 4¾ (5, 5¼)" long for A1. Draw a vertical line 6 (6¼, 6½)" long for B1. Draw a vertical line straight up from C 4¾ (4⅝, 5)" long for C1. Connect A1 to B1, and B1 to C1. Label this piece "Nightie bodice front, cut 1 on fold."

2. Draw a rectangle 9⅝ (10⅜, 11⅛)" long x 4½ (4¾, 5)" wide. Label this piece "Nightie bodice back, cut 1 on fold."

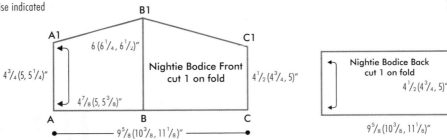

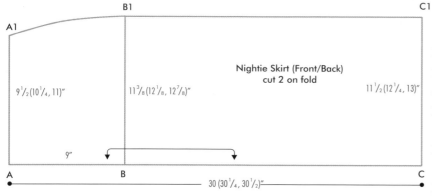

3. Draw a line 30 (30¼, 30½)" long. Label the left end A. Mark B 9" to the right of A. Label the right-hand end C. Draw a vertical line straight up from A 9½ (10¼, 11)" long for A1. Draw a vertical line straight up from B 11⅜ (12⅛, 12⅞)" long for B1. Draw a vertical line straight up from C 11½ (12¼, 13)" long for C1. Draw a soft, hip-shaped curve to connect A1 to B1 or use a hip curve. Label this piece "Nightie skirt front/back, cut 2 on fold."

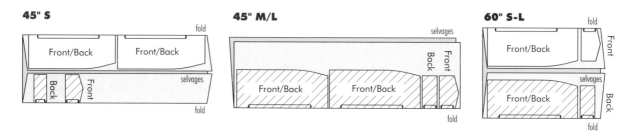

Lay Out Pattern and Cut Fabric

For S in a 45"-wide fabric or S/M/L in a 60"-wide fabric:

1. Fold the fabric in half lengthwise, selvage to selvage with right sides together. Press the foldline. Open up the fabric and smooth on a table right side up.

2. Turn the bottom selvage up, with right sides together so it meets the pressed foldline. Repeat, folding the top down. Now the selvages meet in the middle.

3. Position the pattern pieces printed side up or down on the folds as shown.

4. Pin pattern pieces along the foldline, and cut around three sides.

For M/L in a 45" fabric:

1. Fold fabric selvage to selvage with right sides together and smooth on table.

2. Position pattern pieces printed side down along foldline as shown.

3. Pin pattern pieces along the foldline, and cut around three sides.

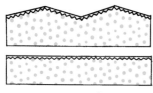

step 1

Sewing Instructions

Sew front and back bodice

1. Finish the top edge of the front and back bodice pieces with a narrow (2.5mm) zigzag stitch length ½" in from the raw edge to prevent fraying. Trim close to stitching, being careful not to cut into stitched thread. Press.

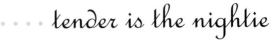

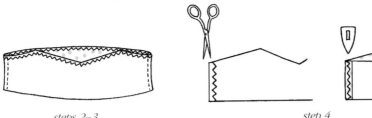

steps 2–3

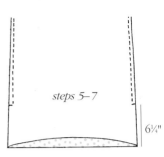

step 4

steps 5–7

6¼"

2. Pin the front bodice to the back bodice with right sides together.

3. Stitch each side seam one at a time, backstitching at beginning and end.

4. Finish bodice side seam allowances by zigzagging them together. Trim the seams, being careful not to cut stitching. Press toward the back of the nightie.

Sew skirt sides and finish side-slit openings

5. Layer the skirt pieces, with right sides together. Pin along side seams.

6. Mark the start of the side opening/slits with disappearing-ink marker 6¼" up from the bottom hem on each side.

7. Stitch along one side seam from the waistband down to the top of the slit opening, backstitching at beginning and end. Reinforce well at end. (Wearing the nightgown will put stress on it.)

8. Press seams open and flat, including the opening down to the hem.

9. Repeat steps 7 and 8 on the opposite side.

10. Finish seam allowances with regular zigzagged-and-trimmed seam finish.

11. Turn the raw edges of each side slit toward the wrong side to create a narrow hem. Press. Pin in place.

step 11

Sew bodice to skirt

12. Slip the bodice on top of the skirt with right sides together, as shown. Pin all the way around the waist. Make sure the side seams line up.

13. Stitch around the waist, backstitching at beginning and end.

14. Finish the raw edge of the waistline seam allowances with a zigzag finish.

15. Press waist seam open and flat, and then together and down toward the hem.

steps 12–13

tip Slide the pinned waistline of the nightie around the free-arm of your machine to avoid accidentally sewing the front and back together.

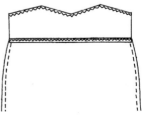

step 15

S·E·W ·

Loop turners make turning any fabric tubes, especially skinny ones like spaghetti straps, a cinch. How's it work? Sew the material right sides together to make the fabric tube and trim your seam allowances to ⅛"–¼" to reduce some of the bulk. Slide the loop turner into the tube, hook it to the opposite end of the tube, close the latch, and pull the hooked end out through the other side. Ta-da! You have yourself a beautifully sewn tube, with little to no effort. Sure, a large safey pin does the same trick, but a loop turner is much easier to pull through thanks to its extra-long wire body. At four bucks or less, it's worth every penny.

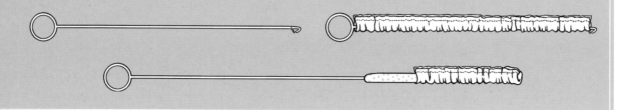

Cut spaghetti straps and attach them to the bodice

16. Cut two straps 16" x 1¼". Fold in half lengthwise and pin, right sides together.

17. Stitch down the center of straps.

18. Using turning tool (see sidebar), turn straps right side out and press with seam at center (this will be underside of strap).

19. Turn ends to right side ½" and press.

20. Pin ends to wrong side of front at topmost points on bodice.

21. Edgestitch straps to bodice and reinforce with plenty of backstitching. (There's nothing more annoying than straps ripping out!)

22. On the back bodice, measure 4" in from each side seam toward the center and mark with chalk. Line up the center point of each strap with that mark and pin.

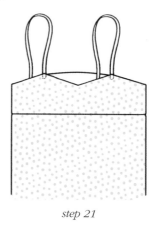

step 21

23. Try on nightie and adjust the length of the straps, if needed, and pin.

24. Edgestitch the back ends of the straps into place, reinforcing well with backstitching.

Trim the bodice

25. Finish the top edge of the bodice with lace. Lay the nightie on a flat surface with the right side of the front facing you. Starting at the left side seam, begin pinning the trim to the wrong side of the bodice. Leave an extra inch at the beginning for tucking under to finish the end (you can cut it away later) and place the trim just under the zigzagged edge, exposing about ½" of lace.

26. Pin lace behind the straps and continue pinning trim to bodice until you're back where you started.

27. Hand-stitch lace to bodice along the edge starting at the left side seam. You will have to pivot at the top of the points of the bodice and at the center front.

step 27

Finish the hem and side openings/slits

28. Turn the nightie inside out. Fold front hem to wrong side ¼". Press. Fold again ½" and press again. Pin in place.

29. Edgestitch along the hem with a zigzag stitch pattern.

30. Repeat steps 28 and 29 on the skirt back.

31. Slipstitch side slit hems by hand.

32. Pin lace to bottom hem, leaving at least ½" showing and turning the ends under to finish neatly. Hand-stitch to the inside of the nightie hem.

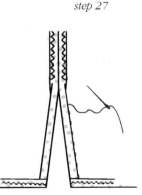

step 31

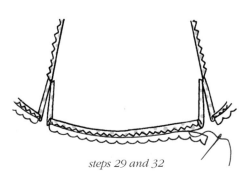

steps 29 and 32

foxy boxers

*N*othing says love like a custom-stitched pair of undies. Use a cotton print with a loved one's favorite food (cupcakes!), animal (bunnies!), or flower (daisies!) all over it. Little dots, paisleys, or stripes are fun, too. These boxers are for boys and girls alike, so make a pair for yourself—you can lounge and sleep in style. Or make a matching pair for the pair of you! Stitching the fly extensions will seem tricky at first, but after you do it once, it makes total sense. When you are done, appliqué a heart on the butt for true love!

Lay Out Pattern and Cut Fabric

1. Lay out single layer of fabric, right side up, and smooth out on table.

2. Position the pattern piece as shown, keeping grainline straight, and pin it in place.

3. Cut out pattern pieces, transferring all the necessary markings.

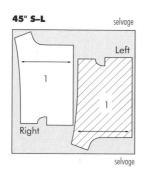

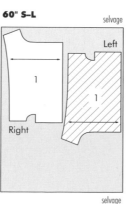

4. Cut out the paper pattern for the left fly template which you will use in the next step to adjust the left side of fly.

level

materials

Fabric Light- to medium-weight cotton, flannel, linen, or silk

Thread in color to match

1"-wide elastic
S (M, L) 1 (1⅛, 1¼) yards

Large safety pin

Pattern (enclosed in box)

yardage
45" or 60"
1⅜ yards for S, M, or L

techniques
Zigzagged-and-trimmed seam finish (page 85), edgestitch (page 93), pivoting (page 36), hems (pages 93–94)

seam allowance
⅝" unless otherwise indicated

pattern pieces
1. Boxer shorts front/back (cut 2)
2. Left fly template

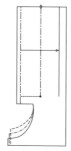

Left fly template

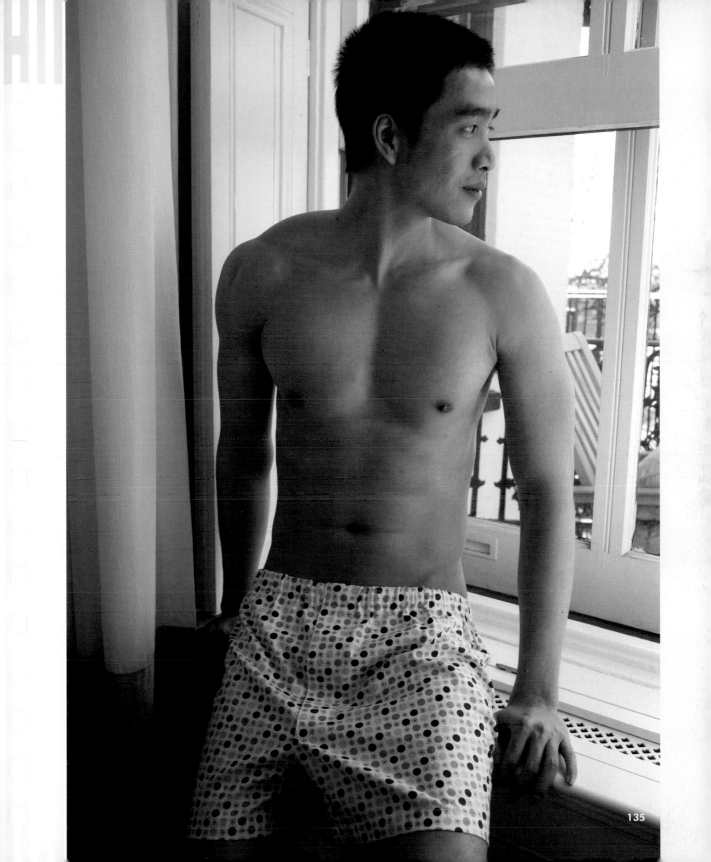

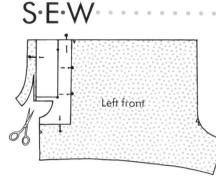

Left front

5. Lay the left fly template on top of the left front/back piece, with the right side of the fabric face up, matching dot and notch at center front. Pin and cut away front excess, as shown. With chalk, mark this piece L, for left front/back, on the wrong side of the fabric.

Sewing Instructions

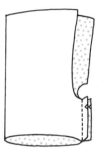

steps 1–3

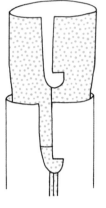

step 4

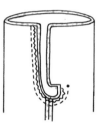

steps 6–7

Sew inner leg seams

1. Fold one boxer shorts front/back with right sides together and pin along inseam, matching notches.

2. Stitch inseam, backstitching at beginning and end. Press.

3. Repeat steps 1 and 2 on other front/back piece.

Sew center seam

4. Turn one boxer side and leg right side out and slip it inside the other with right sides together.

5. Pin the center seam, matching double notches. Make sure the inseams are lining up.

6. Stitch seam up to dot at bottom of fly. Press.

7. Reinforce the seam by stitching another row of zigzag stitches just inside the previous straight seam toward the raw edges. Trim seam allowances, being careful not to cut into zigzag stitching. Press seam flat and to one side.

Finish fly openings

8. Turn boxers inside out. Turn the raw edge of the left fly toward the wrong side ⅜". Press. Fold back again 1⅛" and press again. Pin in place.

9. Edgestitch along the long side of the left fly. Press on both sides.

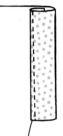

step 9

10. Repeat steps 8 and 9 on the right fly, except that the second fold is 1½".

11. Stitch a short seam from the dot at the bottom of the right fly toward the center front.

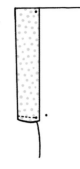

step 11

12. Turn the boxers right side out. Lay the left fly on top of the right fly with right sides of fabric up to create overlapped fly opening. Pin well to keep overlap from shifting while you stitch.

13. Sew a short seam from the dot at the bottom of the left fly toward the center front.

14. Sew across the fly overlap ¼" from the top edge.

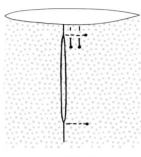

steps 12–14

Create waistband casing

15. Turn boxers inside out. Fold the raw edge of the top toward the wrong side ¼". Press. Fold again by 1⅛" and press again to make casing. Pin in place.

16. Edgestitch waistband casing in place. Press.

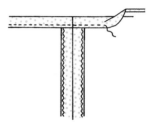

steps 15–16

Insert elastic into waistband

17. Cut the elastic to desired length—usually about 36" for small, 39" for medium, 42" for large. It helps if you can fit it on your model. You want it to be snug. Then add at least an extra 1" for seam allowance.

18. Attach the large safety pin to one end of the elastic. Thread the elastic through the casing, using the pin as a "needle." (Make sure the free elastic end stays outside the waistband!) Try on boxers and adjust elastic to fit.

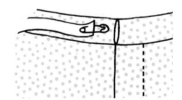

steps 17–18

tip You can also measure a pair of store-bought boxers to help you figure out the right length for the elastic.

19. Overlap the elastic by ½", pin, and stitch, backstitching several times to reinforce.

20. Stitch the waistband opening closed. (Optional: You can stitch a small box here, centered over the fly and pivoting at each corner.)

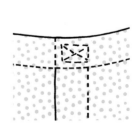

step 20

Finish bottom hems

21. Turn the shorts inside out. Fold the raw edge of each leg toward the wrong side ¼". Turn up by 1¼" and edgestitch hems in place using a zigzag stitch. Press.

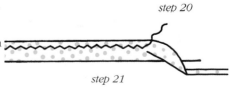

step 21

137

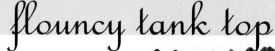

flouncy tank top

materials

Fabric Light- to medium-weight cotton, broadcloth, cotton sateen, eyelet, gingham, piqué, poplin, voile, linen, or silk

Thread in color to match

Hook and eye

Safety pin

Pattern (make your own; pattern paper needed)

yardage

45" fabric	60" fabric
S–L=1¾ yards	S–M=1⅛ yards
	l=1⅜ yards

techniques

Gathering (page 89), edgestitch (page 93), topstitch (page 94), grading seams (page 86), hems (pages 93–94), hooks and eyes (pages 99–100)

seam allowance

½" unless otherwise indicated

Who doesn't love a good gathering? This Flouncy Tank Top features gathering of the flowiest, prettiest kind. It makes you look lighter than air, makes your best curves curvier. (Those hippies were on to something!) Gathering is a great technique to know—it's easy and fun. You get to scrunch and sculpt the fabric, making flat stuff into 3-D fashion. Sew this tantalizing tank with lightweight flouncy fabric, like checked gingham or flowy silk. (Idea: Make the shoulder straps and neckline in a contrasting color or different material altogether.) Wear it with jeans, and you'll be sexy and comfy all summer. Just keep hold of something solid so you don't float away.

Make the Pattern

1. On pattern paper, draw a rectangle S (M, L) 24¼ (24¾, 25¼)" long x 11¾ (12½, 13¼)" wide. Label this piece "Tank front, cut 1 on fold."

11³/₄ (12¹/₂, 13¹/₄)"

Tank Front
cut 1 on fold

24¹/₄ (24³/₄, 25¹/₄)"

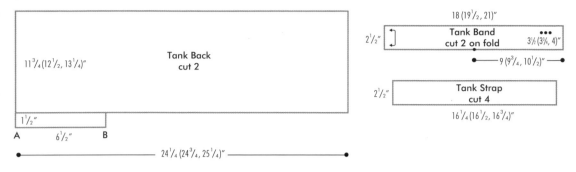

2. Draw another rectangle of the same dimensions. At the lower left-hand corner, draw a 1½" line straight down and label it A. From A, draw a horizontal line 6½" long parallel to the long side of the rectangle. Label the end point B. Connect B to the large rectangle for back opening. Label this piece "Tank back, cut 2."

3. Draw a rectangle 18 (19½, 21)" long x 2½" wide. From the right-hand corner, measure over to the left 9 (9¾, 10½)" and mark for the side seam. Mark dots 3½ (3¾, 4)" in from right edge for straps. Label this piece "Tank band, cut 2 on fold."

4. Draw a rectangle 16¼ (16½, 16¾)" long by 2½" wide. Label this piece "Tank strap, cut 4."

5. Cut out the pattern pieces drawn in steps 1 through 4.

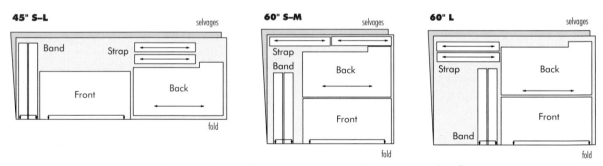

Lay Out Pattern and Cut Fabric

1. Fold fabric selvage to selvage with right sides together, and smooth out on table.

2. Position pieces as shown, either following the foldline or making sure that pieces are parallel to the selvages.

3. Cut out pieces as shown, transferring all necessary markings.

4. Use chalk to mark the band as pieces 1 and 2. (Since they're identical, it won't matter which one is which.)

Sewing Instructions

Sew side seams

1. Layer one back piece to the front with right sides together. Pin along the side edge.

2. Stitch the side seam, backstitching at beginning and end. Press seam allowances open and flat. Press again on the right side. Finish seam.

steps 1–3

3. Repeat steps 1 and 2 with remaining back.

Sew center back seam

4. Fold with right sides together and pin along the center back seam.

5. Stitch from about 6½" from the top of the back opening to the bottom of the tank. Reinforce the seam at the back opening with extra backstitching.

6. Press the seam allowances open and flat, along the entire length of fabric (beyond the seam, to the top edge of the tank). Press again on the right side of the fabric.

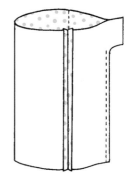

steps 4–5

Finish back opening

7. Turn the tank top inside out. Tuck the pressed seam allowances of the back opening (from step 6) in half to create a double-turned hem. Press.

8. With the tank right side up, stitch ⅜" around the back opening, pivoting at the short end. Press.

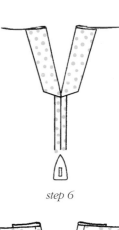

step 6

steps 7–8

Create gathers

9. Set your machine on its longest stitch length and baste along the top edge of the tank (from one side of the back opening across the bustline to the other side of the back opening) ¼" from raw edge. Leave long tails of thread at each end.

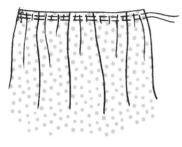

steps 9–11

10. Stitch a second line ⅜" from the first line of stitching. When finished, reset your machine to the regular stitch length.

11. Insert a pin perpendicular to the edge at one end. Wrap the bobbin thread tails around the pin to anchor one end. Gently pull the loose threads at the opposite end to gather in the fabric. Distribute the gathers as evenly as possible. Post-gathering, the front should be 17 (18½, 20)" wide, and each back 7 (8½, 10)".

Make the shoulder straps

12. Pin two shoulder strap pieces with right sides together along one long edge.

13. Stitch the strap seam, backstitching at beginning and end. Press seam open and flat. Trim seam allowance.

14. Repeat steps 12 and 13 on the other long edge.

15. Use a safety pin attached to one end to turn it right side out. Press.

16. Repeat steps 12 through 15 for the second shoulder strap.

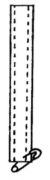

steps 12–15

Stitch bands and shoulder straps

17. Fold the unmarked long edge of one band only toward the wrong side ½". Press.

18. Starting at the back opening, pin the unpressed band to the top of the tank with the right sides together. Extend the ends of the band ½" beyond the finished back opening. (You may have to repin and make adjustments to the gathering for the side seams to line up with the side seam marks.) Stitch the band to the top of the tank. Press the band up and the seam allowances toward the band.

19. Pin the ends of each shoulder strap to the top of the band in the locations marked. The strap ends will line up with the top raw edge of the band and hang upside down, as shown.

steps 18–19

tip When both ends of the strap are pinned in place, lift them up to double-check that they're not twisted, and are sandwiched between the layered bands.

20. With right sides together, pin the remaining band piece over the first band aligning the raw edges and keeping the pressed edge free. The straps should be sandwiched between the two bands. Stitch the bands together at the top edge. Trim and grade the seam. Press the seam open first and then fold the loose band to the back side.

step 20

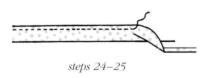

steps 21–22

Stitch the ends of the bands

21. With right sides together, fold the ends of the band back on itself and stitch a ½" seam.

22. Trim the seams. Turn the band right side out and press.

Finish sewing the top band to the shirt front

23. Pin the folded and pressed bottom edge of the band just over the seam allowance. Edgestitch the band to the tank, starting at the back opening. Press.

step 23

steps 24–25

Hem the bottom and attach hook and eye

24. Turn the top inside out. Fold the raw edge of the bottom hem toward the wrong side ¼". Press. Fold again 1" and press again. Pin in place.

25. Edgestitch along the bottom of the hem. Press on both sides.

26. Place hook and eye ¼" down from top edge of band.

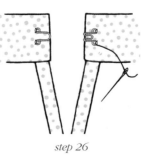

step 26

naughty secretary skirt

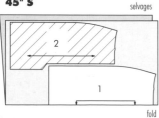

Doesn't this sexy pencil skirt make you want to put on heels, cross your legs (much easier with the back slit!), and take a memo? ("Dear Sir or Madam: I am wearing a very cute skirt.") I designed this—my dream skirt shape—and then I made it in triplicate. You can sew this baby in just about any kind of fabric—cotton, linen, lace, or wool. Wool is perfect for the office, cotton for the office picnic, and hot lace for the company holiday party. And although the pattern is super-straightforward, you will need to sew in an invisible zipper (even the phrase "invisible zipper" sounds sexy and vaguely '50s-ish). If you've made a few projects already, and you are up for a sewing promotion, then this is the project for you. 401(K) not included.

Lay Out Pattern and Cut Fabric

1. Fold fabric selvage to selvage with right sides together, and smooth out on table.

2. Position pattern pieces as shown, following the grainlines. Pin in place.

3. Cut out the skirt pieces, transferring all necessary markings.

level

materials

Fabric Cotton, linen, wool, and blends of these fabrics

Thread in color to match

7" invisible zipper

1 package Wright's double-fold bias tape

Pattern (enclosed in box)

tools

Invisible zipper foot

yardage

45"	60"
S=1¼ yards	S–L=1 yard
M–L=1⅞ yards	

techniques

Staystitch (page 87), darts (page 88), zigzagged-and-trimmed seam finish (page 85), machine basting (page 40), invisible zipper (page 96), edgestitch (page 93), hems (pages 93–94), slipstitch (page 230)

seam allowance

⅝" unless otherwise indicated

pattern pieces

1. Skirt front (cut 1 on fold)
2. Skirt back (cut 2)

45" S

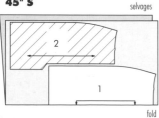

45" M–L

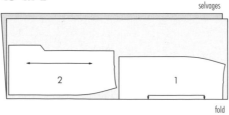

60" S–L

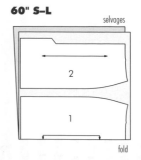

Sewing Instructions

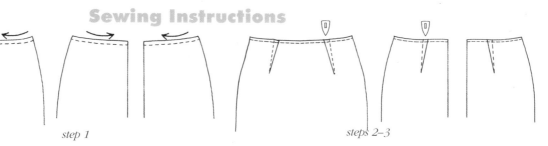

step 1   *steps 2–3*

Shape pieces

1. Staystitch upper edge of the skirt front (what will later be the waistband).

2. Line up notches on skirt front, pin, and sew two darts. Press darts toward the center.

3. Repeat steps 1 and 2 with skirt back pieces.

Finish raw edges of slit extensions

4. Fold back the edges of the slit extensions to the wrong side ¼". Press. Turn back another ¼" and press again. Edgestitch hems in place.

step 4

Insert invisible zipper and stitch center back seam

5. Put the invisible zipper foot on your machine and install an invisible zipper, as detailed on page 96. (Be sure to line up the bottom of the zipper stop with the dot you marked on the skirt pattern pieces.)

6. Swap the invisible zipper foot for a regular zipper foot, and finish sewing the center back seam from the slit dot to the bottom of the zipper. Take a few extra stitches past and alongside the zipper seam to prevent a pucker. Press.

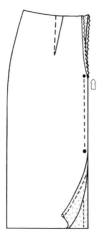

step 6

Sew side seams

7. Layer the skirt front and back pieces with right sides together. Pin each side seam.

8. Stitch each side seam, backstitching at beginning and end. Zigzag and trim the two raw edges of each seam together and press toward the back.

Sew slit extensions

9. Clip right back seam allowance above slit extension, so it will lie flat.

steps 7–8

10. Fold the slit extensions toward the left side of the skirt. Hand-baste the upper edge in place.

11. Turn the skirt right side out and using the free arm of your machine, stitch across the short diagonal line indicated on the left back, to secure the overlapped extensions.

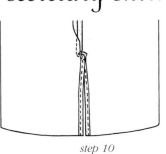

step 10

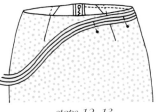

steps 12–13

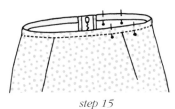

step 15

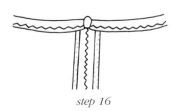

step 16

Attach bias tape for waistband

12. Turn skirt right side out. Unzip zipper and unfold zipper tape at the top of the skirt, so that you're pinning bias tape to zipper tape.

13. Unfold one of the folds of the double-fold bias tape, and starting at zipper tape, pin it along the entire waistline of the skirt, ⅜"

below the top edge with right sides together. Extend an extra 1" of bias tape at the beginning and end of the center back.

14. Stitch the bias tape to the skirt along the pinned foldline. Press the stitching on both sides.

15. Turn the bias tape completely to the wrong side of the skirt.

Keeping the edges of the tape turned under, pin to the inside of waistband, trimming and tucking the ends behind the zipper tape.

16. To finish waistband, zigzag stitch down the middle of the tape, catching the folded edge on the wrong side.

Hem the bottom

17. Try the skirt on and mark the desired length with a pin or chalk. (If you can, get a friend to help you with this.)

18. Measure the distance from the top of the waistband to your mark (for example, 23"), and add 1½" for hem allowance to determine the total length.

19. Using the total length, measure down from the waistband and mark all along the bottom of the skirt.

20. Using a flexible ruler as a guide, connect those hem marks with chalk. (This is your cutting line.)

21. Cut away any excess length, following the cutting line.

22. Turn skirt inside out and fold the raw edge of the bottom hem toward the wrong side ¼". Press. Fold over again 1¼" and press.

23. Edgestitch along the entire hem. Press on both sides.

tip | I like to use a zigzag stitch pattern for this step; it does a good job of attaching the bias tape to the skirt, and it's sew easy!

steps 22–23

level

materials

Fabric Wool and wool blends

Lining Acetate, China silk, or polysatin

Thread in color to match

Three 1" buttons

1"-wide ribbon

Pattern (enclosed in box)

yardage

60" Fabric and lining
S=1⅝ yards
M—L=1¾ yards
Ribbon 3 (3¼, 3½) yards

techniques

Topstitch (page 94), staystitch (page 87), understitch (page 162), hand-stitched hems (page 230), slipstitch (page 230), buttonholes (pages 98–99)

seam allowance

⅝" unless otherwise indicated

pattern pieces

1. Front (cut 2)
2. Side front (cut 2)
3. Back (cut 1 on fold)

*W*ho wears a cape these days? Poets, posh nannies, fancy ingenues, Audrey Hepburn types on the go. That's who. The poncho is très over, but the cape is on the rise. Made of soft, warm wool, Cape Mod wraps around your shoulders like a cozy blanket—only swingy-er and more lovely. I like making this cape in a classic tweed and then lining it with a color like candy. Makes me want to find a handsome man, slap him with my gloves saying, "How dare you!" and then kiss him hard.

Lay Out Pattern and Cut Fabric

1. Fold the main fabric selvage to selvage with right sides together, and smooth out on table.

2. Position pattern pieces as shown, lining up the fold-lines along the folded edge, and checking the grainlines against the fold or selvage. Pin pattern pieces in place.

3. Cut out the pieces as shown, transferring all necessary markings.

4. Repeat steps 1 through 3 with the lining fabric.

60" S-M-L

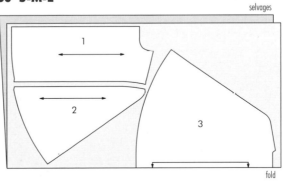

Sewing Instructions

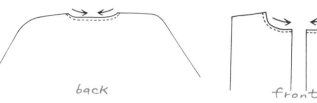

back   front

Staystitch neckline

1. Staystitch the neckline of the cape in both the front and back in the direction shown, ½" from the edge, to keep the fabric from stretching.

Sew front pieces to side pieces

2. Layer one front and one side piece with right sides together, matching notches. Pin along side seam.

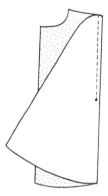

steps 2–3

3. Stitch seam from the top of the shoulder down to the dot, backstitching at beginning and end. (The dot will be the top of the arm opening, or vent.)

4. Press the seam and the vent open and flat as shown.

5. Repeat steps 1 through 4 on the remaining front and side front pieces.

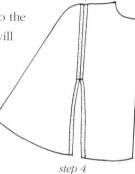

step 4

Topstitch sleeve openings

6. Topstitch around each sleeve opening to finish them, pivoting at the dot as shown. Press.

> **tip** Wool responds well to steam, so you want to use plenty of it when pressing seams.

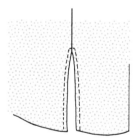

step 6

Sew sides to back

7. Pin one side of the cape front/side front to the back with right sides together, lining up raw edges and matching notches.

8. Stitch the side/back seam, backstitching at beginning and end. Press seam and clip curves.

9. Repeat steps 7 and 8 on remaining side.

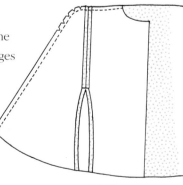

step 8

Sew lining

10. Repeat steps 1 through 9 with lining fabric.

11. Layer cape and lining with right sides together and pin along the front opening and neckline, lining up raw edges. It's a good idea to hand-baste the lining in place before stitching it on the machine.

12. Stitch pinned seams, backstitching at beginning and end of each. Clip neck seam and trim corners. Press seams open first, then flat.

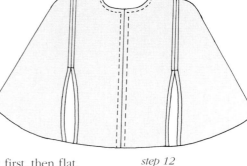

step 12

13. Understitch lining (see page 162) around front edges and neck. (The understitching will keep lining to the inside and flat.) Press.

Add buttons

14. Sew three 1" buttonholes at buttonhole markings.

15. Hand-stitch buttons at button markings.

tip Allow the cape to hang for 24 hours before sewing buttonholes and finishing the hem. This will give the fabric time to stretch.

tip Practice making buttonholes on a scrap of the real fabric and lining. Sew a square of lining to a square of cape fabric, and create a buttonhole through both layers just like you're going to be doing on the actual cape.

Hem the bottom and finish lining

16. Fold the bottom hem toward the wrong side 1½" (amount allowed for hem). Pin and try the cape on to see how you like the length. If too long, cut away excess length, but leave 1½" for hem allowance. Repeat on the lining hem.

17. Fold both cape and lining hems together 1½" to the inside of the cape. Press well.

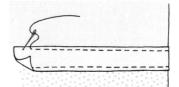

step 17

18. Pin ribbon on top of the raw edge of the cape hem.

19. Hand-stitch the bottom edge of the ribbon to the cape hem only, and hand-stitch the top of ribbon to the lining only, as shown, easing in any fullness. Stitching should not show on outside of cape.

20. Slipstitch the lining to the cape at the arm openings.

steps 18–19

step 20

151

knockout knickers

T his is an homage to the purple corduroy knickers I sewed in my youth. Only now, I wear my knickers at my hips with foxy tights and heels. I love their Oliver-Twist-meets-Marc-Jacobs vibe. You can embellish them with a little hand-stitching on the waistband and cuffs with embroidery floss. Pick out super-cute buttons for the waistband and cuffs. Just don't ask a British person, "Do you like my knickers?" 'cause that means something dirty.

Lay Out Pattern and Cut Fabric

1. Fold the fabric selvage to selvage with right sides together and smooth out on table.

2. Lay out pattern pieces as shown, checking the grainlines from either the fold or selvage to make sure they are parallel.

3. Cut out the knickers pieces as shown, transferring all necessary markings.

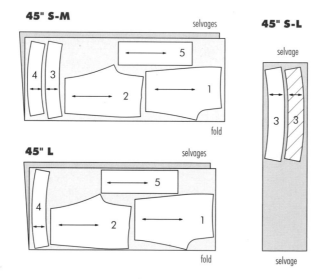

(Layouts for 60" and interfacing on page 154.)

level

materials
Fabric Gabardine, lightweight denim, pinwale corduroy, poplin, or lightweight wool and wool blends
Thread in color to match
Fusible interfacing
7" invisible zipper
2 sew-on hook and eye waistband closures
1 skein embroidery floss
Two ⅞" buttons
Pattern (enclosed in box)

tools
Invisible zipper foot

yardage
45" Fabric   **60"**
S–M=1¾ yards   S=1¼ yards
L=1⅞ yards   M–L=1⅜ yards

22" Interfacing
S=1¼ yards   M=1⅜ yards
L=1½ yards

techniques
Darts (page 88), invisible zipper (page 96), topstitch (page 94), pivoting (page 36), staystitch (page 87), easestitch (page 88), running stitch (pages 228–229), waistband hook and eye closure (pages 99–100), buttonholes (pages 98–99), buttons (page 67)

seam allowance
⅝" unless otherwise indicated

pattern pieces
1. Knickers front (cut 2)
2. Knickers back (cut 2)
3. Waistband front (cut 2 in knickers fabric, cut 2 in interfacing)
4. Waistband back (cut 2 in knickers fabric, cut 2 in interfacing)
5. Knickers cuff (cut 2)

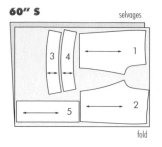

60" S

selvages

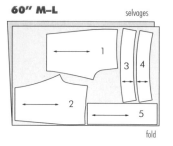

60" M-L

selvages

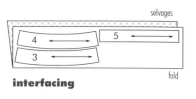

selvages

interfacing

fold

fold

fold

4. Cut two sets of interfacing for the back and front of the waistband.

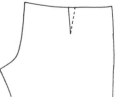

step 1

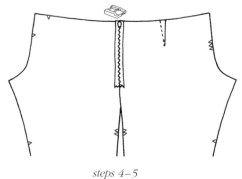

steps 4–5

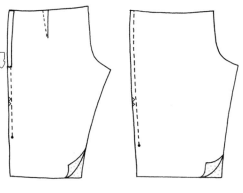

steps 6–7　　　*steps 8–9*

Sewing Instructions

Make darts

1. Sew dart on one knickers back as marked. Press the dart toward the center seam.

2. Repeat on other knickers back piece.

Insert invisible zipper

3. Swap your all-purpose presser foot for an invisible zipper foot.

4. Line up the top of the zipper tape with the top edge of the waistband. Find the markings where zipper ends on the left front and left back pieces and hand-baste the zipper into position.

5. Install the invisible zipper into the left side of the knickers, as detailed on page 96. Put the regular zipper foot on your machine after zipper installation.

Sew outer leg seams

6. Pin outer left leg seam together matching notches.

7. Stitch the left leg seam starting at the dot above the vent opening and ending a few stitches past the zipper stitching, backstitching at beginning and end. Press entire seam allowance, including the slit opening.

8. Pin the front and back of the outer right leg seam together matching notches.

9. Stitch from the waistband down to the slit opening, backstitching at beginning and end. Press as on left leg in step 7.

Finish raw edges of cuff openings

10. Place wrong side of one leg on the ironing board and fold the raw edges of the pressed vent opening by half to create a narrow hem. Pin.

11. Topstitch hem as shown. When top-stitching here, work up one side, pivot, and then work back down. Press.

12. Repeat steps 10 and 11 on the opposite leg cuff.

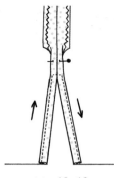

steps 10–12

Sew inseams and center seam

13. With right sides together, pin along the inseam, matching notches.

14. Stitch the leg inseam, backstitching at beginning and end. Press seam.

15. Repeat steps 13 and 14 on right leg.

16. Turn the right leg inside out and slip it into the left leg with right sides together. Pin along center seam, matching notches and keeping inner leg seam allowances open and flat as pressed.

17. Stitch center seam, backstitching at beginning and end. Press seam to open. Trim seam allowances.

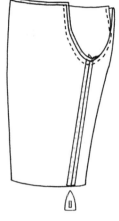

steps 16–17

Make waistbands and attach them

18. Apply fusible interfacing to the wrong side of all four front and back waistband pieces.

19. Staystitch the top and bottom of the waistband pieces to prevent fabric stretching.

20. Pin waistband pieces with right sides together at right side seams, matching notches.

21. Sew the right side seam, backstitching at beginning and end. Press seam.

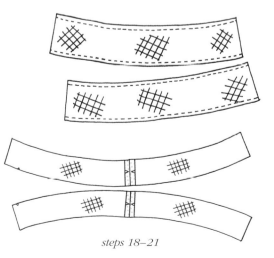

steps 18–21

step 22

steps 23–24

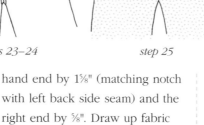

step 25

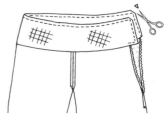

steps 26–27

22. Unzip the zipper. Set your machine to a long stitch length and easestitch around the waistline ⅝" from the edge. (This is in preparation for the eased seam in the next step.) Instead of backstitching, leave long thread ends at beginning and end of seam.

23. Turn the knickers inside out. Starting at the zipper opening, and with the right side of the waistband facing the wrong side of the knickers, pin the waistband along waistline. Extend the left-

hand end by 1⅜" (matching notch with left back side seam) and the right end by ⅝". Draw up fabric on easestitching threads to distribute fullness evenly.

24. Reset to an average stitch length and stitch the inside waistband to the knickers, starting at the left side opening.

25. Turn knickers right side out. Press seams open. Press the seam allowances together, then straight up toward the top of the waistband. Grade seam allowances.

26. Turn knickers inside out. Pin the outer waistband to the inner waistband with right sides together.

27. Starting at the short end of the front waistband, stitch up the side of and across the top of waistband. Pivot again and stitch down the side of the back waistband. Pivot and stitch across the overlap. Press seams open and flat. Trim all waistband seam allowances and clip corners.

steps 29–30

28. Turn knickers and then waistband right side out. (You may need to poke out the top corners of the waistband with a pencil or knitting needle, but do so very carefully.)

29. Fold under the raw edge of the outside waistband ⅝" and pin to the pants waistline. It should just cover the stitching at the waistline.

30. Edgestitch around the entire waistband. Press.

Sew cuffs to legs

31. Iron fusible interfacing to the bottom half of each cuff, as indicated on pattern piece.

32. Turn pants inside out. Starting at the vent opening, pin the right side of the noninterfaced half of the cuff to the wrong side of the pants leg. Match the square markings at the back leg opening and the cuff notch with the pants inseam.

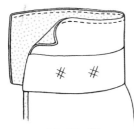

steps 31–32

(If placed correctly, you should have an extra 1⅝" of cuff fabric for the button underlap; refer back to the pattern piece if you are missing either of these marks.)

33. Starting at the chalk mark, stitch the cuff to the leg, backstitching at beginning and end. Press seam allowances open and flat, and then straight down toward the bottom of the cuff.

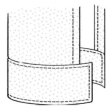

step 33

34. Turn the cuff back by half so the right sides are together and the interfacing is face up. Stitch along each short end and short top edge of underlap ⅝". Press seams open and flat. Grade seam allowances, trim, and clip corners.

35. Turn knickers and cuffs right side out, making sure the corners have sharp points. Press well. Fold the top edge of the cuffs to the wrong side ⅝". Press, making sure to cover up stitching.

36. Edgestitch the top of the cuff to right side of pants as with waistband. Then edgestitch around all sides of cuffs, as shown. Press.

steps 35–36

37. Repeat steps 32 through 36 on right leg and cuff.

Finish the knickers

38. Thread a needle with embroidery floss (removing three strands so it's three strands thick), and hand-stitch along the bottom of the waistband using a running stitch. (In other words, sew a running stitch ¼" up from its edge.)

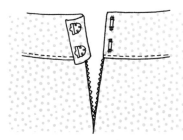

step 38

steps 39–40

39. Repeat step 38 on each of the cuffs, starting at the top left-hand corner and working around all four sides.

40. Make buttonholes on cuffs as marked. Attach the buttons with the leftover embroidery thread.

41. Sew hooks and eyes to waistband, as shown.

step 41

materials

Fabric Dupioni silk, sateen, silk faille, silk shantung, or taffeta; or lightweight linen, wool, or wool blends

Lining China silk, acetate, or polysatin

Thread in color to match

13" invisible zipper

Pattern (enclosed in box)

tools

Invisible zipper foot

yardage

60"
S–L=2⅝ yds.

Lining
60"

Bodice only	**Full**
S–L=¾ yards	S–L=2⅝ yards

***Note:** Line the skirt only if you are using itchy fabric like wool.*

techniques

Staystitch (page 87), darts (page 88), invisible zipper (page 96), slipstitch (page 230), lining (page 162), curved hem (pages 232–233), understitch (page 162)

seam allowance

⅝" unless otherwise indicated

pattern pieces

1. Bodice front (cut 2: 1 in dress fabric, 1 in lining fabric, on fold)
2. Bodice back (cut 2: 1 in dress fabric, 1 in lining fabric, on fold)
3. Skirt (cut 2 in dress fabric and 2 in lining, optional)

I love this dress because of its classic silhouette. The full skirt and fitted waist make a flattering romantic modern retro look. Picture it in a black-and-white movie from the '50s or at this year's Golden Globe Awards. It would work in so many different fabrics for so many occasions. Make it in deep crimson silk for a fancy cocktail party. Make it in navy blue wool and wear it with a cardigan and fancy wool stockings to your board meeting. Beginning seamstresses should save this one until after they have a few projects under their belts. The pattern's challenges include an invisible zipper, a partial lining, and a curved hem.

Lay Out Pattern and Cut Fabric

1. Fold the dress fabric selvage to selvage with right sides together, and smooth out on table.

2. Position pattern piece 3 (skirt) as shown, lining up the foldline along the folded edge, and pin in place.

3. Cut twice for skirt front and back, transferring all necessary markings.

60" S–L

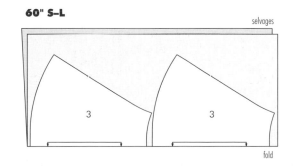

S·E·W

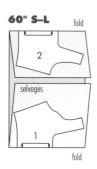

60" S–L fold

2

selvages

1

fold

4. Fold remaining fabric selvage to selvage. Press along foldline. Lay fabric on table and fold each selvage so they line up with the pressed line in the center, and smooth out.

5. Position bodice front (1) and bodice back (2) along foldlines as shown and pin them in place.

6. Cut out bodice pieces, transferring all necessary markings.

7. Repeat steps 4 and 5 with bodice on bodice lining fabric. Repeat steps 1 through 6 with lining fabric for full lining.

Sewing Instructions

Make bodice

step 1

step 2

steps 3–4

front and back

1. Staystitch along the necklines and armholes of the bodice front and back.

2. Sew two darts in the bodice front as marked. Press these darts

down toward the waistline of the dress as shown.

3. Find the side of the front and back pieces without the zipper markings. Pin those two sides

with right sides together to form a side seam.

4. Stitch the right side seam, backstitching at beginning and end. Press seam.

Sew skirt pieces

5. Pin the two skirt pieces with right sides together along one side seam.

6. Stitch the skirt side seam, backstitching at beginning and end. Press seam.

Attach bodice to skirt

7. Layer the skirt and bodice with right sides together as shown, lining them up at the waistline. Line up the right side seam of the bodice with the right side seam of the skirt, and pin along the waistline. (Pin the side seam allowances flat, so they remain open when you sew.)

8. Hand-baste at side seam so bodice and skirt line up.

steps 5–6

9. Sew the bodice to skirt along the waistline, backstitching at beginning and end. Press the waistline seam toward the bodice.

Insert invisible zipper and sew left side seam

tip Cut a small piece of fabric and stitch it on top of the end of the zipper tape, as shown below. This way it won't be scratchy.

10. Put an invisible zipper foot on your machine.

11. Find the zipper-opening dot on the (wearer's) left side of the dress. Pin and then hand-baste the zipper into position.

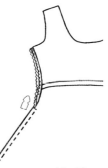

steps 7–9

12. Install the invisible zipper into the dress, as detailed on page 96.

13. Switch to a regular zipper foot and finish sewing the left side seam of the skirt, from the bottom of the skirt to a few stitches past the bottom of the zipper stitching. Put the all-purpose foot back on your machine after zipper installation.

steps 10–13

Sew shoulder seams and prepare armholes

14. Pin bodice front and back at shoulders with right sides together.

15. Stitch one shoulder seam, backstitching at beginning and end. Press seam open and flat. Repeat on the other shoulder.

16. Staystitch along the ⅝" seam line around the armhole openings. Clip the seam allowance to the stitching, being careful not to cut beyond the seam allowance.

17. Press the clipped seam allowance to the wrong side around the entire armhole, using the staystitching as a pressing guide.

Make a pretty belt with satin ribbon and a silk flower.

steps 14–15

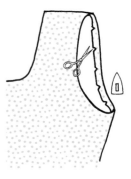

steps 16–17

161

step 19

Make the dress lining

18. Repeat steps 1 through 4 and 14 through 17 for a bodice-only lining with lining fabric. For a fully lined dress, repeat steps 1 through 17, skipping steps 10 through 13. Instead of installing a zipper, simply press back the seam allowances in the lining that run along the zipper area by ⅝".

Sew lining to dress

19. Turn main dress right side out. Turn bodice lining inside out and slip over the main dress, so the two are lined up everywhere—especially at the shoulders and neckline—with right sides together. Pin lining to dress around the neckline, carefully matching seams at shoulders.

20. Stitch slowly around the neckline. It's important that you stick to the ⅝" seam allowance around the entire neck so that the dress will hang correctly. Press.

21. Clip curves as shown. Trim seam allowances.

22. Understitch the lining around the neck to keep it from rolling (see sidebar, below).

tip Since fabrics for lining tend to be a bit slippery, you'll want to use plenty of pins to pin the lining to the dress. Then I suggest hand-basting it in place before stitching on your machine.

step 21

understitching

When a seam line is pressed to form an edge and it also encloses the seam allowances (as it does with the neckline of the dress), you'll often have to do a little understitching to keep the lining or facing lying flat and where it belongs—on the inside of the garment. Understitching is as easy as 1-2-3. First, grade, clip, or notch the seam allowances and then press them together and toward the facing or lining. With the right side up, edgestitch ⅛" on the lining fabric along the seam line. Since you've already pressed the seam allowances over to this side, you'll be stitching through them, thus stitching them to the underside of the garment. Last, fold the project fabric and the lining so the wrong sides are together, press again, and you're done!

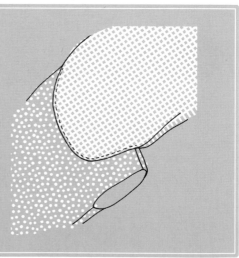

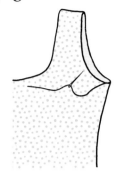

23. Slipstitch the lining to the dress around the armholes and the outside edge of the shoulder straps.

step 23

Hem the bottom

24. Try on the dress. Decide on a length, adding a 1¼" hem allowance. Then mark and trim the hem to an even length.

tip Allow the dress to hang for 24 hours to allow for any stretching of the fabric before finishing the hem.

25. Turn raw edge of hem under by ¼". Press. Turn by 1" and press again.

26. Pin and then hand-sew hem with a slipstitch.

27. Repeat steps 24 and 25 on the lining, making the lining 1" shorter in length than the main dress, so it will be hidden to the inside.

steps 25–26

Finish the dress

28. Slipstitch the lining around the zipper opening to the zipper tape, making sure the lining fabric is clear of the zipper teeth. Press.

29. When lining bodice only, press back bottom raw edge of the lining by ⅞". Slipstitch the edge of the lining to the waistline, as shown.

30. When fully lining dress, hand-tack the lining to the dress at the waistline side seams.

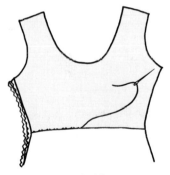

step 29

tote-ally awesome

eed a good beginner project? Sure, there are the pillows—but those are for people who *lie* down. These Tote-ally Awesome totes are for people who are on the go and *carry* things. (Cut to *West Side Story*–like rumble between pillow makers and tote sewers.) But seriously, you get to practice sewing seams, hems, linings—on a small and manageable scale. You play with pockets, make handles out of fabric or ribbon. Mix and match the elements until you trot off into the sunset toting your dream bag.

Cut and Mark Fabric

For front/back of totes (in 3 styles)

1. Fold the tote front/back fabric selvage to selvage with right sides together. Smooth out on table. (**Note:** For long-handled tote you'll be laying the handle piece on a single layer of 60" fabric.)

Measure, mark, and cut the following out of fabric, using the selvage as your straight edge, so the fabric is cut on grain (see page 49).

level

finished measurements

Long-handled tote 10" x 11", 1" x 50" handle

Hand tote 12" x 12", 1" x 14" handles

Shoulder tote 13" x 10½", 2" x 32" strap

materials

Fabric Lightweight canvas, denim, upholstery fabrics, wool, or wool blends

Optional lining Lightweight canvas, cotton, and cotton blends

Thread in color to match

Double-fold bias tape

Trims ribbon, lace, twill tape, etc.

Buttons (optional)

tools

Loop turner or large safety pin

yardage

Main fabric with optional pocket
½ yard at least 45" wide

Lining fabric (optional)
Same as main fabric

If use fabric for handles, add ⅛ yard for long-handled tote and shoulder tote

Option: *Substitute webbing or ribbon for handle fabric as follows:*
Long-handled tote, 1" wide   2¼ yards
Hand tote, 1" wide   1 yard

techniques

Patch pockets (page 167), topstitch (page 94), seam finishing (pages 85–86)

seam allowance

½" unless otherwise indicated

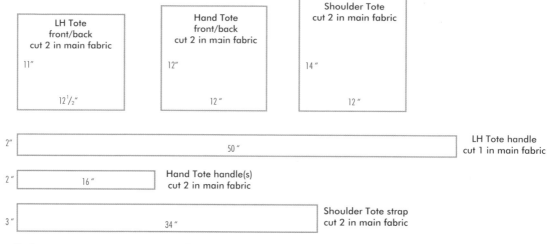

LH Tote
front/back
cut 2 in main fabric

11"

12½"

Hand Tote
front/back
cut 2 in main fabric

12"

12"

Shoulder Tote
cut 2 in main fabric

14"

12"

2"   50"   LH Tote handle
cut 1 in main fabric

2"   16"   Hand Tote handle(s)
cut 2 in main fabric

3"   34"   Shoulder Tote strap
cut 2 in main fabric

Long-handled tote:

2A. 11" x 12½" rectangle for front/ back (cut 2)

3A. 2" x 50" rectangle for handle (cut 1 on single layer of fabric)

Hand tote:

2B. 12" square for front/back (cut 2)

3B. 2" x 16" rectangle for handles (cut 2)

Shoulder tote:

2C. 14" x 12" rectangle (cut 2)

3C. 3" x 34" rectangle (cut 2)

Lined bags:

4. Cut front/back in contrasting fabric for lining.

Sewing Instructions

Add patch pockets (optional)

1. If you choose to have pockets (see sidebar, opposite page), add them to the front/back of your tote as the first step, with the wrong side of the pocket sewn to the right side of the back/front fabric and/ or lining.

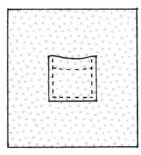

step 1

Sew the tote front/back together at sides

2. Layer front/back pieces right sides together. Pin. Stitch a side seam. Repeat on remaining side.

3. Press side seams. If you plan to line your tote, leave the seam allowance as is. If you are not lining your tote, then neaten your seams with the seam finishing of your choice.

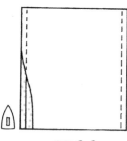

steps 2–3

Shoulder tote

patch pocket (OPTIONAL)

1. Make a square or rectangle the size of the pocket you desire, plus ½" seam allowance added on three sides for a turn-under hem and 1¼" for the double-turned hem at the top of the pocket.

2. Staystitch ½" on two sides and the bottom.

3. Press back the raw edge of the top of the pocket by ¼". Fold the top over, right sides together 1". Press. Stitch the sides of the top of the pocket with ½" seams. Turn the top of the pocket right side out and press.

4. Fold the sides and bottom to the wrong side on the staystitching and press.

5. For proper pocket placement, use your chalk and ruler and draw your seam allowances on the top (½" on three sides, and 1" on the top) so you'll know where your pocket will be after

you sew the sides, top, and bottom of tote. Pin the pocket in the desired location, lining it up visually with the sides of the bag. Measure up and/or over from the bottom and sides of tote to the pocket to check that it's straight—the distance around all four sides should be equal for a centered pocket. Readjust as needed, and then pin well.

6. Topstitch the pocket on three sides, back-stitching at the top to reinforce where the pocket is attached to the front/ back or inside of the tote.

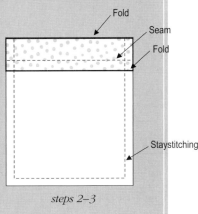

steps 2–3

Sew the bottom of the tote

4. Pin the bottom raw edges of the front/back with right sides together. Stitch. Press seam allowances open and flat. Trim corners. Finish as in step 3.

Sew the top of the bag

5. Turn the tote inside out and slip it onto the ironing board. Fold back the top edge by 1" and press well. Tuck the raw edge of the fabric in half toward the inside of the fold and press again to create a double-turned hem. If you're not planning on lining the tote, pin and edgestitch ⅛". (Or if you prefer, you can edgestitch and repeat with topstitching for two lines of decorative stitching.) Press on both sides.

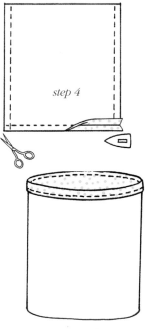

step 4

step 5

Hand tote

Make lining (optional)

6. Take contrasting fabric and repeat steps 1 through 5.

Make fabric handles

7. For long-handled tote: Press back the raw edges of the fabric to the wrong side by ½". Fold the handle in half lengthwise and press to set the foldline. Pin.

8. Edgestitch around all four sides. Press.

9. For hand tote or shoulder tote: Layer two handle pieces and pin them right sides together. Stitch along one long edge. Press seam open and flat from both sides.

10. Repeat step 9 on the opposite edge.

11. Turn handle right side out with a loop turner or safety pin and press well.

12. Repeat steps 9 through 11 with remaining handle pieces.

Attach handles

Handles can be sewn on the outside or the inside of the tote. Instructions for both are explained below, but feel free to play designer and mix and match handle options.

13. To stitch handle on outside of tote: Press back the handle ends by ½". Set your machine to a short stitch length.

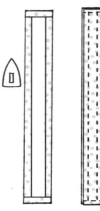

steps 7–8

handling it
HANDLE ALTERNATIVES

Think you can only use fabric handles on your tote? *Au contraire.* You can make handles from twill tape, grosgrain ribbon, or webbing in whatever width or length your heart desires. Pink or fold back the raw edges of the trim and then attach either to the inside/outside of the bag or sandwich them between the tote and lining. Stitch small boxes with an X, sew buttons to hide stitches, and/or machine-embroider stars for a tote that is sew cute!

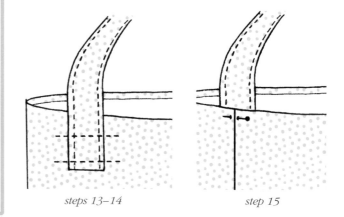

steps 13–14   *step 15*

14. For hand tote: Mark center front and center back. Measure and mark 3" on either side of this mark for handle placement. Pin 1" below the top edge of the bag. Stitch. Press. For extra strength, stitch again as shown opposite in steps 13–14.

15. For long-handled tote: Line up the center of the handle with the side seams. Pin 1" below the top edge of the bag. Stitch. Backstitch and stitch again. Press.

16. For shoulder tote: same as step 15.

17. To stitch handle on inside of tote: If you'd rather not see the handles on the outside of your tote, pin the raw ends of the handle(s) in the desired locations 1" below the top edge on the inside of the bag. Sew.

Drop the lining fabric into the bag and stitch it in place

18. Turn the lining wrong side out and slip it into the right-side-out tote, wrong sides together. Pin well, lining up the side seams. Use the free arm on your machine to topstitch ¼" around the top and attach the lining. Be very careful not to stitch the handles to the bag! Press.

step 18

Variation: *Sew two lines of stitching at different seam allowances, or use a decorative stitch pattern such as a zigzag in a contrasting thread color.*

Long-handled tote

level

measurements
10" square (when tied);
16" (from bottom to top of tie)

materials
Fabric Brocade, cotton, dupioni silk,
silk faille, or satin
Lining Canvas, lightweight corduroy,
or denim; something heavy enough
to hold the shape of the bag

Thread in color to match

1 sew-on snap size 3

Pattern (make your own, pattern
paper needed)

yardage
45" Fabric
¾ yard

Lining
¾ yard

techniques
Grading seams (page 86),
pivoting (page 36), clipping
curves (page 87), French seam
(pages 85–86), snaps (page 100)

seam allowance
½" unless otherwise indicated

This pretty kimono print bag reminds me of something out of old Tokyo, complete with a big beautiful tie like a geisha's obi. But it's great for holding your twenty-first-century essentials—cell, wallet, Netflix to mail—in modern style. No fancy sewing maneuvers required. Simply stitch along the body of the bag and handles, taking your own sweet time around the curves. (Remember how to pivot?) Finish the bottom with a neat and strong French seam. Tie the handles into a nifty knot at the top, and go drink saki with someone you love. P.S. This bag is also super-cute in denim!

Make the Pattern

1. Draw a horizontal line 18¾" long on pattern paper. Mark an A at the left end of the line, then mark a B 9" to the right, and a C 2¾" to the right of B. (This is where the handles will end.) Label the right end of the line D.

2. At A, draw a vertical line 1⅛" up and mark the top A1. At B, draw a vertical line 2½" up and mark it B1. At C draw a vertical line 5⅝" up and mark it C1. At D, draw a vertical line 5⅛" up and mark it D1.

3. Connect A1, B1, and C1 for the handle, holding your flexible sewing ruler on its edge to create a subtle curve as shown.

4. Connect C1 and D1 for the center seam.

5. Label this pattern piece "Tokyo tie bag, cut 4 on fold (2 in main fabric, 2 in lining)."

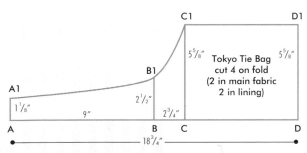

Lay Out Pattern and Cut Fabric

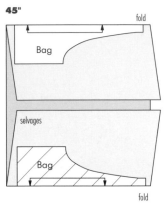

1. Fold the fabric in half lengthwise, selvage to selvage with right sides together. Press the foldline. Open up the fabric and smooth on a table right side up.

2. Turn the bottom selvage up, with right sides together so it meets the pressed foldline. Repeat, folding the top down so that the selvages meet in the middle.

3. Position the pattern piece printed side up on the top fold as shown.

4. Pin pattern piece along the foldline, and cut around three sides.

5. Flip pattern piece over and repeat step 4 on the bottom foldline as shown.

6. Repeat steps 1 through 5 with the lining fabric.

Sewing Instructions

Stitch main bag and lining

1. Layer the two pieces of the main fabric with right sides together. (The long part will be the ties and the boxy part will be the bag; the boxy part is constructed by sewing two short seams, which will run down the center of the bag on both sides.) Pin.

2. Stitch seam, backstitching at beginning and end.

3. Press seam open, turn right side out, and press again.

steps 1–2

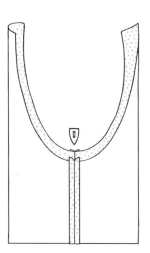

step 3

4. Repeat steps 2 and 3 on the other side.

5. Repeat steps 1 through 4 with the two lining fabric pieces.

Connect main bag to lining

6. Slip the main fabric bag into the lining fabric bag with right sides together, matching center seams. Pin.

7. Start at a center seam of the lining and stitch around the top and handles as shown.

8. Grade seam allowances and clip corners and curves. Press.

Finish bottom with French seams

9. Turn the bag right side out, wrong sides together. Pin bottom edge and stitch across the bottom using ¼" seam allowance. Grade, being careful not to cut too close to the stitching, which would weaken the seam.

10. Turn the bag wrong side out, pin bottom edge, and stitch across the bottom again using ½" seam allowance. (The graded seam will be encased in the new seam.)

11. Turn bag right side out and tie the top into a square knot. (You know: right over left, left over right.)

Sew on a snap

12. Hand-sew the corresponding pieces of a snap to each center seam ¼" below the top edge of the bag.

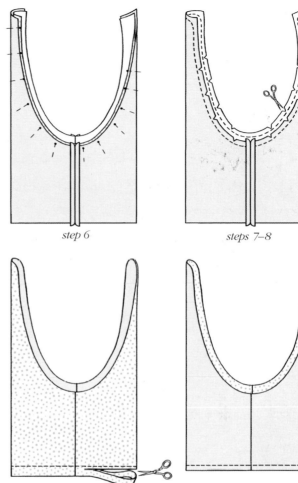

step 6   *steps 7–8*

step 9   *step 10*

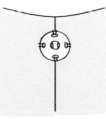

step 12

hobo bag

Y ou will be the chicest hobo at the campfire when you pull your can of beans and harmonica out of this cute bag. Just kidding. You can sew this classic slouchy carryall in a weekend. Make it girly with a tiny print or preppie with stripes and plaids. Stitch up a new one every season. Toss it in the wash when it looks tired. I love this shape because it's big enough to tote a laptop and myriad daily necessities, but still looks stylish.

Make the Pattern

1. Draw a rectangle 15" long x 11" wide on pattern paper. Cut out the pattern piece. Mark foldline, along one of the long sides. Label this piece "Hobo bag body, cut 4 on fold (2 in main fabric, 2 in lining)."

2. Place the rectangle with the bottom foldline toward you. Use a French curve to round off the upper right corner as shown. Mark and cut corner.

3. Draw a rectangle 20" long x 3¼" wide on pattern paper. Cut out the pattern piece. Label this piece "Hobo bag handle, cut 2 (1 main fabric, 1 lining fabric)."

level 🧵🧵🧵

measurements
19" wide x 14" high

materials
Fabric Canvas, corduroy, cotton duck, denim, or wool
Lining Lightweight canvas, poplin, or printed cotton

Thread in color to match

20" all-purpose zipper

Pattern (make your own; pattern paper needed)

tools
French curve

yardage
45" fabric
¾ yard

Lining
¾ yard

techniques
Basting (machine and hand) (pages 40 and 229), zipper (page 95), topstitch (page 94)

seam allowance
½" unless otherwise indicated

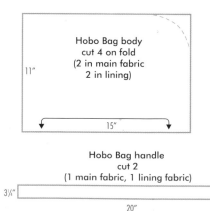

Hobo Bag body
cut 4 on fold
(2 in main fabric
2 in lining)

11"

15"

Hobo Bag handle
cut 2
(1 main fabric, 1 lining fabric)

3¼"

20"

S·E·W ·

Lay Out Pattern and Cut Fabric

1. Fold the fabric in half lengthwise, selvage to selvage with right sides together. Press the foldline. Open up the fabric and smooth on a table right side up.

2. Turn the bottom selvage up, with right sides together so it meets the pressed fold-line. Repeat, folding the top down so that the selvages meet in the middle.

3. Position the pattern piece printed side up on the top fold as shown.

4. Pin pattern piece along the foldline, and cut around three sides.

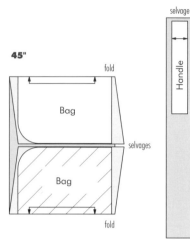

5. Flip pattern piece over and repeat step 4 on the bottom foldline as shown.

6. Cut out handle piece going through one layer of fabric.

7. Repeat steps 1 through 6 with the lining fabric.

Sewing Instructions

Sew in zipper

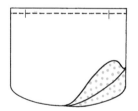

steps 1–2

1. Layer the two main fabric pieces with right sides together, pin, and baste along the straight edge (top) using a ½" seam allowance. Press open.

2. Mark 2½" in from each side with chalk or disappearing-ink marker. (This is for zipper.)

3. Mark a line 1½" from the bottom of the zipper. Lay bag in front of you with seam allowances open and flattened. Place closed zipper right side down and centered on top of the seam allowances, with the top end of the zipper pull aligned with one marking on the bag seam and the new marking on the zipper aligned with the opposite mark on the bag seam. Pin the zipper to the seam allowance *only* (not the main bag fabric), lining up the raw fabric edge with the zipper tape, as shown. (Zipper will have 1½" of unsewn tail at the bottom end.)

4. Hand-baste the zipper to the seam allowances only.

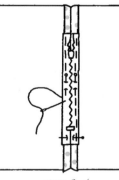

steps 3–4

5. Put a zipper foot on your machine and stitch the zipper to one of the seam allowances *only*, ½" away from the zipper teeth and stopping 1½" from the bottom end. To do so, you'll need to keep the rest of the bag material to the left of the machine.

6. Flip the bag over, so the fabric is once more to the left, leaving just the seam allowance on the throat plate. (Move the position of the zipper foot as needed.) Stitch as in step 5.

7. Remove all basting from the top of bag, including the zipper. Put the all-purpose presser foot back on your machine.

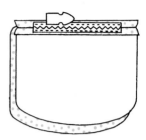

step 6

Make the main bag and lining

8. Layer the two main fabric pieces with right sides together and pin along the sides and bottom of the bag.

9. Sew from top corner down one side, across the curved bottom and up the other side, backstitching at beginning and end.

10. Press seam open, grade seam allowances, and clip curves. Turn right side out and press again.

11. Repeat steps 9 and 10 with lining fabric.

12. Turn the lining inside out and fold the top edge toward the wrong side ⅝". Press.

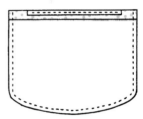

steps 8–9

Make and attach bag handle

tip Mark the center of each handle with a small chalk mark before pinning. It will help you line it up perfectly!

13. Pin the two handle pieces (one in bag fabric, one in lining fabric) along the long edges with right sides together.

14. Stitch each edge, backstitching at beginning and end.

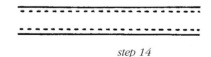

step 14

15. Press seams open and trim seam allowances to ⅛".

16. Turn right side out with loop turner or safety pin (see page 132) and press again.

step 15

17. Topstitch along the outside edges of the handle, ¼" in from the edges.

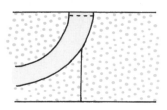

step 19

18. Pin the short ends of the handle to the side seams of the bag, with right sides together. (The center of the handle end should line up with the side seam.)

19. Sew handle ends into place with a ⅜" seam allowance. Reinforce with backstitching.

Sew in lining

20. Slip the lining inside main bag with wrong sides together. Pin lining in place ¼" below the zipper's teeth.

21. Topstitch around top edge of bag through both main fabric and lining fabric.

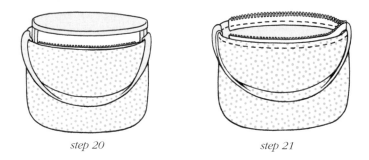

step 20 *step 21*

Make zipper stop

22. Cut two 1" squares of fabric. With right sides together, stitch ¼" from edge around three sides. Fold open end back ½" and press.

23. Turn zipper stop right side out and slide onto bottom end of zipper. Topstitch close to the edge of four sides.

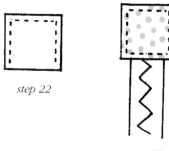

step 22

step 23

level

finished measurements
About 70" (shown) or desired length

materials
Fabric Gauze-type prints, Batiste, lawn, voile, or silk

Thread in a neutral color

Cardboard or heavy cardstock
(for template)

yardage
You need scraps larger than 4" x 4". If you are buying new fabric and want to create this scarf, you need a minimum of ½ yard in a fabric at least 45" wide and in at least two different colors.

Scrap Scarf template — 3½" x 3½"

Here's a great way to use up leftovers, especially light and floaty fabrics. It's called a Lucky Scrap Scarf because you put all your leftover scraps into a paper bag and pull them out one at a time—forming a pattern by the luck of the draw. You'll be surprised how pretty chance can make things—with unexpected repeats and combos. Both sides of the material will show, so it's good (but not essential) to use stuff with two right sides, like silk solids. The edges will fray, but let 'em! The effect is like a colorful feather boa. And you can make one in an hour or so! Then wear your scarf indoors or out. It'll bring you good luck either way!

Lay Out and Cut Fabric

1. Fold fabric selvage to selvage and smooth out on table.

2. Using cardboard or a heavy cardstock, create a 3½" x 3½" square template.

3. Starting at the selvage—so you know the grainlines are perfectly straight—trace around the template with your disappearing-ink marker until you have the desired number of swatches and then cut the fabric. (I used about 70 swatches; you can always use less).

4. Throw the swatches into a large paper bag.

Sewing Instructions

Assemble scarf sections

1. I prefer to pin the swatches into sections rather than pin the whole scarf all at once. It keeps things easy to manage, and also allows you to play around with the design. Start by drawing swatches at random from the bag and arranging a line of squares on top of one another as shown until you've created a 10" section. They can be right side or wrong side up and should overlap by at least ½".

steps 1–3

2. Lay your ruler down over the row of squares, going down the center (this will help hold them in place). Carefully mark a line down the center with disappearing-ink marker.

3. Pin along either side of the line, with pins running the same direction as the marked line, pinheads toward you.

4. Repeat steps 1 through 3 to create four or more 10" swatch sections.

5. Connect the sections with pins to prepare the scarf for stitching.

Stitch down the center of the swatches

6. Set your machine to straight stitch. Sew one long line from one end of the scarf to the other. Take your time and work slowly and carefully, keeping all edges of fabric flat as it feeds through the machine.

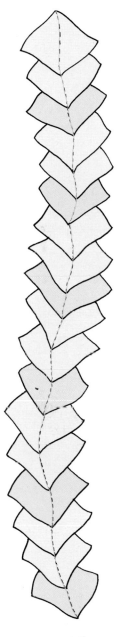

step 6

curtain call

Curtains are the classic beginner sewing project—incredibly easy and incredibly practical. Curtains keep out both light and peeping eyes, while adding yards of personality to a room. A curtain is really just a rectangle of fabric that's hemmed on four sides with some rod-friendly magic at the top. A folded-over tunnel (known in the home decor world as a casing) is easy as pie. You can also stitch fabric loops at the top to slip over the rod. This project requires careful measuring and planning, so it's a good idea to read through the directions and make your design choices before shopping.

tip Curtains have a big impact on a room, especially any wild prints or bold color. Purchase ½ yard and hang it up in the window to see how it looks, how the light changes it, and how it grows on (or off) you before investing in more yardage.

To measure: For the width, measure the span of the rod or the width of the window starting at the outer edge of the casement. For length, measure from the top of the rod to the place where you want the curtain to end. Another trick for finding the right size for your windows? Measure sample curtains at your favorite store or at a friend's house and knock them off—they're the perfect pattern!

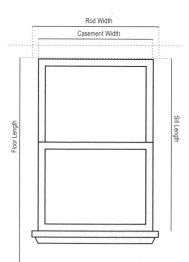

Rod Width
Casement Width
Floor Length
Sill Length

level

measurements
Depends on the window. Curtain shown here is a single panel 53" x 80".

materials
Fabric Canvas, corduroy, cotton, linen, velvet, or silk
Thread in color to match
Optional supplies (trim or other notions to finish)

tools
Yardstick

estimating yardage
Width
Double the finished width figure (left) for heavier-weight fabrics. Triple it for lightweight fabrics. Add on another 2"–3" for each side hem. For two panels, that would be 4 side hems or another 8"–12".
Length
Add an extra 4"–8" to the length measurement (left) for the bottom hem. Add another 12" for the casing at the top.

Note: *If you're making more than one panel or want to cover a window wider than 60", go for an extra-wide drapery fabric that's made specifically for this job, or you might have to piece your material, which is a real pain.*

techniques
Hems (pages 93–94), edgestitch (page 93)

seam allowance
½" unless otherwise indicated

> ## cutting fabric for curtains
>
> The bigger the window and the heavier the fabric, the more difficult the draperies will be to handle as you cut and sew. And if you want the fabric to hang straight down (and trust me, you do) you must use the selvage to measure and draw a perfect rectangle on the fabric. Using a yardstick and chalk, measure your desired curtain length along the selvage and mark those points A and B. (When you measure, you'll need to move away from the cut edge about 3" to compensate for the unevenness of the cut fabric.) From point A, draw a line straight up with chalk—that is your desired width, mark that end C. Now measure the width up from point B and mark that D. Connect all the dots with chalk and you should have a perfect rectangle. Cut the fabric along your chalk lines, going slowly and adjusting the large piece of fabric on your surface as you go. Last, draw a straight line along any remaining selvages and trim them away.

Sewing Instructions

Sew side hems

steps 1–3

1. Fold one side edge toward the wrong side 2" to 3" to create desired width and press. Repeat on the other side edge.

2. Fold again toward the wrong side, creating a 1" to 1½" double-folded hem. Press and pin in place. Repeat on other side hem.

3. Edgestitch along both side hems. Press.

4. Repeat steps 1 through 3 on second panel.

5. Choose either a casing or loops option for the top of your curtain and follow the applicable instructions below.

> **tip** If you're working with a large piece of fabric, line up two tables or use the floor. Also, support the extra fabric with a chair or stool when stitching it on the machine.

Sew the top (casing option)

A casing is a tunnel of fabric that the curtain rod slips through, causing the fabric to gather into soft folds. The casing can be plain or it can have a heading that extends above the rod.

6. Measure the circumference of the rod and then add an extra 1" (for ease and seam allowance). Or pin the fabric over the rod to measure and add 1" to this amount. This step may involve some trial and error—you want the casing to be narrow enough to gather, but not so narrow that it doesn't slide easily along the rod.

7. Fold the top raw edge toward the wrong side ½" and press. Fold again by the amount of fabric you figured in step 6. Press again and pin in place.

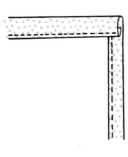

steps 6–8

8. Edgestitch, working from the wrong side of the curtain. Press to set stitching.

Sew the top (loops option A)

A looped top can make a plain curtain more interesting—like straps on a dress. The number and spacing of the loops depends somewhat on their width and the weight of the fabric. Here's a guideline.

Start by measuring the circumference of your rod. Basically, the bigger the rod, the longer you'll want your loops to be. A good rule of thumb for an average-size window would be to make loops about 2" to 3" wide and 10" long. (When folded, this will be 5" long.) With those proportions, leave at least 2" to 3" or more between the loops. Then do the math: For example, how many 3"-wide loops, spaced 5" apart, will fit in your 53"-wide curtain top. Remember, you'll want one loop at each end. (Psst! The answer is 7.)

5A. Finish the top edge of curtain with a 1" double-folded hem. Follow steps 1 through 3.

> **tip** If you're not sure what dimensions you should use for your loops, visit your favorite home goods store and take a close look at their curtain display.

6A. Cut seven strips of fabric about 7" wide x 11" long.

7A. Press back sides, top, and bottom of loop to wrong side by ½". Fold loop in half lengthwise wrong sides together, and press to set fold. Pin. Topstitch on each long edge. Press. Repeat with other loops.

8A. Use chalk and a sewing ruler to mark the location of each loop on the curtain.

9A. Pin both ends of the loop to either side of the curtain, 1¼" below the top edge. Check both sides to make sure placement is correct.

10A. Stitch loops to top of curtain using a 1" seam allowance. Press.

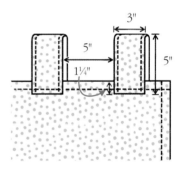

steps 5a–10a

Sew the hem

11. Make a double-folded hem 4" to 6" wide for long curtains, using an extra 8" to 12" of fabric at the bottom. The extra fabric adds weight to the hem and helps it hang better. For shorter or lightweight curtains, use just 4" of fabric to make a 2" hem. Again, for a double-folded hem, repeat steps 1 through 3.

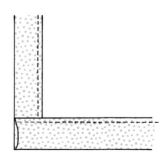

step 11

the envelope, please

*a*nd the winner is . . . this envelope pillow that lets you pop in the cushion in a jiff. It takes less than an hour to sew and makes a great basic pillow structure that you can embellish with embroidery, appliqué, or any award-winning doodads. Or you can just let some gorgeous fabric take the spotlight.

12½"	A cut 1			12½"	B & C cut 2
	16½"				11¼"

Cut and Mark Fabric

1. Measure, mark, and cut one 16½" x 12½" rectangle from fabric using the selvage of the fabric as your straight edge. (You want the pillow fabric to be cut on-grain.)

2. Use chalk on the wrong side of the fabric to mark this piece as A.

3. Measure, mark, and cut two 11¼" x 12½" rectangles from fabric.

4. Use chalk on the wrong side to mark one piece as B and the other as C.

Sewing Instructions

Make envelope backs

1. Fold under one long edge of B ¾" and press. Fold again ¾" and press again. Pin in place.

2. Edgestitch along the fold. Press.

3. Repeat steps 1 and 2 with piece C.

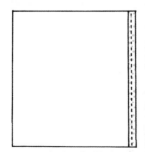

steps 1–3

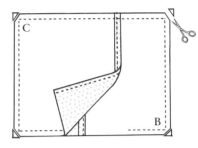

steps 4–5

Assemble pillow

4. Place B on top of A with right sides together, lining up the raw 12½" edges at one end. Repeat with C, lining up the raw edges and overlapping B at center back. Pin around outer edges.

5. Stitch all four edges of the rectangles, pivoting at the corners. Press. Clip corners.

6. Turn pillowcase right side out and insert pillow form through "envelope" opening.

level

measurements
18" square

materials
Fabric Solid color for pillow back and border (home decor fabrics as on page 187)

Fabric Floral print for pillow front center (home decor fabrics as on page 187)

Thread in color to match

Pillow form (18" square)

yardage
Solid fabric ⅝ yard (54"-wide decorator fabric used for sample)
Floral fabric ⅝ yard

techniques
Pivoting (page 36), clipping corners (page 87), slipstitch (page 230)

seam allowance ½"

Note: *If your fabric is napped or has a directional print or pattern, make sure your pieces are all running in the same direction.*

bloom and border pillow

If you're a new seamster, then gather ye rosebuds right here with this perfect starter project. Let the cute flowery fabric do all the work—not you. A super-simple patchwork border frames a fabric blossom. If you're feeling as frisky as a bunny in a peony patch, make the border out of four different nonmatching scraps. Now hop to it!

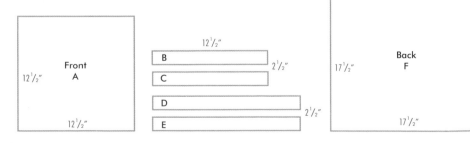

Measure and Cut Fabric

1. Measure and cut one 12½" square from floral fabric.

2. Use chalk on the wrong side of the fabric to mark it A.

3. Measure and cut two 2½" x 12½" rectangles from solid fabric and mark them B and C.

4. Measure and cut two 2½" x 17½" rectangles from solid fabric and mark them D and E.

5. Measure and cut one 17½" square from solid fabric and mark it F.

Sewing Instructions

Assemble pillow front

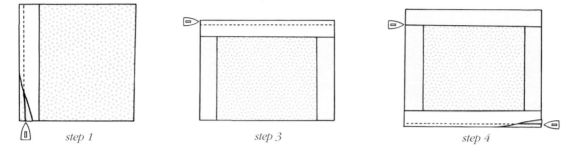

step 1 *step 3* *step 4*

1. Pin the long side of B to A with right sides together. Stitch. Press seam toward the solid rectangle.

2. Repeat step 1 on the opposite side of A with C.

3. Pin the long edge of D to the patchwork piece you just created with right sides together. Stitch. Press seam allowance toward the solid rectangle.

4. Repeat step 3 with E.

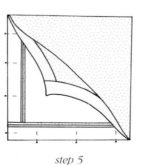

step 5

10" opening

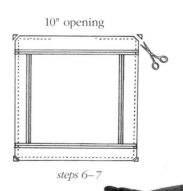

steps 6–7

Finish pillow

5. Pin the assembled patchwork pillow front to F with right sides together.

6. Stitch around all four sides, pivoting at the corners, and leaving a 10" opening on one side. Press.

7. Clip corners and turn right side out. Slip pillow form into the cover and slipstitch the opening shut.

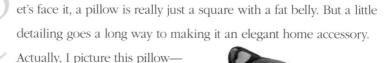

piper's pillow

measurements
16" square

materials
Fabric Solid color or printed (home decor fabrics as on page 187)
Piping (with ³⁄₈" seam allowance)
Thread in color to match
Pillow form (16" square)

yardage
Printed fabric ½ yard
(54"-wide decorator fabric)
Solid fabric ½ yard
(54"-wide decorator fabric)
Piping 1⅞ yards

techniques
Notching corners (page 87), clipping corners (page 87)

seam allowance ½"

Let's face it, a pillow is really just a square with a fat belly. But a little detailing goes a long way to making it an elegant home accessory. Actually, I picture this pillow— with its neat piped trim—in the party cabin on a yacht.

Cut and Mark Pieces

1. Measure and cut one 15½" square from each fabric using the selvage as your guide. (You want the pillow to be cut on-grain.)

2. Use a seam ripper to remove 1" of stitching from one end of the piping. Peel back the fabric and trim away 1" of the cording inside, being careful not to cut the fabric.

3. Use a fabric marking tool to draw a line ⅛" inside all four edges on the right side of the printed fabric square.

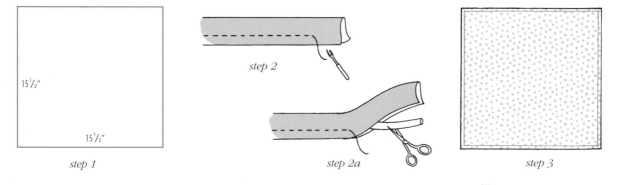

15½"

15½"

step 1

step 2

step 2a

step 3

Sewing Instructions

Prepare and sew on piping

1. Pin the piping, starting with the trimmed end, around the edges of the square of printed fabric on the right side, with the raw edge of the piping even with the marked lines. (Cord of piping should be toward the center of the square.)

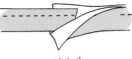

step 3

2. Cut V-shaped notches into the seam allowance of the piping to round each corner. When the ends come to touch, let them overlap 1" and then cut the untrimmed end.

3. Wrap the loose fabric of the trimmed end of the piping around the newly cut end and pin in place.

4. Use a zipper foot to stitch piping to the fabric, along the stitch line of the piping.

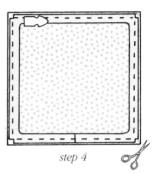

step 4

Assemble pillow case and insert pillow form

5. Pin the pillow front and back with right sides together.

6. Stitch around all four sides, leaving a 7" opening.

7. Clip corners. Turn case right side out and slip pillow form into the case. Slipstitch the 7" opening closed.

7" opening

steps 5 6

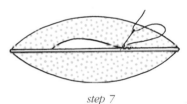

step 7

zip-o-riffic pillow

level

measurements
12" x 27"

materials
Fabric (home decor fabrics
as on page 187)

Thread in color to match

9" metal zipper

Pillow form (12" x 27")

yardage
*1 yard (54"-wide decorator fabric
used for sample.)*

techniques
*Pivoting (page 36), installing
a zipper (page 95), clipping
corners (page 87)*

seam allowance *½"*

Do you have zipper phobia? Are you a zipper virgin? Then today you can become a woman, a seamstress even! This pillow includes a super-easy zipper (you don't even have to buy it a drink). Make it your first. You'll get the hang of it in no time, and your pillow will have a super-neat and tidy closure. You'll want to do it again and again with all your wild scraps. Make a whole set—that'll really add some zip to your decor.

Measure, Cut, and Mark Fabric

1. Measure and cut one 12½" x 27½" rectangle. (This will be the pillow front.)

2. Use chalk on the wrong side of fabric and mark it A.

3. Measure and cut one 12½" x 20" rectangle and one 12½" x 8½" rectangle. (These will be for the pillow back.)

4. Use chalk on the wrong side(s) of fabric and mark the 12½" x 20" rectangle as B and the 12½" x 8½" rectangle as C.

12½" A 27½"	12½" B 20"	12½" C 8½"

Sewing Instructions

Prepare back pieces for zipper

1. Layer B and C with right sides together. Pin them together along one 12½" edge.

2. Stitch the pieces together, but at 1¾" into the seam, backstitch. Increase the stitch length and baste the seam for the next 9". Stitch the remaining 1¾" of the seam normally, with average stitch length. Backstitch. Press the seam open.

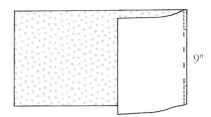

9"

step 2

Install zipper

3. Place the assembled pieces wrong side up on your work surface. Place the zipper facedown over the basted portion of your back seam with the zipper teeth centered over the stitching. Pull down your zipper tab ¼" and pin the zipper tape in place. Hand-baste.

4. Attach your machine's zipper foot. With chalk or disappearing-ink marker, mark on the right side of the fabric where you want to begin and end the 9" topstitching around the zipper opening.

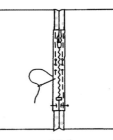

step 3

5. Starting at the bottom mark, right side up, stitch across the bottom of the zipper (it will be ¼" away from opening). Stop with your needle in the down position, through the fabric. Lift your presser foot and pivot your fabric to continue stitching along one side of the zipper teeth, ¼" from the opening/seam line, using your zipper foot as a guide, until you have sewn to the top of the zipper.

6. Start again at the base of the zipper and stitch along the opposite side of the zipper as in step 5. You may need to remount your zipper foot so it is set to the other side.

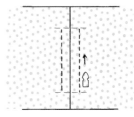

steps 4–6

7. Use a seam ripper to remove all basting stitches to reveal the zipper underneath. Open the zipper on the pillow back.

Sew pillow front and back together

8. Take the pillow front (A) and pin it to the pillow back with right sides facing and raw edges even.

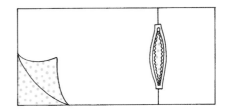

steps 7–8

9. Stitch around all four sides and clip corners.

10. Turn pillowcase right side out through the zipper hole and slip pillow form inside.

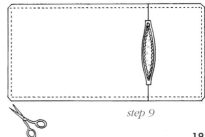

step 9

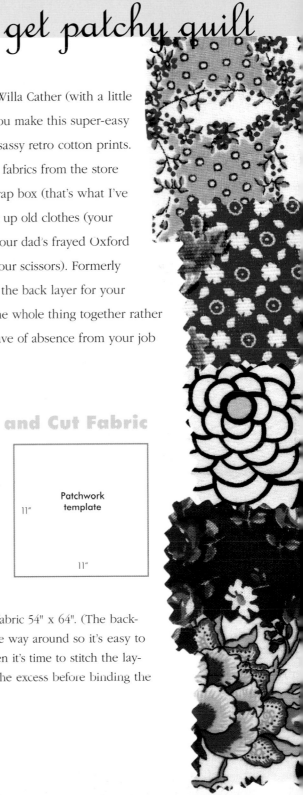

level

measurements
50" x 60"

materials

Fabric Medium-weight cotton or wool Twin-sized flat bed sheet or quilt-backing fabric (extra wide)

Thread in color to match

Light- to medium-weight cotton batting (at least 52" wide x 62" long)

Yarn (1 skein) for ties

3 packages Wright's double-fold bias quilt binding

tools

Yardstick

Masking tape

Quilter's safety pins (They're bent, which makes them easy to pin through the quilt layers.)

Chenille needle (large enough to sew yarn)

yardage

Patchwork material at least 45" fabric 2½ yards (total)

Backing material
1½ yards of fabric 64" wide or pieces from 45" fabric

Quilt binding 220 yards

techniques
Edgestitch (page 93)

seam allowance ½"

C hannel your inner Willa Cather (with a little Doris Day) when you make this super-easy patchwork quilt in sassy retro cotton prints. Play mix-and-match with cool fabrics from the store or grab material from your scrap box (that's what I've done here) or even better, cut up old clothes (your niece's outgrown baby gear, your dad's frayed Oxford shirts—nothing is safe from your scissors). Formerly loved bedsheets work well as the back layer for your quilt. And colorful yarn ties the whole thing together rather than quilting, saving you a leave of absence from your job to get the thing done.

Lay Out Pattern and Cut Fabric

1. Draw an 11" x 11" square on a piece of card stock. Cut along lines. This is your patchwork template.

2. Using disappearing-ink marker and ruler, draw and cut thirty 11" squares of fabric using template.

Patchwork template

11"

11"

3. Create (or find) a piece of fabric 54" x 64". (The backing fabric is cut 2" wider all the way around so it's easy to line up the patchwork top when it's time to stitch the layers together. You'll trim away the excess before binding the edges.)

Sewing Instructions

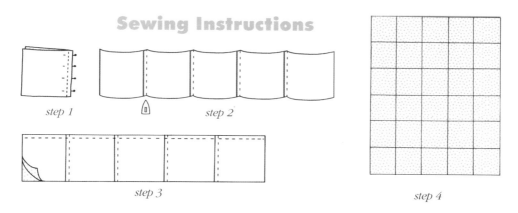

step 1   *step 2*

step 3   *step 4*

Sew squares together for patchwork top

1. Place two squares on top of each other with right sides together, pin along one side, and stitch. Press seam allowances together and to one side.

2. Repeat with four more squares as shown, creating rows that are five patches long.

Sew rows together

3. Pin row 1 to row 2 along the lengthwise edge with right sides together and stitch. Press seam allowance to one side.

4. Repeat step 3 for row 2 and row 3 and the rest of the rows until all rows are connected.

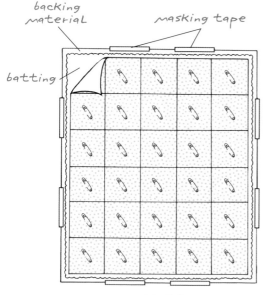

backing material

masking tape

batting

Assemble the layers (make a quilt sandwich)

5. Lay backing fabric on a large, flat surface wrong side up and smooth it out. (Chances are your work table isn't big enough, so find a space on the floor without carpet.) With masking tape, tape it in place, along the length and then the width.

6. Center the batting on top of the quilt backing and smooth it out as well, working from the center out to the edges.

7. Center the patchwork fabric on the batting with right side up.

8. Use quilter's pins to attach the layers together, pinning every 3" to 4" to temporarily hold the fabric and the batting together.

steps 5–8

Tie yarn through the layers

9. There are 20 intersections where patches touch at corners to tie off with yarn. (Don't count outer edge intersections.)

10. Cut 20 pieces of yarn—each 10".

11. Thread the large chenille needle with the yarn. Do not knot the ends.

12. Insert the needle into the quilt top at one intersection and push the needle through all three layers, leaving a 2" tail. Bring the needle back up through the quilt top about a ¼" away from where you entered. Tie the ends into a secure knot. Snip the yarn at each end to 1" or desired length.

13. Repeat step 12 on all intersections (except the outer edges), removing the safety pins as you come to them.

Trim the quilt

14. Trim away the back so it is even in size to the patchwork top. (You may want to use your yardstick and disappearing-ink marker to draw the necessary cutting lines.)

Bind the edges

15. Cut a 60" piece of bias quilt binding. Pin the seam binding to one long edge of the quilt, wrapping it around all three layers. Remember to put the wider side of the quilt binding to the back. Pin.

16. With right side up, edgestitch the binding using a zigzag stitch. Press.

17. Repeat steps 15 and 16 for remaining long edge.

18. Cut and pin a 51" strip of quilt binding to a short side as in step 15, tucking the raw edges under ½" at each end.

19. Edgestitch the binding to quilt, using a zigzag stitch. Press.

20. Repeat steps 18 and 19 on remaining short edge.

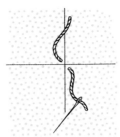

step 12

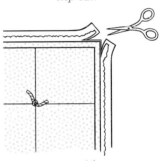

step 12a

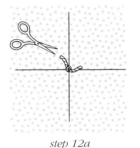

step 14

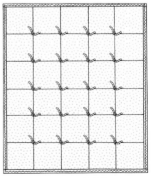

steps 15–20

handy no-frills apron

Once the frilly garment of oppression, now you wear it his-or-her style and you wear it by choice. And who wouldn't choose this super-practical—yet appealing—helpmate? Whether you're transplanting orchids, mixing a remoulade, painting a nude, or painting your house, this apron is tough enough to protect your clothes, but cute enough to impress anyone who sees you in action. For a more masculine look, choose a guy-friendly fabric and bias-tape binding.

Make the Pattern

1. Draw a horizontal line 32" long on pattern paper. Label left-hand end of the line A and the right end C. Measure 9½" to the right of A and mark it B.

2. At A draw a 5½" line straight up and mark it A1. At B, measure and draw a 16" line straight up. This is B1. Repeat at C for C1.

3. Connect B1 and C1 with a straight line 23" long.

4. Use the edge of your flexible sewing ruler to draw a curve to connect A1 and B1. Cut out the pattern piece.

5. Label the pattern piece "Apron front, cut 1 on fold."

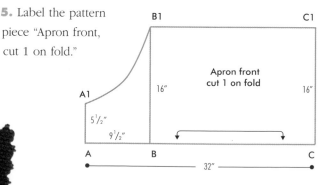

level

measurements
One size fits most. Adjust length and ties as desired
Apron 11½" wide at top, 32" wide at bottom, 32" long

materials
Apron fabric
Medium-weight canvas or denim

Pocket fabric (contrasting color or pattern in cotton or linen)

Thread to contrast bias tape

Thread to match apron pocket

Wright's extra-wide double-fold bias tape (3 packages)

2 buttons (⅝") (optional)

Pattern (make your own; pattern paper needed)

tools
Yardstick

yardage
Apron 1⅛ yards at least 45" wide

Pocket 1 yard at least 45" wide

techniques
Pivoting (page 36), zigzag stitch (pages 38–39), pocket (page 167)

seam allowance
½" unless otherwise indicated

6. Draw a rectangle 29" x 20".

7. Mark the long side as the foldline. Label pattern piece "Apron pocket, cut 1 on fold."

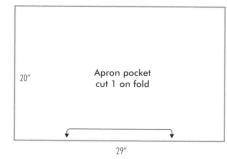

20"

Apron pocket
cut 1 on fold

29"

Lay Out Pattern and Cut Fabric

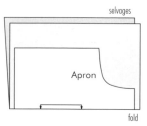

selvages

Apron

fold

1. Fold the apron fabric in half with right sides together.

2. Position the apron pattern piece on the fold as shown. Pin in place.

3. Cut around three sides, through both layers of fabric.

4. Repeat with pocket on pocket fabric.

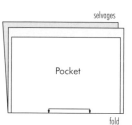

selvages

Pocket

fold

Sewing Instructions

Sew bias tape to apron sides

1. Cut a 60" length of bias tape. Slip bias tape onto the apron, with the wider tape width in the back, so the raw edge fits snugly in the fold. Pin well.

2. Using a zigzag stitch, sew the bias tape in place, stitching close to the edge of the bias tape to enclose the raw seam. For a better-looking zigzag stitch, begin and end (i.e., backstitch) on a straight-stitch setting.

3. First bind the sides of the apron, the bottom, then the top of apron.

4. Cut two lengths of bias tape equal to 70" for all-in-one ties.

5. Measure and mark 24" down from top edge. (This is the length of one neck tie.)

6. Slip bias tape around the curve of apron (underarm), lining up mark with top edge. Pin well. There should be 28" free at the end as shown.

7. Zigzag stitch along entire bias tape, backstitching at beginning and end.

8. Repeat steps 5 through 7 on other side.

steps 1–8

practice tip Using the same fabric as your apron, practice sewing a short length of bias tape to a raw edge. Also play around with the length and width of the zigzag until you're happy with how it looks.

Assemble and attach pocket

9. Fold the raw edges of the sides of the pocket toward the wrong side ½". Press.

10. Repeat step 9 on the top and bottom of the pocket.

11. Fold the pocket in half lengthwise and press, keeping all edges as pressed in steps 9 and 10.

12. Edgestitch all four sides of pocket using a straight stitch and matching thread. Press. (Pocket is double fabric.)

13. Center pocket on apron front. Pin well.

14. Topstitch pocket to apron around sides and bottom, pivoting at corners.

Stitch pocket detail

15. Lay apron flat on a table. Measure and mark with disappearing-ink marker a point 6½" over from the top left-hand corner of pocket, or A. Measure 3¾" to the right of A and mark that B. Measure over 3¾" and mark that C. From C measure another 8" to the right and mark D. At each of these marks, draw an 8" line down and perpendicular to the top edge, to A1, B1, C1, D1, as shown. Draw a straight horizontal line to connect A1 to D1.

16. Sew along each marked line through all layers using a straight stitch and matching thread. Press.

Sew buttons (optional)

17. Hand-stitch one decorative button at each top corner.

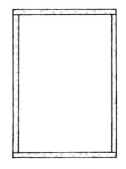

steps 9–10

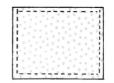

steps 11–12

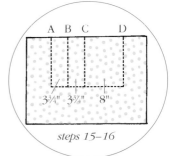

steps 13–14

steps 15–16

den of pin pincushion

Couldn't be easier! And so cozy! It's like making a little upholstered chair for your pins to rest in. Great for first-timers, you can keep this adorable little cushion at your side every time you sew—filling you with pride. Make it in a circle or a square. Make one for all your fellow seamsters. You can seriously churn out four or five of 'em in an hour, once you get the hang.

And they're small enough to stitch by hand in front of the TV. Dig into the scrap bin for material, but use something on the heavy and durable side—like old jeans denim—'cause it's gonna get poked!

Measure and Cut Fabric

1. For a round pincushion: Trace around a CD on both the front and back fabrics and cut out the two circles.

1A. For a square pincushion: Measure, mark, and cut out a 4" x 4" square from both the front and back fabrics.

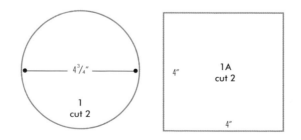

1
cut 2

4"   1A
cut 2

4"

level

finished measurements
3" square or 3¾" circle

materials
Fabric Cotton, denim, felt, linen, or wool

Back fabric Felt or wool

Thread in color to match

Polyfill (for stuffing .08 ounce)

Embroidery floss in contrasting color

Button

tools
CD to trace (for circle)

Embroidery needle

yardage
Pincushion front ⅛ yard
Pincushion back ⅛ yard
(Scraps are even better!)

techniques
Pivoting (page 36), whipstitch (page 230), hand-sewing buttons (pages 231–232)

seam allowance
½" unless otherwise indicated

Note: *Because this is a small-scale project, you don't need to worry about fabric grain—just merrily cut the shapes out.*

S·E·W

2" opening

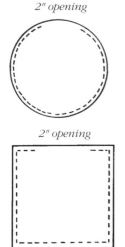

2" opening

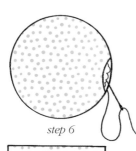

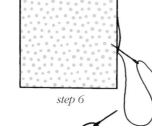

step 6

step 6

Sewing Instructions

Sew the front to the back

1. Mark a 2" opening on the wrong side of the top fabric piece. This will be the opening to turn your "pillow" right side out. It's also where you'll insert the stuffing.

2. Place circles or squares with right sides together, lining up along raw edges. Pin well.

3. Machine-stitch around the edges, starting at one end of the opening mark, and pivoting at the corners or curves. Reinforce well with extra backstitching. Press.

4. Turn pincushion right side out and press, tucking in the raw edges of the opening to the wrong side.

Stuff pincushion

5. Stuff the pincushion with the polyfill, adding it bit by bit until you have the desired thickness and cushiness. (It should be rather full/dense.)

Stitch opening closed

6. Use regular sewing thread and an embroidery needle to slipstitch the opening closed, tucking in the raw edges as in step 4.

Embellish

7. Cut an 18" piece of embroidery thread and thread your needle. (You'll want all six strands.) Tie a good size knot (see page 227 for the Rupp-alicious knot) and pass the needle through the center back to the center front, and pull tight.

8. For a circular pincushion: loop the thread around the sides of the cushion over to the back and then back up through the center, forming one "petal." Repeat until there are six petals in all.

8A. For a square pincushion: as above, except you'll loop the thread from the center out and around the four sides. When complete, tie a knot at the back.

9. Attach the button at center front using a doubled strand of embroidery thread and you're done!

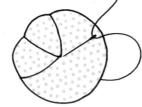

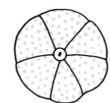

steps 7–9

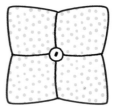

step 8A

level

measurements

11½" tall, 16½" wide, 7½" deep
(To fit 11" x 14¾" x 5¾" machine)

materials

Fabric Oilcloth

Thread in color to match

1 package Wright's double-fold bias tape in matching color

tools

Teflon foot (makes stitching vinyl easier)

yardage

⅔ yard at least 47" wide

techniques

Pivoting (page 36), trimming corners (page 87)

seam allowance ½"

*I*t's kind of like a tea cozy for your sewing machine. But instead of keeping your machine warm, it keeps it clean, and prevents dust and fuzz from getting into the works. And in the process, discover the joy of oilcloth—a most colorful and useful fabric. The cozy looks miles better than the factory-issue plastic cover. You just might find yourself sewing cozies for everything in sight!

Measure and Cut Fabric

1. Measure, mark with chalk right on the oilcloth, and cut out the following rectangles:

A One 8½" x 17½" (top),

B Two 8½" x 12½" (short sides),

C Two 12½" x 17½" (long sides) for cover, as shown.

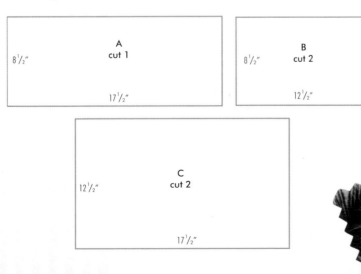

A
cut 1

8¹/₂"

17¹/₂"

B
cut 2

8¹/₂"

12¹/₂"

C
cut 2

12¹/₂"

17¹/₂"

Make and bind hole for handle (optional)

1. Take A and mark the center of the rectangle on the wrong side. Center that rectangle on the top of your machine with the right side facing down. Using chalk or a disappearing-ink marker, mark a hole for the handle of the machine. Remove the cover and measure the handle to double-check your marked hole. Cut the hole, adding a bit extra. (For example, my handle is ½" x 6", so I made the opening ¾" x 6½".)

2. Wrap the bias tape around the hole, with the wider half of the fold to the back, sandwiching the raw edge of the oilcloth inside. Pin. Overlap the ends by ½" and trim off excess tape. Stitch in place along the outer edge of bias tape.

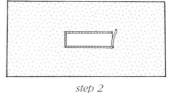

step 2

Sew side seams

3. Pin one B to one C (with right sides) together along one 12½" edge. (This will be a side seam of the cover.) If your fabric is printed, make sure the print orientation is the same on both pieces.

4. Attach the Teflon presser foot to your machine and set your stitch length to 3.5 or 4. Stitch the seam together, ending ½" from the top edge.

5. Pin the remaining B to the remaining C, with right sides together and raw edges even. Make sure your print orientation matches again.

6. Stitch seam, ending ½" from the top edge.

7. Pin the remaining C to the 12½" raw edges of both B rectangles, with right sides together, as shown. Make sure your print orientation matches the other sides.

8. Stitch both seams, ending ½" from the top edges. The four sides should form an oilcloth box with no top or bottom.

9. Finger-press all of your seams open. DO NOT use an iron, as it will damage the oilcloth.

Sew top in place

10. Pin A (top) to the top edge of the assembled sides, with right sides together and raw edges even. Pull the unstitched ½" at the corners of the sides apart, to fit around the top edge.

11. Stitch around all four sides of the top edge, pivoting at corners. Finger-press the seam allowances toward the sides and turn cover right side out.

Make and trim slit for cords

12. Slip cover over your machine, and using the marker, mark an opening on the side for the cords.

13. Remove cover from machine. Double-check the size of the slot against the actual measurements of the height and width of your cords. (Mine are about 3" tall and ½" wide, so I cut an opening 3" x ¾".)

Bind bottom and slit to finish

14. Pin bias tape around the side cord opening.

15. Stitch along the top edge of the bias tape. Trim off any excess tape.

16. Repeat steps 14 and 15 on the bottom edge of the cover, overlapping the ends as in step 2.

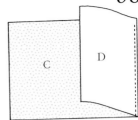

steps 3–4

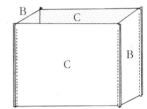

steps 5–6

steps 7–8

step 9

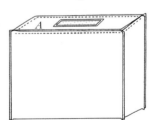

steps 10–11

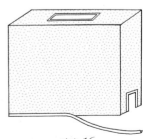

step 16

sew very pretty card

materials

Blank folded cards
(4¼" wide x 5½" long)

Matching envelopes

Fabric scraps Cotton prints

Fusible interfacing

All-purpose thread

Embroidery floss

Ribbon scraps

Buttons

tools
Glue stick

yardage

Fabric scraps
(at least 3" square)

Fusible interfacing
(leftovers or ¼ yard)

Ribbon scraps
(about 6")

techniques
Interfacing (page 90), pivoting (page 36), hand-sewing buttons (pages 231–232)

There's something very satisfying about sewing on paper. Maybe it's because you finish in about two minutes or less! The Sew Very Pretty Card is also sew very easy. And it's a great way to have fun in your scrap pile, use up leftover trim, and show off your favorite buttons. The fusible interfacing prevents fraying, and the technique is basic appliqué. This is also a good chance to play with those enticing stitch settings like a zigzagged or scalloped border. I decorated a standard blank greeting card here. But gift tags, place tags, menus, journal covers, even file folders can all get gussied up with machine stitching. Be sure to change your needle when you're done because it'll be dull from piercing the cardstock. You might want a designated paper-only needle—especially since you'll be sewing on paper again and again. It's that addictive.

S·E·W

step 1

tip You can use these steps to appliqué clothes and accessories, too.

Cut Fabric

1. Choose a design to cut out from a scrap of fabric. Either take a pretty part of a print or make your own shape.

2. Cut out the shape carefully to create the appliqué.

Sewing Instructions

Apply fusible interfacing

1. Pin the glue side of the interfacing to the wrong side of the appliqué. Trim interfacing to match.

step 2

2. Apply interfacing to fabric with a warm iron.

Sew appliqué to card

3. Using the longest possible stitch length and an all-purpose thread in a contrasting color, stitch the fabric appliqué to the front of the card. You can let the feed dogs pull the paper through, pivoting at the corners and curves. You can also set your machine for free-form embroidery by either dropping your feed dogs or applying a feed dog cover—see your sewing machine manual for guidance—and then stitching in any direction or design desired. There's no wrong way to do this! Have fun experimenting.

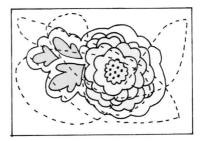

step 3

Decorate envelope

4. Cut a length of ribbon the same length as the envelope flap. Adhere ribbon to envelope flap lightly with glue stick. With flap open, machine-stitch along sides of ribbon.

5. Hand-stitch one or more buttons in place with embroidery floss.

Note: You can't sew across the envelope because the stitches will block the card from going inside. But you can sew the ribbon or another appliqué to the envelope flap.

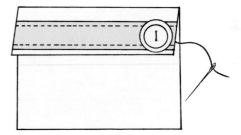

steps 4–5

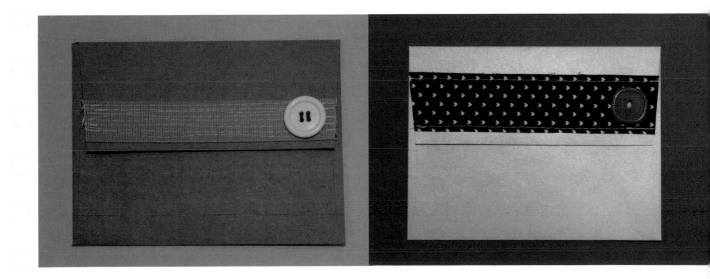

power tie

Once upon a time, the necktie was a gift of last resort—a generic male offering. But if you make it yourself out of elegant or unexpected fabric, it becomes a true power tie. The pattern is unisex, so you can also make one for yourself in a tiny pink plaid and harness the girl-power of Annie Hall. Make one in denim for casual Fridays. And how cool is a tie made of corduroy? (Answer: Very.) There's not a ton of material or even sewing—just be careful with measurements and ironing and your tie will reign supreme.

Lay Out Pattern and Cut Fabric

1. Lay out main fabric flat, and smooth out on the table. Place the tie front and back pattern pieces diagonally as shown, lining up the grainline arrows so they are parallel to the selvage. (This way the pattern will be cut out on the bias.) Pin pieces in place.

2. Cut out the tie pattern, transferring all necessary markings.

3. Repeat steps 1 and 2 with the lining fabric and lining front and back piece(s).

4. Cut out the interfacing pattern pieces on the bias as shown.

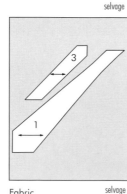

Fabric

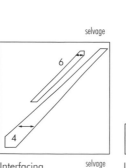

Interfacing

Lining

level

materials

Main tie fabric Broadcloth, brocade, calico, chambray, corduroy, denim, poplin, satin, silk, or wool

Contrasting lining fabric Cotton prints or silks

Thread in color to match

Lightweight fusible interfacing

½" extra-wide double-fold bias tape, twill tape, or ribbon

Embroidery floss

Pattern (enclosed in box)

yardage

Main fabric
1⅛ yard (at least 45" wide)
Lining fabric ¼ yard
Interfacing
1 yard (at least 35" wide)

techniques

Interfacing (page 90),
slipstitch (page 230)

seam allowance ⅜"

pattern pieces

1. Tie front (cut 1)
2. Tie front lining (cut 1)
3. Tie back (cut 1)
4. Tie front interfacing (cut 1)
5. Tie back lining (cut 1)
6. Tie back interfacing (cut 1)

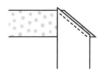

steps 1–2

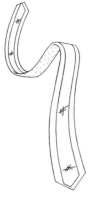

step 3

Sewing Instructions

Stitch the tie front to the tie back

1. Pin front and back of the tie at the center seam (narrowest part) with right sides together, matching notches to form one continuous tie piece. Position the pieces so that the edges of the tie match at the seam line, not at the points.

2. Stitch the seam, backstitching at beginning and end. Trim seam and press open.

Apply the interfacing

3. Center the fusible interfacing on the wrong side of the tie, lining them up with the diagonal seam and with the tie ends. The interfacing will be about ⅝" from the ends of the tie (at the seam allowance).

Stitch lining to ends of tie

4. Pin the tie front lining to the tie front with right sides together.

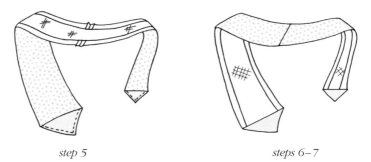

step 5   *steps 6–7*

5. Stitch the two angled ends.

6. Trim seams and point and press open. Turn end right side out and press the edges flat.

7. Repeat steps 4 through 6 to sew the tie back lining to the tie back.

Stitch sides together

8. Fold the tie in half lengthwise with right sides together. Pin.

9. Stitch, leaving an opening between the notches. Reinforce well with backstitching at each end of the opening. (Turning the tie right side out is stressful for the seam and the thread could break.)

10. Press seam open and trim.

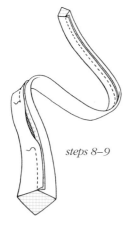

steps 8–9

11. Turn the finished tie right side out, and press again, with the seam line in the center as shown.

12. Slipstitch the opening closed.

Make tie keeper for the back

13. Cut a piece of ¼" wide bias, twill tape, or ribbon 2½" long and press ends under.

14. Mark the center of the tape, using your sewing ruler and disappearing-ink marker. Pin into place, lining up your mark with the center seam line on the back of the tie front.

15. Stitch by hand with a few overlapping straight stitches at each end, hiding your knots, and be careful that stitches don't go through to the front.

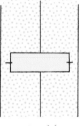

step 12

step 14

tie one on

Follow these directions with the tie around your neck and looking in a mirror:

1. Place tie around neck so the narrow end is 2" to 3" shorter than the wide end. Lap the wide end over the narrow end.

2. Bring the wide end under and over the narrow end.

3. Bring the wide end through the loop around your neck.

4. Bring the wide end through the knot and pull it so the tie fits comfortably around your neck and the knot is where you want it.

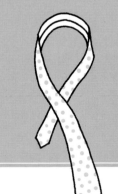

unforgettable elephant

Remember how you had one stuffed animal that you adored above all the rest because it was cushy and extra-charming? Now you can make that critter for someone else. How many kids do you know with homemade stuffed animals? It's nicer than making a cake or some brownies. (Try cuddling with those at night!) There are a few pieces to this one, but the scale is small, so you can put her together before you know it. Make a pair (mommy and baby) so they won't get lonely. Denim and corduroy are good fabrics for this puffy pachyderm. I like to line her ears with tiny flower fabric on the inside. If you're traveling or your machine is on the fritz, this project is easy to hand-stitch—for extra homemade love.

Lay Out Pattern and Cut Fabric

1. Fold main fabric with right sides together and smooth out on table.

2. Position pattern pieces, checking grainlines. Pin pattern pieces in place.

3. Cut out pieces on folded section: two bodies and two ears. Cut one underside, one tail, and one head inset on single layer.

4. Fold accent fabric as shown, right sides together.

5. Position ear piece and pin in place.

6. Cut out two ears.

7. Clip notches where indicated on all pattern pieces.

(See layouts on next page.)

level

measuremws

mommy
approximately 9¼" high x 11" long

baby
approximately 5½" high x 7½" long

materials
Main fabric Calico, canvas, chenille, corduroy, or wool
Accent fabric (for lining ears)
Cotton, felt, or wool
12-ounce bag poly-fill
Embroidery thread
Two ⅜" buttons
Pattern (enclosed in box)

yardage
at least 45" wide

Mommy	Baby
Main fabric	**Main fabric**
½ yard	⅜ yard
Accent fabric	**Accent fabric**
⅜ yard	¼ yard

techniques
Clipping curves (page 87), trimming seams (page 86), trimming corners (page 87), slipstitch (page 230), whipstitch (page 230)

seam allowance ¼"

pattern pieces
1. Body (cut 2)
2. Underside (cut 1)
3. Head inset (cut 1)
4. Ear (cut 4: 2 in main fabric, 2 in accent)
5. Tail (cut 1)

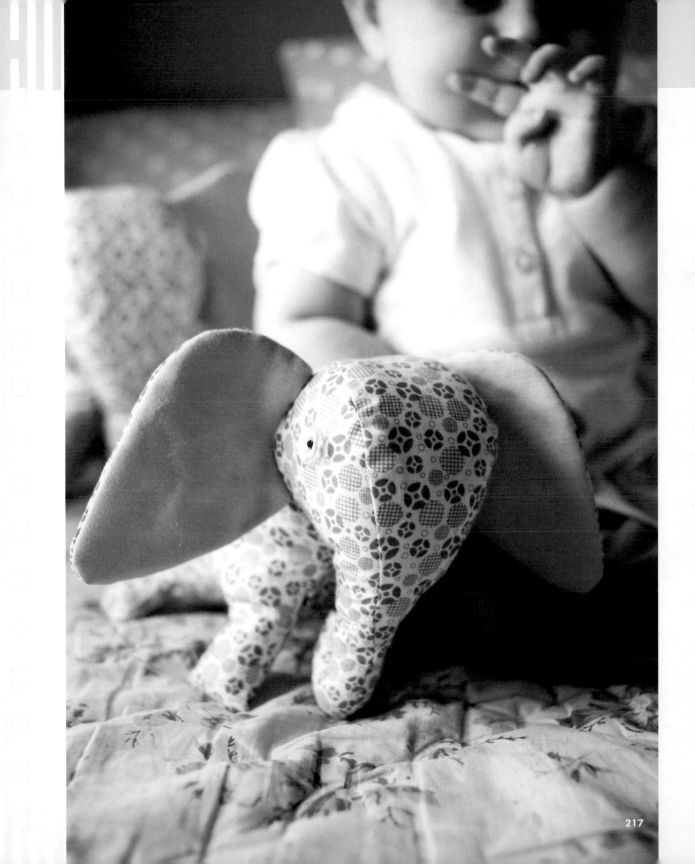

Mommy

Baby

accent
fabric

main fabric

accent
fabric

main fabric

Sewing Instructions

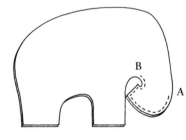

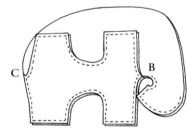

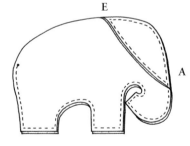

steps 1–2

steps 3–4

steps 5–6

Assemble elephant sides and underside

1. Pin the two body pieces right sides together along the edge of the trunk from mark A to B.

2. Stitch together between the markings, backstitching at beginning and end.

3. With right sides together, pin the underside piece to the body pieces along the edges of the legs between B and C, matching notches as you go and gently pulling on the fabric to make pieces fit.

4. Stitch between B and C around all four legs. Clip as necessary.

Add head inset and attach tail

5. Pin the head inset to the body pieces matching A and E with right sides together.

6. Start stitching at the top end of trunk (A) and stitch along both sides of the head inset ending at E. Press.

Attach tail

7. Fold the tail piece in half, right sides together. Pin.

8. Stitch the long edge and the least angled short end. Press.

9. Trim seam allowances and turn tail right side out.

10. Pin tail to the right side of one body piece at the tail placement mark.

11. Pin and stitch the two body pieces together, sandwiching the tail and leaving an opening between D and E. (The opening is for the stuffing.) Trim seam allowances and press.

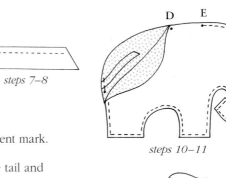

steps 7–8

steps 10–11

Stuff elephant

12. Turn the elephant right side out and stuff with poly-fill, making sure you push fill into the legs and trunk evenly.

13. Slipstitch the back opening closed.

steps 12–13

Add eyes and ears

14. Pin one main ear and one accent ear with right sides together and raw edges even.

15. Stitch around all edges, leaving an opening for turning. Trim seam allowances and turn ear right side out. Press.

16. Press ear opening seam allowances to the inside. Close ear opening with slipstitch.

step 14-15

17. Repeat steps 14 through 16 for second ear.

18. Whipstitch ears in place on elephant head where marked.

19. Hand-stitch buttons to elephant's face for eyes. (If making this for an infant, make eyes with embroidery thread instead.)

level

measurements

The finished size will vary according to the size of your dog. The coat pictured here is 14½" wide x 19" long.

materials

Main coat fabric Canvas, denim, fleece, vinyl, or wool

Lining fabric Cotton or cotton blends, fleece, or wool

Muslin (for testing pattern)

Thread in color to match

Closure supplies 2 buttons, 2 snaps, or ¼ yard 2"-wide hook-and-loop tape

Pattern (make your own; pattern paper needed)

tools

French curve

yardage

at least 45" wide

These measurements are based on the length from your dog's neck to her tail. There's 1" added for the seam allowance.

Dog Center Back Measurement	Main and Lining Fabric
11" (XS)	½ yard
16" (S)	¾ yard
21" (M)	1 yard
26" (L)	1⅛ yards

techniques

Pivoting (page 36), edgestitch (page 93), trimming corners (page 87), clipping curves (page 87). Optional: buttonhole (pages 98–99), snaps (page 100), hook-and-loop tape (page 68)

seam allowance

½" unless otherwise indicated

*I*magine designing and custom-tailoring a coat for your favorite pooch. After creating the pattern on paper, I recommend making it in muslin first and adjusting it on your dog. Once you figure out what works for your woofer, you can sew a whole wardrobe. Take a look at any dog coats you may already own. Maybe incorporate what you discover—fancy buttons, a good fabric choice. Give your dog treats when you're measuring and trying the jacket on, and make a fuss over her. Tell her how pretty she looks and what a good doggy she is! I did this with my Chihuahua Rita, and now she wags her tail when she sees a tape measure coming her way.

Measure

Use a tape measure on your dog (don't forget the treats!) to take these measurements:

Center back. Measure from the base of the neck (where the collar sits) to the base of the tail, plus 1".

Width. Distance from the top of one front leg across the back to the other leg, plus 1".

Belt. At the widest part of dog, the distance from the middle of the body around the belly to the same point on the opposite side, plus 1".

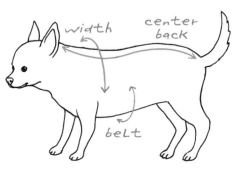

chest

Chest. Space between the front legs, plus 1". This measurement will help you make the overlapping edges of the front.

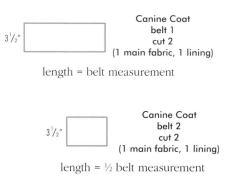

3½" [rectangle] Canine Coat belt 1 cut 2 (1 main fabric, 1 lining)

length = belt measurement

3½" [rectangle] Canine Coat belt 2 cut 2 (1 main fabric, 1 lining)

length = ½ belt measurement

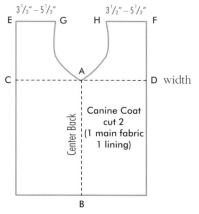

3½" – 5½"   3½" – 5½"
E   G   H   F
C – – – – – – – – – – – – – – – – D width
A
Center Back   Canine Coat cut 2 (1 main fabric 1 lining)
B

Make the Pattern

1. Draw a straight vertical line on the pattern paper, equal to the *center back* measurement. Label it "Center back," with the top end as point A, and the bottom end as point B.

2. Use A as the center and draw a horizontal line the length of the *width* measurement (forming T shape). Label ends C and D. Draw a line parallel to C–D with B as the center.

3. Connect the ends of the horizontal lines to form a rectangle.

4. Draw a vertical line equal to the *chest* measurement, starting at C. Do the same on the other side at D. (This extends the sides of the coat for a chest overlap, which

wraps around the doggie's front.) Mark the top of these points E and F.

5. Decide on a width measurement for the chest overlap. It will be between 3½" to 5½", depending on your dog's size. On your pattern, draw a horizontal line equal to this width from E and F toward the center of the coat on each side. Label ends G and H.

6. Use your French curve to connect G and H by passing through point A for the curved neckline. Label this piece "Canine coat, cut 2 (1 in main fabric, 1 in lining fabric)."

7. Draw a rectangle whose length equals your *belt* measurement and

whose width is 3½" (or desired width). Label this piece "Canine coat belt 1, cut 2 (1 in main fabric, 1 in lining fabric)."

8. Draw a rectangle with a length equal to half the length of Belt 1. (The width stays the same.) Label this piece "Canine coat belt 2, cut 2 (1 in main fabric, 1 in lining fabric)."

Note: *You make two belts that get sewn at the sides of the coat and meet underneath in the middle of doggy's belly. They overlap and attach with snaps or hook-and-loop tape.*

9. Cut out the pattern pieces.

Lay Out Pattern and Cut Fabric

1. Lay fabric right side up and smooth out on the table.

2. Position the pieces as shown, lining up the long edge of the pieces so they are parallel with the selvage. Pin in place.

3. Cut around the coat and belts.

4. Repeat steps 1 through 3 with lining fabric.

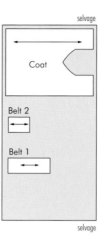

Sewing Instructions

Make the belts

1. Pin one main fabric belt piece and one lining fabric belt piece with right sides together.

2. Stitch around three sides, leaving one short end open.

3. Trim seams and corners. Turn right side out through the unstitched end. Press again.

4. Repeat steps 1 through 3 with the remaining belt pieces.

5. With right side up, edgestitch around the edges of one belt, finishing it on three sides. Repeat for the second belt.

steps 1–5

Attach belts to coat

6. Place the main fabric coat piece on the table right side up with the neck opening at the top. Pin the open end of one belt to the side of the coat as marked, with the right sides of the coat and belt together.

7. Stitch the belt end in place using ⅜" seam allowance. (Keep rest of belt straight with a couple of pins so it doesn't shift when you're stitching.) Reinforce with backstitching. Press.

8. Repeat steps 6 and 7 with remaining belt on the other side of the coat.

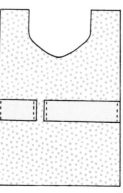

steps 6–8

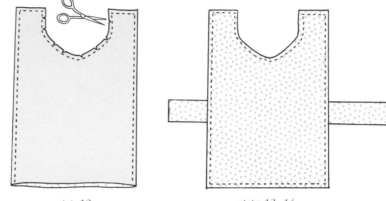

| steps 9–11 | step 12 | steps 13–14 |

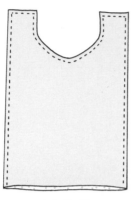

Sew the body of coat

9. Fold the belts in across the center back and pin to keep them from shifting.

10. Lay lining on top of the coat with right sides together (the belts will be hidden inside), and pin well around edges, leaving the tail end (or bottom) open.

11. Start at a bottom corner and stitch around one long side edge, pivoting carefully around the neck, and then stitch back along the opposite side.

12. Press seams open. Trim. Clip curved neck.

13. Leave the coat inside out and turn back the raw edges of the tail end to the wrong side ½". Press. Turn coat right side out and press again. (The raw edges of the bottom will be tucked in toward each other.) Pin closed.

14. Edgestitch the bottom opening closed. Then continue to edgestitch around the entire coat. Press.

Attach closures

15A. Faux-button closure (as shown): Hand-sew decorative buttons on the outside of coat at chest and belt overlaps, and snaps on the inside. (The heavier the fabric, the bigger the snap you'll need.)

15B. Hook-and-loop tape: For a more casual coat, cut two 3" lengths. Pin to chest and belt overlap in desired locations. Attach with a ⅛" seam allowance.

Last, but not least, take your dog for a high-stylin' stroll on Park Avenue.

Note: Hook-and-loop tape does not work well with fabrics that snag, such as the wool shown here. Check that your fabric is hook-and-loop-tape-friendly before using this type of closure.

hand-sewing 101

*L*ots of people (mainly ones who don't sew) think that machines have made hand-sewing obsolete. Simply not true! Let me tell you a little secret: Almost any sewing project requires *both* the machine and the hand in action. There are times when hand-sewing is simply *better* than stitching on a machine. For one thing, it offers much more control. When I make a patchwork pillow, for instance, I'll sew the squares by hand to make sure they stay perfectly put when I sew them on the machine. Similarly, you might *baste* (instructions to follow) a sleeve in place to make sure it fits into the armhole. Stitching by hand really cuts down on any number of unhappy surprises, like zippers that don't line up, or piping that's shifted away from an edge. And hand-sewn details often determine the quality of a finished item.

You can skip this tutorial if you're one of those lucky few who learned sewing at home or took home ec. If not, enjoy this little primer of stitches that will help you sew seams, hem, and even do appliqué with the stitches you learn here. Try each one until it becomes second nature (which won't take long, since hand-sewing is easy and repetitive). Several inches of practice can get you into the groove. But a journey of a thousand hand-stitches starts with threading the needle and tying a little knot. Let's learn how.

one basic techniques

Equipment

You need a few hand-sewing essentials: needles, thread, embroidery scissors, pins, measuring and marking tools, and scrap fabric or an old tea towel to practice on. (Or pick up ½ yard of gingham at the fabric store and use its grid as a stitch guide.)

Threading the Needle

Unwind a piece of thread from the spool until it's about the length of your arm (or 18"). Cut the thread at an angle with your embroidery scissors, so it slips more easily through the eye of the needle. Take a *sharp* from your needle variety packet. Or just choose a medium-length needle with a rounded eye. Draw the thread end through the eye. Note to the needle-threading challenged: If you're having a tough time or the thread is fraying, cut the end again and wet it with your tongue. Be patient—it might take a few tries. Reminder: Never bite or tear the thread. We're civilized craftspeople, not wild animals!

You work most stitches using a single strand of thread, with one end longer than the other. The shorter side is the tail; the longer side will be sewn into the fabric and gets the knot. As you sew, adjust the length of the tail to prevent it from getting sewn into the fabric.

the silver savior NEEDLE THREADER

Ever wondered about that Susan B. Anthony—looking metal thingy in your hotel sewing kit? It's a needle threader. It's got two parts: the handle, which has the lady in relief, and the wire. First stick the bent piece of wire through the eye of the needle. Then, take your thread and poke it through the bent wire loop (really, shaped more like a diamond than a loop), leaving a 3" tail so it doesn't slip out. Gently pull on the handle so the wire comes back through the eye, taking the thread with it. Now go sew!

Warning: The needle threaders found in free sewing kits are not meant for much more than a single use. I've broken dozens. But you can pick up higher-quality versions at a fabric store. There are even special threaders for the sewing machine.

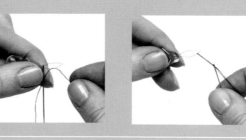

tying the knot

You need to secure the thread at one end with a knot, or your stitches would pull right through the fabric into oblivion. To knot your thread for most sewing tasks:

1. Pinch the long thread end between the thumb and index finger of your left hand.

2. Use your right hand to wrap the thread around your index finger.

3. Roll the wrapped piece of thread off your index finger by dragging it across your thumb.

4. Catch the knot between your index finger and thumb and pull the long end of the thread with your right hand.

the secret Rupp-alicious parlor-trick knot

When you need a super-strong knot that can hold its own with bulky material or the backside of a button, try this. Then impress your friends with your magicianlike sleight of hand.

  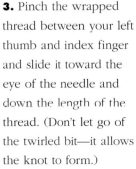

1. Hold the threaded needle horizontally in front of you, pointing left, thread dangling. Lay the long thread end on top of the needle, along the shaft with the cut end pointing toward the eye—basically making the thread form a

circle. Pinch the thread end and the needle shaft with your right index finger and thumb.

2. Wrap the thread that's near the point around the needle two or three times with your left hand.

3. Pinch the wrapped thread between your left thumb and index finger and slide it toward the eye of the needle and down the length of the thread. (Don't let go of the twirled bit—it allows the knot to form.)

S·E·W

twist and shout
TRICKS TO GET RID OF TWISTS

Having trouble with twists in your thread? Turn the work upside down with the needle and thread still attached, making sure to leave a fairly long tail. The needle will immediately start to spin around like a mini-tornado, and should untwist the thread without flinging itself off in the process. If this happens, rethread.

If the thread continues to twist, tie a knot where you are and start a new thread. Thread weakens as you sew. The more it's pulled through fabric, the more likely it is to misbehave. Of course you might have a bunk spool of thread. In that case, give it to your kitten as a toy and get a better brand.

Pinning for Hand-Sewing

Whether you are making a hem or a seam or just basting, you need to pin the fabric in place. Arrange your cut pieces of fabric with right sides together as for machine sewing. With hand-sewing, you have the option of pinning perpendicular to the edge or parallel to the edge with the pinheads facing toward you so you don't get pricked. Remove pins as you reach them, and stick them in your pincushion!

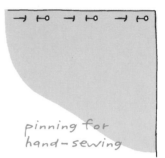

pinning for hand-sewing

Hand-Sewing Rules

1. Stick to a thread length of 18" to 24". Anything longer is likely to tangle and fray.

2. Work stitches from right to left unless instructed to do otherwise. (Reverse the direction if you're left-handed.)

3. Discreetly hide your knots. When starting, bring the needle through the fabric from the back (a.k.a. "wrong") side. In the case of a hem, go from underneath the finished edge. (The smaller the stitch, the stronger the stitching.)

4. Keep tension loose enough to avoid puckering the fabric.

Basic Hand-Stitches
running stitch

What for: Also known as a *straight stitch,* the *running stitch* looks like a line of dashes. It's so simple, you probably already know it—even if you claim you've never sewn in your life. Running stitch works for any type of seam, although it's not as strong as a backstitch. Use it to attach trims, pockets, patches, and more. I also love the look of hand-sewn straight stitches in brightly colored embroidery floss.

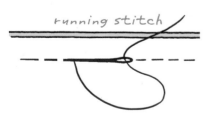

running stitch

How to: Working from right to left, rock the point of the needle in and out of the fabric several times before pulling the needle and thread

. . . .

through. Keep the stitches and spaces between them as even and as small as possible. For permanent seams, use stitches ⅟₁₆" to ⅛" long. For gathering or easing, ⅛" works fine.

basting stitch

What for: You *baste* to temporarily hold two or more fabric layers in position for final stitching. "Isn't that what pins are for?" you ask. Yes and no. Sometimes pins can't hold well enough or just plain get in the machine's way—like when you insert a zipper.

How to: This is the same basic stitch as the running stitch, but this time you take a much bigger stitch, ¼" to ⅜" long. Basting stitches can even get a little sloppy because they aren't going to hang around for very long. When basting, use a contrasting thread, as it'll be easier to spot when you're tearing it out. And stay within the seam allowance—again, for easy removal. Secure the end with a knot.

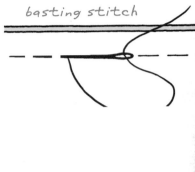

basting stitch

backstitch

What for: Stronger and more durable than the running stitch, the *backstitch* will rival a sewing machine stitch for strength and durability. It's the go-to stitch for most hand-sewn seams.

How to: Bring the needle up through the fabric (point A). Take one stitch about ⅟₁₆" to the right and back down through the fabric (point B). Then pull the needle up through the fabric two stitch lengths over to the left (at point C). Continue working in a straight line, making one stitch backward to the left, two stitch lengths forward to the right. Stop and take a look at your stitches. The ones on top should look like sewing machine stitches. The ones on the underside should be twice as long and overlap.

backstitch

Finishing a Stitch

Finish either with a few backstitches or a knot. When you get near the end of your rope (when your thread is about 3"), make a tiny backstitch on the wrong side, leaving a small loop. Pass your needle through the loop and pull tight. Repeat on top of the stitch you just made. Cut thread with scissors.

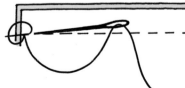

finishing a stitch

S·E·W ···

Hemming Stitches

Many experienced sewers believe in sewing their hems by hand. I'm one of them. I think they add a sweet and extra special "handmade" touch.

You form some hems by turning the edge under twice. For others, you finish the raw edge with pinking shears or sew on *seam binding* or *bias tape*.

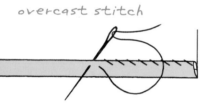

overcast stitch

overcast stitch (or whipstitch)

What for: This is how I always did my hems when I was a kid. The *overcast stitch* is the easiest and fastest way to hem or to join two finished or folded edges together. Who doesn't

tip If you hold the needle perpendicular to the hem as you go, you'll get diagonal stitches, which are the purtiest.

have a pair of pants in need of shortening? Even nonsewers seem to instinctively know how to work this stitch, often called a *whipstitch*.

hemming tips As a general rule, hems should be discreet and the stitches invisible. Keep them on the down-low by using a thread color that matches the fabric as closely as possible. If your hems pucker or look lumpy, loosen up! Pulling thread tight when you're stitching does not make for happy hems.

How to: Work with the hem facing you, garment inside out. Start by bringing the needle up through the edge of the hem (to hide the knot). Take a tiny stitch into the single layer of skirt or pants fabric that the hem is meeting. Though it's painstaking work, picking up a single thread in the fabric will make the hem nearly invisible on the front. Then, tuck the needle behind the hem edge (about ⅛" from the fold) and pull the needle through. Make your stitches about ⅛" apart.

slipstitch

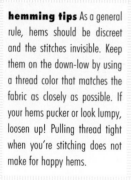

slipstitch

What for: The *slipstitch* is an almost invisible stitch formed by slipping the needle inside the fold of the hem. In addition to hemming, this stitch works particularly well for attaching one folded edge to a flat surface, as in the case of pockets or linings, or to repair torn seams. You'll use it on the Girly Go-To Dress, page 159, to stitch the lining around the armholes.

How to: Draw the needle out through the folded edge of the hem. Take a small stitch in the main fabric. Then slip the needle back into the fold of the fabric. Keeping the needle inside the fold, bring the needle out through the edge about ¼" over and pull it through. Continue in the same fashion with stitches approximately ¼" apart.

Buttons

Sewing on a button is like being able to boil water or make a piece of toast. It's beyond easy and so essential. Buttons fall into two categories: ones with holes and ones with shanks. The shank is that nub on the back of the button—usually a curved piece of metal or a plastic rectangle—that raises the button above the surface of the fabric. Suits, coats, and things made with thick or heavy fabric need shank buttons. (If you've ever worn a jacket that won't stay shut, it may need a shank button instead of a hole-y button.) Buttons with holes are called sew-through. Shirts, skirts, pants, blouses, dresses, and pajamas don't need shanks—sew-through buttons are better for thinner fabrics.

thread tip Although most sewers use all-purpose thread in a shade slightly darker than the fabric, I sometimes use bright embroidery floss in a contrasting color. It looks sweet, and it's thicker—and therefore stronger—than regular sewing thread, making it more likely to hold.

attaching a sew-through button

Learning this basic task should be required for Living 101.

1. Bring a double-threaded needle (complete with knot) from the underside of the fabric and up through one hole in the button and back down through the other.

2. Keep sewing until the button feels secure. (I'd do at least six stitches just to be safe.)

3. Make a knot on the underside, then make a few small stitches over it to secure the button. Clip the threads.

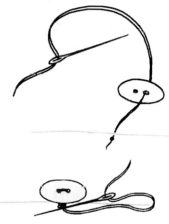

Note: *To attach a four-hole button, sew the same way, using a parallel, cross, or square stitch configuration.*

button positioning system BPS GUIDE

When replacing buttons on commercial garments, look for leftover thread or holes where the first one was sewn so you can put the new one right back where it belongs. If you can't tell where the original was, carefully pin or hold the garment closed and insert a pin through the center of the buttonhole as shown, and rub chalk against the pin. This is where you want to place the button. Use your sewing gauge to make sure it's equidistant from buttons above and below, and that it's the same distance from the edge of the fabric. Oh, and look at the thread on the other buttons and try to match that color.

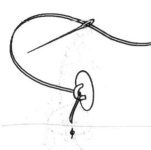

attaching shank buttons

Sewing on a shank button is even easier than a flat two-holed button.

1. Bring the knotted double-threaded needle from the underside of the fabric and through the shank. Put the needle back down into the fabric to the wrong side and pull. Repeat at least a half-dozen times.

2. Secure the thread by making a few small stitches and then making a knot.

3. Clip the threads.

---

make it button play

Take a run-of-the-mill dress shirt and replace the buttons with snazzier ones. Buttons can really change the look and quality of a garment—swapping them is akin to a complete reinvention! **Warning:** Bring the shirt or other item with you when shopping to be sure you get the right size and color.

✳ Dig around in your closet, or the closets of friends or loved ones, for clothing with missing buttons and fix whatever comes your way. When you're done, they'll love you even more!

---

two   mending and altering by hand

Making Ch-Ch-Changes

One of the best things about learning to sew is the ability to fix or change clothing you already own. Mending and altering can be as satisfying as creating something from scratch. Repairs and renovations also help you learn a ton about how garments are put together. The trick to mending is to imitate what's already in place by using the same thread color and stitching technique. The most common clothing repair is taking up or letting down a hem. As with most things, the more times you play little Miss Fix-It, the better you'll be.

how to shorten a skirt

Skirt hems usually have a slight curve, while pant hems tend to be straight across and easier to sew. The more curved the hem, the more work to prepare it for stitching. Follow these steps carefully, and you'll be fine:

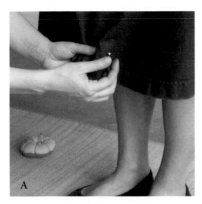

A

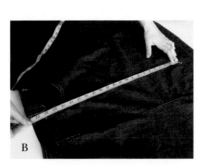

B

C

1. Put the skirt on with the proper shoes—high heels or flat sandals, or both—to help you decide which length looks best.

2. Place a pin in the front where you'd like the skirt to end (A). This is probably the only time I'd advise you to err on the conservative side and leave it slightly longer. You can always shorten the skirt more, but once you cut the fabric away, there's no going back.

3. Lay the skirt flat on a table and measure down from the waistband to the pin (B). Throw in an extra ½" just to be safe. Then add the width of the original hem plus ¼" to this number and write it down.

4. Measure this amount against your skirt, and tear out or cut off the original hem if necessary.

5. Hold the tape measure from the waistline down to the pin and mark this desired length every 3" to 4" with chalk around the bottom of the skirt.

6. Turn your flexible ruler on its side edge and bend it into a gentle curve. Trace the curve with chalk to connect the marks (C).

7. Turn the skirt up to the desired length and pin and try it on again in front of a mirror. (Remember that the finished product will be shorter.) Make adjustments if necessary and then cut the excess fabric off

along the chalk line with the skirt lying flat on a table.

8. Turn the skirt inside out. Tuck the raw edge under ¼" and press. Then turn up the hem to the original hem length. Press well with an iron.

9. Pin every 2" to 3" at a right angle or parallel to the edge.

10. Start at a side seam (to hide your knot) and hem with a whipstitch. Watch out for puckers and lumps. Don't pull too tightly on the thread.

11. When you're done, press to set the stitches and take out any unevenness in tension. It really will make a difference.

drop it like it's hot: letting down a hem

First, check out the hem to make sure there's enough fabric to let down. How can you tell? Most hems on store-bought clothing are turned-and-stitched, which means the hem can be twice as long as it looks. If, for instance, you want a pair of pants to be 1 inch longer and the current hem is 2 inches wide, it's quite likely you'll have a happy ending. Here's what to do:

1. Undo the old hem by cutting the thread with your seam ripper (A). Be careful not to cut the fabric.

2. Press out the crease (B). This is the trickiest part of lengthening because the hemline on manufactured clothing can be super-stubborn. Steam helps as does pressing with a damp cloth. If there's any discoloration, you can cover it up with embroidery or sew a pretty piece of ribbon on top.

3. Redo the hem by pressing it up to the desired length, tucking under by ¼", and stitching with your favorite hem stitch (C). If there's almost enough fabric but not quite, machine stitch a seam binding or hem facing (such as Hug Snug) to serve as the edge of your hem.

Changing Pant Lengths: Sew Easy!

Ever try buying pants the perfect length, right off the rack? Not easy. If you're sick of paying a tailor $20 to lose an inch, learn to DIY. Basic altering is *sew* easy and doesn't require much time or talent. To shorten unlined pants:

1. Tear out the original hem carefully, using a seam ripper (see page 37).

2. Measure the width of the original hem from bottom crease to edge and write this number down. Hem sizes vary depending on style and fabric. In general, you want your new hem to be the same width as your old hem because it's already been calculated to match the drape and weight of the fabric.

3. Try the pants on in front of a full-length mirror. Put on shoes and a belt (if you plan to wear one) to get the correct length. Cuff one pant leg under until it looks right, and then pin it in place at each side seam. (**Note:** Standard-length pants rest on the top of the shoe, but you know what you like.)

4. Take off the pants and measure the length of the upturned cuff from the fold to the raw edge. Jot this number down as well.

5. Turn the pants inside out and lay them flat on a table. Turn the pant leg up to the desired length (the measurement you just wrote down) and pin. Repeat on the second leg.

6. Press the pant leg bottoms in place. Pin every few inches. Turn pants right side out.

7. Try on the pants again to double-check the new length. Make adjustments if necessary.

8. Turn the pants inside out again. Using your chalk and sewing ruler, mark the measurement from step 2. For example, if the original hem was 2" of fabric, draw a line 2" above the pressed hem. Cut away excess fabric.

9. Tuck the raw edge under about ¼"; press and pin.

10. Choose a hemming stitch (see page 230). Starting at a side seam, hem around both cuffs.

11. Press the finished hems and pat yourself on the back for a job well done!

hemology
UNDERSTANDING HEMS

The width of a hem depends on the weight and type of fabric, plus the style of the garment. A straight hem can have an allowance up to 3". A curved hem can be 1½" to 2". Soft, sheer fabrics, no matter what the style, are usually rolled rather than turned up (which makes them more difficult to sew).

Go to your closet right now and spend ten minutes checking out hems. See if you can identify any of the stitches or methods. It can be an eye-opening experience!

Resources

Fabrics, Notions, and Patterns

Most of the stores listed below have either locations nationwide and/or online stores for you to shop. Make sure to seek out local retailers in your area as well! For most of the projects in this book, I shopped at New York City's Mood—where the *Project Runway* contestants shop—or at B & J Fabrics, which has a well-edited and gorgeous array of designer textiles. For trim and buttons, I went to M & J Trimming.

Clotilde
Boasts a very impressive array of sewing products and pattern-making tools.
800-545-4002
clotilde.com

Crafter's Vision
The place to look for deals on fabric.
craftersvision.com

Create for Less
Basic sewing supplies at a discount.
createforless.com

Denyse Schmidt Quilts
Shop for Free Spirit cotton prints designed by the über-talented quilter.
dsquilts.com

Fabric Tales
A great source for Japanese fabric, craft books, and sewing patterns.
fabrictales.com

fabric.com
This online fabric superstore also sells notions and patterns.

Hancock Fabrics
All-in-one fabric store that offers classes and sewing machines in 42 states.
877-FABRICS
hancockfabrics.com

Jo-Ann Fabrics
Well-known chain with 940 locations and frequent sales.
joann.com

M & J Trimming
The place to buy trims, tapes, and buttons.
mjtrim.com

Oilcloth International, Inc.
Where I bought the material for the sewing machine cozy.
323-344-3967
oilcloth.com

Reprodepot Fabrics
My go-to site for vintage-inspired printed fabrics and alternative patterns.
877-RETROFAB
reprodepot.com

superbuzzy.com
Japanese fabric and notions, fun craft supplies, and other cute stuff!

Textile Arts
Shop here for Marimekko fabrics.
store.txtlart.com

labels

heirloomlabels.com
Custom-printed woven labels for your creations.

shimandsons.typepad.com/ shimandsons/2006/11/ made_by_hand.html
Instructions for how to make your own labels with rubber stamps DIY-style.

patterns

McCall Pattern Company: Butterick, McCall's, and Vogue
Search by state for retailers or shop the online catalog with free shipping.
mccall.com

sewingpatterns.com
The largest selection of commercial sewing patterns, often at a discount.

Simplicity/New Look
Order patterns, learn sewing basics, or try free projects.
simplicity.com

vintage fabrics and sewing patterns

eBay
The number one auction site for vintage textiles and sewing supplies.
ebay.com

rustyzipper.com
Thousands of vintage fashion sewing patterns dating from the 1940s to 1980s.

sewfunpatterns.com
Impressive collection of antique patterns from as early as 1900 through 1940s.

vintagemartini.com
Victorian through 1960s with a link to a vintage sewing patterns web ring.

Your Support Groups

If you want to hook up with other sewers, there are myriad websites, blogs, and sewing groups out there. Here is my highly selective list.

craft websites

craftster.org
A forum for people who love to make things.

getcrafty.com
Meet like-minded crafters in the sewing message boards.

supernaturale.com
"Making art out of everyday life."

whipup.net
Craft-a-longs, sewing tutorials, reviews, and so much more.

favorite blogs

Honestly, there are so many inspiring blogs out there, it was hard to choose a few! Visit any one of the sites listed and follow the links for even more goodness, including sew-a-longs.

angrychicken.typepad .com

chocolatachuva .blogspot.com

craftlog.org

sewiknit.blogspot.com

periodicals

Adorn
"The crafty girl's guide to embellishing life."
adornmag.com

Craft
"The new magazine for the new craft movement."
craftzine.com

Sew Stylish
"Basic training to unleash your creativity."
besewstylish.com

Threads
"For people who love to sew."
tauton.com/threads

sewing organizations and groups

American Sewing Guild
Search for a sewing group in your area.
asg.org

Home Sewing Association
Not-for-profit trade organization offers free sewing projects and a sewing educator database.
sewing.org

patternreview.com
Popular message boards, sewing machine reviews, and database of sewing topics.

sewing.meetup.com
A worldwide networking site for "meeting other local people who like to do all sorts of sewing, including garments, home decorations, and crafts."

sewing machine companies

Bernina
Free online classes in the form of PDFs, message boards, online gallery, and list of charitable organizations you can sew for, with over 500 dealerships in the U.S.
berninausa.com

Brother
Helpful online model consultant plays matchmaker.
800-4A BROTHER
brother.com

Elna
Use its model comparison tool and search for a distributor.
elna.com

Husqvarna/Viking
Wide array of free downloadable patterns, and video instruction for basic sewing techniques.
husqvarnaviking.com/us

Janome
Janome means "eye of the snake" in Japanese. Search their handy sewing technique archive by category or visit the help desk.
janome.com

Kenmore
I've been super-happy with my user-friendly Kenmore machine, and you can go to Sears to see them for yourself.
sears.com

Pfaff
In business for 140 years, Pfaff sold its millionth machine in 1910. The site features tons of free downloadable patterns.
pfaffusa.com

Singer
Order manuals, presser feet, and sewing books online, plus find basic sewing instruction, factory-refurbished machines with warranty, troubleshooting, and stitch reference guides.
singerco.com

White
Available in store at Jo Ann's and Hancock Fabrics, or visit the website for a PDF guide to choosing the right machine for you.
whitesewing.com

Glossary

Appliqué Technique of sewing one piece of fabric on top of another either by hand or machine, usually with a zigzag or buttonhole stitch. The piece is often a smaller cut-out design or motif, which is placed right side up on the right side of the larger main fabric.

Backstitch 1. A few machine stitches sewn backwards by holding down the reverse lever at the beginning and end of a seam to secure and reinforce the threads. 2. A strong hand-sewing stitch done generally from right to left, in a "one step backward, two steps forward" fashion.

Bar Tack A reinforcing seam made by setting sewing machine to a zero stitch length and sewing in place.

Basting Long stitch made by hand or machine to hold fabric together temporarily. This stitching is often removed after sewing, but not always.

Batting Layer of cotton or polyfill placed between the top and backing fabric of a quilt to add warmth and height.

Bias The diagonal direction on a piece of cloth. This line is where the fabric stretches the most, which is why curved areas on a garment, such as necklines and armhole facings, are often cut

out on the bias. **True bias** is at a precise 45 degree angle to the lengthwise and crosswise grains of a woven fabric.

Bias Binding (aka Bias Tape) A strip of fabric cut on the bias grain of fabric, used to envelop the raw edge of a hem or seam or to make piping. It can be bought prepackaged in different widths and folds, or made from scratch.

Blind Hemstitch A tiny handstitch or a machine stitch used to stitch hems invisibly.

Bobbin Small metal or plastic spool that holds the lower thread on a machine. The bobbin thread links with the needle or upper thread to create a lockstitch.

Bobbin Case Metal case that holds the bobbin in the lower area (a.k.a. shuttle race) of a sewing machine.

Bolt Large unit of cloth wound on a cardboard tube or flat box for display in a fabric store. A shopper's yardage is cut from the bolt by the retailer.

Butthonhole Foot Presser-foot attachment on a machine that automatically sews buttonholes to match a button put in its sliding tray.

Casing A tunnel or tube made by

folding over the top of a project to hold curtain rods, elastic, or drawstrings.

Clip (Clipping) To cut a short distance in a seam allowance with the point of the scissors. Done to prevent the distortion of curved seams, or to cut diagonally across corners to reduce bulk.

Crosswise grain Direction of the widthwise threads on a fabric that runs from selvage to selvage, or horizontally.

Cutting Line A solid printed line on a pattern used as a guide for cutting.

Dart Tapered, stitched fold of fabric used to give shape to a garment to better fit the contours of the body.

Directional Stitching The stitching of seams in the correct direction of the grain so that the fabric will not stretch during sewing or wearing.

Drape The quality of a fabric that causes it to fall into graceful folds, as with a soft silk. Not all fabrics have this property.

Dressmaker's Carbon Special paper with colored coating on one side, used with a tracing wheel to trace or transfer pattern markings to fabric.

Ease 1. The even distribution of fullness when joining a longer section of fabric to a shorter one

without forming gathers or tucks.
2. In patternmaking, ease is the amount of sizing added to allow movement or for design purposes.

Easestitch Long machine stitch used to ease in fullness.

Edgestitch A line of stitching ⅛" from a folded edge or a seam line.

Facing A piece of fabric used to back the main fabric positioned on the inside of a garment to finish raw edges such as necklines, armholes, and jacket openings. Linings are also facings.

Flywheel Hand wheel on the upper right-hand side of a sewing machine that is used to manually raise or lower the needle. (Always turn it towards you!)

French Curve Measuring tool used to create curved lines on patterns.

French Seam A self-enclosed seam with a neat, narrow finish. It's to completely enclose the raw edges.

Fusible Interfacing A chemically treated interfacing designed to be fused to another fabric with the heat of the iron. It adds body, shaping, and support.

Gathering Stitch Two parallel lines of running stitch or machine basting used to make gathers.

Grading Trimming the seam allowances of a seam to different widths to eliminate bulk.

Grain The lengthwise and crosswise directions of the threads in woven fabrics. When these threads are cut at right angles, the fabric is "on grain."

Grainline The line that follows the grain of a fabric.

Grainline Arrows Marked on patterns to indicate where the pattern pieces should be placed in relation to the grain of the fabric.

Hem 1. The method of finishing a raw edge of fabric by turning it under twice and stitching.
2. The bottom edge of a garment or home furnishing.

Hemline (Hem Foldline) Foldline along which a hem is marked and the hem allowance is folded to the wrong side for stitching.

Interfacing A specially designed fabric joined to the back of fabric to give added shape and support at specific areas such as waistbands, collars, and cuffs. See fusible interfacing.

Lengthwise Grain The direction of fabric weave that runs parallel to the selvage and is the strongest direction.

Lining Fabric layer sewn inside a garment to add weight to the drape, comfort, or warmth, and/or to conceal the seam allowances.

Lockstitch The type of stitch made automatically by a household sewing machine. A top thread interlocks with a bobbin thread, creating a strong line of stitching.

Loop Turner Long wire tool with a hook at one end for turning narrow pieces of sewn tubing from the wrong side to the right side.

Muslin Inexpensive undyed cotton fabric used by designers to test patterns.

Nap The raised surface texture of a fabric made by short fibers that brush in one direction, such as velvet or corduroy. Napped fabrics must always be cut in the same direction.

Nonwovens Material used in sewing that are not woven or knit, such as leather, faux suede, and felt.

Notch 1. A triangular shaped mark on a pattern used to match adjacent pieces. 2. To cut a V-shaped wedge in the seam allowances of curved seams to reduce bulk when the item is turned right side out.

Notion Any article other than fabric used in sewing, such as needles, thread, zippers, buttons, etc.

Patchwork Anything made with different pieces of fabric.

Pattern Markings Symbols printed on a pattern to indicate the grain, the placement of a pattern on the fold, and construction details like notches, darts, buttonholes, etc.

S·E·W ·

Pattern Piece The piece of tissue or paper printed with pattern markings.

Pinking Finishing a raw edge of fabric with pinking shears, which create a zigzag cut to help prevent fraying. This is the quickest and easiest seam finish.

Piping Fabric-covered cord used as trim.

Pivot To turn the fabric on the machine while the needle is still in the fabric. Used to stitch a sharp corner or for freeform stitching.

Placket A finished opening used in a garment to make it easy to put on.

Preshrink Washing a piece of fabric so it will shrink before you cut out your pattern.

Press Cloth Cloth placed over fabric to prevent marking during ironing.

Presser Foot Part of a sewing machine lowered onto fabric to hold it in place as you stitch. The most common types you'll use are all-purpose, buttonhole, and zipper.

Raw Edge The cut sewn (not sewn) edge of fabric.

Right Side The outer side of the fabric designed to be seen in a finished garment.

Running Stitch A short, even handstitch, similar to basting, but permanent.

Seam A line of stitching that joins two pieces of fabric.

Seam Allowance The amount of fabric between the seam line and the edge of fabric, generally ⅝".

Seam Guide Marks on the throat plate of a sewing machine used to help you sew seams at the proper distance from the fabric's edge.

Seam Line The line designated for stitching a seam around the edge of a piece of a fabric. Most often ⅝" from the seam edge.

Seam Ripper Sharp hook-ended tool used for taking out stitches.

Selvage The finished side edges of a length of fabric parallel to the lengthwise threads.

Shank The stem of a button.

Sharp Long needles used for most hand-sewing.

Slash A cut on fabric in a straight line that's longer than a clip, such as a finished slit in a garment that is faced.

Slipstitch A handstitch used primarily for hemming and repairing torn seams.

Staystitch Machine stitching just inside a seam allowance to stabilize fabric and prevent stretching.

Straight Stitch Plain stitch on a sewing machine used for seaming, staystitching, edgestitching, topstitching, understitching.

Tack Tiny hand-stitches taken on top of each other to hold two pieces of cloth together.

Tailor's Chalk Fabric chalk used to make marks that can be brushed off.

Tailor's Ham Hard cushion used when pressing hard-to-reach fabric as with curved seams.

Take-Up Lever Part of a sewing machine that controls the thread as it is fed to the needle.

Tension The degree of tightness or looseness of the upper (needle) and lower (bobbin) threads that interlock on a sewing machine. When the two are balanced, the threads are drawn into the fabric to the same degree to create a perfect stitch.

Topstitch A stitch sewn on the right side of a garment about ¼" from a finished edge, often with a long stitch, to emphasize a seam or finish a hem.

Tracing Wheel Tool with a spurlike wheel used with dressmaker's carbon to transfer marks from a pattern to fabric.

Trim To cut away excess fabric.

Understitch Line of machine stitching through a facing and seam allowances sewn close to the seam line, to prevent it from rolling to the right side.

Warp The lengthwise threads of woven cloth. Warp threads run

parallel to the selvage and are the strongest direction of the fabric.

Weft The threads of a woven fabric that run across a woven fabric, or selvage to selvage. Also known as the crosswise grain.

Wrong Side The back of a fabric, or the side that you do not see on a finished project.

Zigzag Stitch A Z-shaped machine stitch often used to finish raw edges or secure hems.

Zigzagged-and-trimmed finish Make a zigzag stitch on either side of a seam, about ¼" from the raw edge, then trim away the excess fabric.

Zipper Foot Narrow sewing machine presser foot used to sew zippers.

Quiz Answers from page 45

1. Lockstitch

2. C

3. Tension disks

4. False. Most fabrics are fine with a standard needle, but knits, leather, and other fabrics require special needles.

5. Toward you, or counterclockwise

6. 2.5mm to 3mm

7. D

8. Your manual

9. A

10. False. Like your car or your own human body, you need to check it and tune it up yearly

Index

How did you do?

After you sew a thing or two, I'd love to know how it all turned out! Please send digital pictures to my website, www.makeworkshop.com, so I can post them and give you props. You can also give other readers ideas and inspiration—just like in a workshop! I'll also be posting updates and alternate versions of the projects, so check back often. Or if you have a question about a pattern, go to the website for the latest 4-1-1.